Raising Up a Prophet

RAISING UP A PROPHET,

THE AFRICAN-AMERICAN ENCOUNTER WITH GANDHI

Sudarshan Kapur

BEACON PRESS
Boston

Beacon Press
25 Beacon Street
Boston, Massachusetts 02108-2892

Beacon Press books
are published under the auspices of
the Unitarian Universalist Association of Congregations.

99 98 97 96 95 94 93 92   8 7 6 5 4 3 2 1

Text design by Diane Levy

Library of Congress Cataloging-in-Publication Data

Kapur, Sudarshan.
    Raising up a prophet : the African-American encounter with Gandhi
/ Sudarshan Kapur.
      p. cm.
    Includes bibliographical references and index.
    ISBN 0-8070-0914-8 (cloth)
    ISBN 0-8070-0915-6 (pbk.)
    1. Afro-Americans—Civil rights. 2. Civil rights movements—
United States—History—20th century. 3. Gandhi, Mahatma,
1869-1948—Influence. 4. Nonviolence—History—20th century.
I. Title.
E185.61.K344 1992
323.1′196073—dc20   91-34682

To Vincent Gordon Harding
teacher, brother, and friend

Contents

Acknowledgments

EVER SINCE the need for this study was demonstrated to me in early 1981, a host of people have helped me in a variety of ways. My intellectual debts are enormous. One of the many insights that I have gained from my teachers is that in interpreting the past we need to be faithful to the dreams, hopes, and courage of ordinary people in human struggles for justice. Professor Vincent Gordon Harding has been a major influence in helping me to understand and appreciate this perspective. It is a perspective which informs *Raising Up a Prophet*. Thanks are also due to him for the invaluable guidance he provided me as chairperson of my dissertation committee and for his timely interventions, which made it possible for me to have access to sources which would otherwise have remained unavailable. As a member of my committee, Will B. Gravely, Professor of Religious Studies at the University of Denver, was a source of great encouragement and support. With his encyclopedic mind and penchant for detail and his great love of African-American religion and history, he put me on research trails which have borne rich results. Dana Wilbanks, Professor of Christian Ethics at the Iliff School of Theology, also served on my committee. He made me acutely aware of the need for careful analysis. I am indebted to them all.

A considerable portion of the basic research for this book was done during my stay at the Center for the Study of World Religions in Cambridge, Massachusetts. While I was there, the W. E. B. Du Bois Institute for Afro-American Studies at Harvard University became home away from home. I am grateful to the late Professor Nathan Huggins and to Dr. Randall K. Burkett, director and assistant director of the Institute, for the use of workspace and a stimulating environment. It was there that I first met the late Professor St. Clair Drake and Professor George Shepperson. They were both extremely generous with their time and wisdom. This work is richer and better for their interventions. Dr. Thomas Jarl Sheppard Mikelson, Dr. Bridglal Pachai, the Reverend Glenn Smiley, Lerone Bennett, Jr., Daniel Berrigan, S.J., Professors David Carrasco, Robert Hill, Darlene Clark Hine, James D. Hunt, Charles Long, George Makechnie, Aldon D. Morris, Michael R. Winston have all shown interest in my work and provided valuable insights.

Robert Hill and Thomas Mikelson have read an earlier version of *Raising Up a Prophet*. I am thankful to them for their critical comments and suggestions. They have alerted me to aspects of the larger story which I might have otherwise neglected. Will Gravely, Vincent Harding, and James Hunt have gone through the manuscript. I have been helped by them in ways too numerous to list.

Perhaps at no time have I appreciated the magnificent role that librarians play in the advancement of knowledge and the furtherance of scholarship than during the course of my research for this book. I wish to thank Professor Michael Winston and Dr. Thomas C. Battle of Howard University's Moorland-Spingarn Research Center for giving me access to the Benjamin E. Mays and William Stuart Nelson Papers. I was also given supervised access to the Mordecai Wyatt Johnson Papers. The staff at the Moorland-Spingarn Research Center was most helpful, especially Ms. Karen L. Jefferson and Ms. Esme E. Bhan. With considerable care and interest they and their colleagues guided me through hard-to-get-at materials. Ms. Wilma Mosholder of the Swarthmore College Peace Collection was most helpful with the Fellowship of Reconciliation Papers. The staff at the Mugar Memorial Library at Boston University has given me generous help and advice with the Howard Thurman Papers. I also wish to thank the staff at the University of Denver's Penrose Library for their cooperation and valuable help. Mrs. Katie Fisher at the Ira J. Taylor Library has been patient and prompt with her assistance.

Mrs. Margaret Manion has given skilled and timely help with typing. Vivek Pinto has provided valuable assistance and given generously and tirelessly of his time. As the final deadlines approached, their efforts proved of critical importance. My research assistant, Ms. Vereene Parnell, my brother, Raj Kapur, and my nephew, Eknath Ghate, have all worked to move the process along. I am grateful to them for their support in my work.

I could not have asked for greater support and encouragement than I have enjoyed from Beacon Press. I have been immeasurably aided by a patiently persistent and appropriately demanding editor, Ms. Deborah Chasman. Ms. Chris Kochansky has also given outstanding help with the manuscript. Without such help the final results would not have been as satisfactory.

My immediate and extended family has had much to do with the completion of this book. The spirit of my birth mother Swaran Lata Kapur has gently guided me in this project and kept me faithful to my task. My parents, Shiv Lal Kapur and Sheila Kapur, have been consistently kind and generous. Without the constant loving support and encouragement of my companion and encourager, Sita, and children Rahul and Vatsala, this work could not have materialized. To them and many, many more, I am deeply grateful.

Finally, this book owes much to the people of India, who demonstrated the efficacy of *satyagraha* for social change movements everywhere. It owes even more to African-Americans, who by their decades-long exploration of the nonviolent alternative nurtured the ground upon which flowered the black-led nonviolent freedom movement of the 1950s and 1960s. Not only is theirs the primary voice in the story narrated here, they are the reason for this endeavor. Therefore, this book is also for them.

Introduction

BUILDING ON the struggles of earlier generations, the modern African-American freedom movement (1955–1968), in the short span of slightly more than a decade, forced an otherwise unready and unwilling nation to move toward becoming a free and open society. The leap forward was the direct outcome of countless non-violent initiatives of thousands of committed and courageous African-Americans. The courageous witness of those determined social activists, which galvanized a whole generation into action, has since inspired nonviolent activists from the Philippines to China to Eastern Europe.

In recalling that momentous post-Montgomery decade, a stream of powerful and moving images of ordinary African-Americans acting individually and in concert comes to mind: Mose Wright in a Mississippi courthouse surrounded mostly by hostile local whites, facing a white judge and an all-white jury, pointing to the white abductors of his nephew, Emmett Till; fifteen-year-old Elizabeth Eckford, one of the "Little Rock Nine," walking to Central High School in Little Rock, Arkansas, to the hate-filled objections and shouts of "Lynch her! Lynch her!" of white segregationists; Diane Nash's gentle, though forceful, confrontation of mayor Ben West in Nashville, which compelled him to respond from the heart and to admit that segregation is morally wrong; the Reverend C. T. Vivian's challenge of Dallas County Sheriff James G. Clark, Jr., and his men on the steps of the courthouse, when Vivian was beaten for trying to get black people to register to vote. These are images which encapsulate the power and the essential meaning of nonviolent resistance.[1] Yet as we recall these and other images of resistance, we are perforce taken even further back in time to explain fully the roots of the modern African-American nonviolent resistance movement, for the nonviolent activism which blossomed in this country in the 1950s and 1960s was nurtured by an earlier generation of African-Americans who had made direct and significant connections with Mohandas Karamchand Gandhi and the Indian independence movement.

The religiously grounded methodology of nonviolent resistance which Gandhi developed and tested has been applied in struggles for justice, peace, and social transformation in various parts of the world. But since World War II no single group has developed Gandhian ideas more creatively than African-Americans. Beginning with the Montgomery bus boycott in 1955, under the leadership of Martin Luther King, Jr., Southern-based African-Americans and their white allies eventually demonstrated the power of revolutionary nonviolence and its capacity to transform persons, institutions, and perceptions. As a result, nonviolent resistance emerged with a new vitality, just as Gandhi had predicted a generation earlier.[2]

However, when we seek an understanding of this important historical process by which one culture's experiences in social change are adapted to the life of another, there is relatively little guidance in the literature, either scholarly or popular. The essential historical connection generally made between the Indian independence movement and the modern African-American freedom movement is almost always limited to a focus on King's "discovery" of Gandhi in his seminary years, specifically as the result of his hearing, in 1950, a lecture on Gandhi delivered by Mordecai Wyatt Johnson, president of Howard University.

One problem with this scenario is that while its basic historical facts are correct on one level, it obscures a much richer story. To confine ourselves to such an approach keeps us focused too narrowly on King, developing an elitist approach to a story which should involve the preparation of an entire people. It is the experience of the African-American people and the possibilities of their prior knowledge of and experience with Gandhian methodology which are largely missing from earlier approaches to this story.

This work assumes that most often a dialectical, creative relationship exists between a leader and the community which that person represents. Thus viewed, a leader is the product of a movement of social change as well as the co-creator of a people's movement. From these assumptions emerges a more helpful way of dealing with the questions of social change and movement of ideas across cultures; the leader may be seen as a representative of the inner urgings and outer manifestations of a people in struggle.

The essential task of this study is to look at the African-American community in the years of Gandhi's greatest activity, from the early 1920s to 1947, and ask in what ways African-Americans became aware of Gandhi and his movement and the implications of that movement for their own North American situation of segregation, discrimination, and disenfranchisement. Such an approach does not assume any simple causal relationship between Gandhi's movement and the post-Montgomery African-American struggle for freedom. Whatever its precise debt to Gandhi and the Indian independence movement, the modern African-American freedom movement was grounded in its own understanding of religion in general, and of Christianity in particular. The religious ground on which they stood and their understanding of Jesus provided African-Americans access to Gandhi's nonviolent movement, for Gandhi also defined his struggle as a religious one and suggested that he too, a Hindu, followed the way of Jesus. In addition to their own traditions of civil disobedience to unjust systems, which began on the slave ships, African-Americans in the post–World War II freedom movement drew upon the essential teachings of their Christian faith as well as upon Gandhian principles of nonviolent direct action. The liberating role of Jesus and the teachings of the Sermon on the Mount, though not always central in every aspect of their historic struggle, often guided their thoughts and actions.

Under King's leadership of the Montgomery bus boycott, Christian teachings and the Gandhian concept of nonviolence were joined in a powerful and effective way. As King stated in *Stride Toward Freedom*, "Christ furnished the spirit and motivation, while Gandhi furnished the method."[3] In those tumultuous decades of the 1950s and 1960s, African-Americans seemed to appropriate Gandhi's teachings relatively quickly and successfully. It is my hope that this study will change, widen, and enrich our understanding of the African-American freedom struggle in the twentieth century and provide greater clarity about the ways in which struggles for transformation may be shared across cultural and political boundaries.

Raising Up a Prophet attempts to explore the prior basis for Gan-

dhi's appeal in the African-American community. It seeks out a set
of pre–1950s traditions upon which King and others built in an
attempt effectively to apply Gandhian concepts of nonviolent social
change. Were ordinary, literate African-Americans aware of Gandhi
and his nonviolent methods of resistance? If African-Americans were
drawn to the Mahatma prior to the Montgomery boycott, what was
the basis of such attraction? Assuming its existence, what was the
content and nature of the debate within the African-American community over the issues of Gandhian nonviolence and its relevance
to their situation in America?

These questions can be summarized as a search for some of the
ways in which African-Americans were prepared for the coming of
King and the nonviolent freedom movement, especially through
the application of the Gandhian concept of *satyagraha,* nonviolent
resistance based on truth and non-sentimental love of the opponent.
Many members of the early generations of twentieth-century African-Americans, I found, had a grasp of both the revolutionary
nature of the Gandhi-led Indian freedom movement and the moral
basis of Gandhian nonviolence. Even more important was their
discussion, exploration, and experimentation with Gandhian nonviolence in the decades preceding the Montgomery bus boycott;
those earlier roots helped to establish a viable basis for the successful
adoption of nonviolence by African-Americans in the decades of the
1950s and 1960s.

This book was largely shaped by the variety of means by which
African-Americans were introduced to Gandhi and carried out their
discussions of the man and his movement. Over the early decades
of the twentieth century there were several important vehicles.
Among the pioneers were outstanding African-American leaders like
W. E. B. Du Bois (1868–1963) and Marcus Garvey (1887–1940),
who drew the attention of their communities to the struggles of
colored peoples in other parts of the world and specifically to the
Indian movement. Du Bois expressed his solidarity with the oppressed of the world through his voluminous writings, through
speeches before a wide range of African-American communities
throughout the United States, and especially through his editorship,
between 1910 and 1934, of *The Crisis,* the influential official organ
of the National Association for the Advancement of Colored People
(NAACP). Therefore, Du Bois's writings are an important source.

Garvey's extensive but relatively short-lived organizing was rooted in and consciously tied to worldwide struggles of oppressed people. His organization, the Universal Negro Improvement Association (UNIA), and its widely read newspaper, *The Negro World*, offered him and his associates a popular platform from which to launch and propagate international concerns.

Probably the most significant and extensive means by which African-Americans throughout the country were informed of the Mahatma and his struggle against British domination was through the coverage of the Indian independence movement in African-American newspapers and journals. Before the desegregation actions of the 1950s and 1960s, the white-owned newspapers in the United States—insofar as they dealt with the African-American community at all—were essentially interested only in crime stories and other sensational matters. Rarely did they make the effort to inform and educate their readers about the hopes and aspirations of people of color in the United States or elsewhere. In contrast, African-American newspapers played a crucial role in the shaping of their people's lives and consciousness. The significance of the African-American press was described in 1944 by Gunnar Myrdal in *An American Dilemma*.

> *The press defines the Negro group to the Negroes themselves* [Myrdal's italics]. The individual Negro is invited to share in the sufferings, grievances, and pretensions of the millions of Negroes far outside the narrow local community. This creates a feeling of strength and solidarity. The press, more than any other institution, has created the Negro group as a social and psychological reality to the individual Negro.

Myrdal stressed that "its existence, its popular spread, and its content are a testimony of Negro unrest. Its cumulative effect in spurring race consciousness must be tremendous." The role of the African-American press became even more significant with "the rising Negro protest and the increase of Negro literacy."

> Practically all Negroes who can read are exposed to the influence of the Negro press at least some of the time. . . . Newspapers are commonly passed from family to family, and they are sometimes read out loud in informal gatherings. They are available in barber shops, and sometimes in churches, lodges and pool parlors. Their contents

are passed by word of mouth among those who cannot read. Indirectly, therefore, even aside from circulation figures, this press influences a large proportion of the Negro population.[4]

The African-American press was a major force in educating and molding opinion. As Myrdal wrote, "Together with the church and the school—and in the field of interracial and civic opinions, more than those two institutions—it determines the special direction of the process through which the Negroes are becoming acculturated." But, as the sociologist Brewton Berry argued in 1959, the African-American press did more than acculturate its community. Berry declared that "the Negro press . . . has been a powerful instrument in molding Negro opinion behind the crusade of full citizenship. . . . However, it has performed a variety of functions, and certainly protest has been one of its most characteristic and effective."[5]

The unique and vital role the African-American press played in the life of its community, especially in the pre-television age, was well understood and discussed by the newspapers and journals themselves. For example, in January 1932, the *Atlanta Daily World* listed a host of reasons why an African-American newspaper should be published. African-American newspapers, it argued, publish "the good that Negroes do . . . in addition to the bad"; these papers tell their readers what is going on in their churches and lodges "with respect" and without ridicule. It insisted that "in no other way can the interests and rights of Negroes individually and collectively be preserved."[6]

In its coverage of the rising post–World War II anticolonial struggle being carried out by the colored peoples of Asia and Africa, the African-American press played a major role, including the transmission to its readers of significant news and opinions regarding Gandhi and the Indian movement. The importance of the African-American press as the communicator of information and as a forum for popular discussions concerning the Indian struggle led by Gandhi cannot be overestimated. Therefore, in the course of my exploration of the place of the Gandhian movement in the African-American consciousness prior to 1955, I have analyzed coverage concerning the Gandhi-led Indian freedom movement in twelve respected and widely read African-American journals.

I have selected a representative sample of African-American newspapers and journals providing a religious, regional, and political balance. Beginning with the rise of Gandhi as a national leader and ending with the emergence of King in Montgomery, the survey covers the years from 1919 to 1955. These journals are: the *A. M. E. Church Review*, the *Atlanta Daily World*, the *Baltimore Afro-American*, the *Chicago Defender*, *The Crisis*, the *Journal of Religious Thought*, the *Journal of Negro History*, the *Journal of Negro Education*, *The Negro World*, the *New York Amsterdam News*, the *Norfolk Journal and Guide*, and the *Pittsburgh Courier*.[7]

However, it is also important to note that another crucial way in which African-American communities learned about the Indian independence movement and Gandhi's concept of nonviolent resistance was through pre–World War II visits to India by a number of black leaders. Some of these leaders met with the Mahatma at his ashram (religious and political community): Howard Thurman (1900–1980), the celebrated preacher-mystic-theologian, and his wife, Sue Bailey Thurman (1903–); the Reverend Edward Carroll (1910–), a church leader; William Stuart Nelson (1895–1977), the editor of Howard University's *Journal of Religious Thought;* Benjamin E. Mays (1895–1984), president of Morehouse College; Channing H. Tobias (1882–1961), member of the Board of Trustees of the NAACP in the early 1940s and others. These African-Americans probed Gandhi on his ideas of nonviolence and the meaning of direct action, discussed with him the problems of training individuals or communities in the task of carrying out the nonviolent antisegregationist struggle, and reflected with Gandhi on the applicability of nonviolent resistance to injustice on a mass scale in the United States.[8]

In the pre–1955 period, a number of Gandhians from India also brought the message of the Mahatma and his movement to African-Americans, as did Charles Freer Andrews (1871–1940), a British Christian missionary, friend, and biographer of Gandhi, in 1929. In 1934, Madeleine Slade (1892–1982), another British disciple and co-worker of Gandhi, communicated the meaning and the relevance of his work to African-American students and faculty at Howard University as well as to the wider community. In the early 1940s, Krishnalal Shridharani (1911–1960), a veteran of the 1930 Salt March, established important working relations between the two movements through participation in several campaigns for racial justice, including the early activities of the Congress of Racial Equality. In 1951, four years after India regained her independence and as many years before the Montgomery bus boycott, Ram Manohar Lohia (1910–1967), a onetime colleague and follower of Gandhi, came to the United States on a six-week lecture tour. He visited several African-American communities. In public addresses and private conversations, Lohia advocated jail-going and civil disobedience to black Americans in their struggle.[9]

Given the fact that the African-American struggle was grounded in religion, I have also explored the religious and social context in which the Gandhian concept and practice of *satyagraha* was communicated to and appropriated by African-Americans. Within the category of religion, Christianity, especially before 1955, held pride of place among the overwhelming majority of African-Americans. Faith in the redemptive power of suffering and the love ethic of Jesus constituted for African-Americans vital elements of their worldview. I will argue here that the Gandhian notion of *satyagraha,* based on the principles of *ahimsa* (non-injury or non-killing) and *satya* (truth), struck a favorable chord because it affirmed a very important aspect of African-American popular spirituality.

I approach this task from a fundamentally historical perspective, primarily because that method demonstrates the ways in which African-American attention to Gandhi and the Indian freedom movement developed over time. Events in the Indian independence movement, such as the noncooperation movement of 1921–1922 and the Salt Satyagraha of 1930–1931, constitute an important historical context for this inquiry and are examined in the light of the developing African-American freedom movement and its periodic discussions of the appropriateness of Gandhian methods for its situation. Questions pertaining to the meaning of *satyagraha* are incorporated into the descriptive and narrative sections of this work, especially as such questions entered the African-American discussions of the time.

The two freedom movements had their own inner and outer pressures, "stages" of development, needs, and immediate as well as longer-term goals. Sometimes their objectives became one—over Mussolini's invasion in 1935 of Ethiopia, for instance, or in the post–World War II period, when the United Nations considered the questions of human rights. Most often the two struggles moved on their own separate courses, at their chosen speeds, and in response to the urgencies of a given moment. Nevertheless, I hope to demonstrate that the African-American communities were aware of the workings of the Gandhi-led movement in the Indian subcontinent.

Having said that, I recognize that both elements of my approach carry their own difficulties. Developments in the two movements cannot always be fitted into a chronological order. Because what follows is an attempt to narrate African-American responses to Gandhi, his concept of nonviolent resistance, and the Indian independence movement, accounts of the Indian-based events need to be controlled so as not to get in the way of that narration. As I proceed with this exploration, it will become clear that a significant and historic interplay between movements, people, and events took place during the years from 1919 to 1955. Consequently, this must permeate the spirit as well as the actual telling of that story.

Finally, for nearly four decades, African-Americans explored the possibility of raising up a Gandhi-like leader. They appreciated the miracles the Mahatma was making for his people in their struggle against Britain. Some were quick to recognize the need for a leader who might combine the way and the vision of Jesus just as Gandhi had done. African-Americans did not wait idly by for a prophet to deliver them to the promised land. Rather, by way of discussion, debate, and activism in the decades leading up to the Montgomery bus boycott, they helped to create the circumstances that made possible the emergence of Martin Luther King, Jr. In thought and action they were hard at work. In the process they raised a prophet who at a critical moment in their ongoing struggle helped an entire nation to move closer to freedom.

Denver
January 1992

=1=

The Awakening of a Global Alliance

IN AN ADDRESS he prepared for the Pan African Congress of 1900, the scholar-philosopher-activist W.E.B. Du Bois expressed the conviction that "by reason of sheer numbers and physical contact" people of color were bound to shape the history of the twentieth century. In 1903 he wrote in *The Souls of Black Folk* that "the problem of the twentieth century is the problem of the color-line,— the relation of the darker to the lighter races of men in Asia and Africa, in America and the islands of the sea." Three years later, noting the Russian defeat in the Russo-Japanese War, Du Bois said it was only a matter of time before "the brown and black races" too would stand up and challenge the imperial nations, and in an undated and unpublished essay titled "India's Relation to Negroes and the Color Problem," he went to the heart of the need for solidarity among the darker peoples of the world in general, and between East Indians and African-Americans in particular:

> The problem of the Negroes . . . remain[s] a part of the world-wide clash of color. So, too, the problem of the Indians can never be simply a problem of autonomy in the British commonwealth of nations. They must always stand as representatives of the colored races—as the yellow and black peoples as well as the brown—of the majority of mankind, and together with the Negroes they must face the insistent problem of the assumption of the white peoples of Europe that they have a right to dominate the world and especially so to organize it politically and industrially as to make most men slaves and servants.[1]

The theme of international racial solidarity was an integral part of the influential Du Boisian philosophy, and it continued to inform and challenge his community. Towards the end of World War I, when the future of India and Egypt became a focus of worldwide attention, Du Bois again was moved to express his identity with them. In an article written in June 1919, Du Bois argued that "the sympathy of Black America must of necessity go out to colored India and colored Egypt" because the foreparents of these people "were ancient friends, cousins, blood-brothers, in the hoary ages of antiquity." Pressing his readers to recognize the essential unity of the colored people of the world, he wrote, "We are all one—we the Despised and Oppressed, the 'niggers' of England and America."[2]

There is no obvious way of determining how responsive his readers were to such urgings, but the tradition of African-American solidarity with other peoples of color was not new to the twentieth century nor was it confined to Du Bois. It extended back at least as far as the first half of the nineteenth century, to David Walker's militant *Appeal to the Colored Citizens of the World . . .* (1829) and Martin Delany's powerful novel, *Blake* (1859). The theme was regularly reinforced by racially conscious African-American church leaders and other informers of the popular black consciousness. Throughout, parallels were drawn between their situation in the United States and that of colored people in other parts of the world.

The internationalist vision was also kept alive by the leading African-American protest organization, the National Association for the Advancement of Colored People (NAACP). Under attack from sections of the black community for its espousal of the cause of African nations at the Versailles Peace Conference, the NAACP organized a mass rally in New York in early 1919 to respond to criticism. The poet, novelist, and NAACP secretary James Weldon Johnson defended his organization's efforts to "bring Africa to the attention of the Peace Conference and the civilized world." Johnson reminded his critics that the NAACP's current interests were not "the result of any passing flash of enthusiasm." The internationalist concern was rooted in realism, he argued, adding that it was also inspired by a moral vision which demanded African-Americans share in the sufferings of others. According to Johnson, "It will be a lamentable condition when the American Negro grows so narrow and so self-centered in his own wrongs and sufferings that he has no sympathy for the wrongs and sufferings of others"; when such a day arises "he will have forfeited the right to demand that others be interested in him."[3]

By the outset of the twentieth century, then, Du Bois and other black leaders were articulating a familiar theme in African-American life. And with the coming of World War I, the truth of these insights was rediscovered and acted out on the world stage. Participation in the war was perhaps the single most important event which led thousands of African-American soldiers to deepen their identification with the struggles of the peoples of Asia, Africa, and Latin America. In *The Other American Revolution,* Vincent Harding argues that when the United States and European powers drafted African-Americans and nonwhite colonial peoples in World War I, they "affirmed in many black minds the basic unity there was between their situation in America and the oppression of nonwhite peoples in Africa and the rest of the world." The over a third of a million African-Americans who fought to make the world safe for democracy soon learned that their nation had no intention of honoring citizenship rights for them. Black soldiers also realized that in some ways they had greater liberty in Europe and North Africa than they enjoyed at home. They returned home to continued legal segregation, disfranchisement, economic exploitation, humiliation, and harassment. Racist violence increased with the revival of the Ku Klux Klan in 1915. Lynchings multiplied—there were as many as 222 in 1917, and all the lynchers went free.[4]

At the same time, the war had provided African-American soldiers with a "clearer international context and focus to the struggle for black freedom in America." African-American soldiers returned home determined to create a new reality for themselves and their families. "They did not want to return to a prewar normalcy, but to move forward to a new basis for democratic living in the United States," writes John Hope Franklin in *From Slavery to Freedom.* It was in this setting of renewed resistance at home and new awareness of the world that African-American church leaders, intellectuals, educators, and writers informed and educated African-Americans about the connection of their struggle with that of oppressed people everywhere.[5]

This theme was put forward by Hubert H. Harrison, one of his community's most important self-educated intellectuals, who taught on the streets and in the lecture halls of Harlem. In his well-organized and cogent lectures, Harrison often said that while he deplored the human costs of World War I, he hoped for "a free India and an independent Egypt; *for nationalities in Africa flying their own flags and dictating their own internal and foreign policies"* [Harrison's italics]. An important dimension of the expanding sense of African-American solidarity with other peoples in the aftermath of World War I was the specific interest certain African-American leaders took in the Indian freedom movement and in the vision and life of Mohandas Karamchand Gandhi. In an essay he published in September 1917, Harrison urged "the Negro of the Western world . . . [to] follow the path of the Swadesha [*sic*] in India," referring especially to Gandhi's call for Indian self-reliance. The same year, speaking before a group of socialists in New York, Du Bois likewise made a call for Indian independence.[6]

Meanwhile, the Indian political scene had become extremely volatile. The 1905 partition of Bengal was unpopular and generated nationwide protests, including the boycott of British cloth. With the founding of the Muslim League the following year to further Muslim interests, the nationalist movement faced its most serious challenge. The arrest and exile of the nationalist Bal Gangadhar Tilak in 1907 for his uncompromising opposition to British rule added to the national mood of uncertainty. Tilak returned home in 1914, the same year Gandhi left South Africa after having won a victory of sorts in his *satyagraha* struggle there. By that time India had been forcibly taken into the European war on the side of Britain. Over a million Indian soldiers and noncombatants who participated in the war effort on the European and African fronts came back with their worldviews changed forever.[7]

Although the African-American interest in India was not unique in American history—contact with India had been initiated by the New England transcendentalists by the nineteenth century—in the new century African-Americans became the major U.S. contact point. Indeed, in the first three decades of the century, the teachings of African-Americans like Du Bois and Harrison were regularly reinforced and supplemented by personal encounters with Indian visitors to the United States who sought out African-American contacts. Political freedom and social reform were now uppermost in the minds and hearts of a great many of the leading members of Indian society, especially in light of the British decision to achieve administrative efficiency by dividing the politically vibrant province of Bengal in eastern India. Responding to the 1905 partition of Bengal, the burgeoning Indian nationalist movement sent several activists to establish bases overseas. In 1913, the *Ghadr* (Revolution) Party was founded in San Francisco. The Ghadr was committed to forcing the British out of India through whatever means necessary. Their goal was to keep the resistance going while remaining out of British clutches, and the United States seemed a place of safe haven. The party's representatives in the United States also took upon themselves the task of educating the people about India and its freedom struggle. The Ghadr received considerable support from Germany. Because of the party's anti-British stance the United States did not welcome the Ghadr; many of its members were hounded out by the government.[8]

At the same time, Lala Lajpat Rai (1865–1928), who would soon develop close contacts with several American black leaders and become a supporter of Gandhi, came to the United States. A founding member of the Hindu reformist movement, *Arya Samaj*, an outspoken opponent of British rule, and a prolific writer, Rai was the first major representative of the Indian freedom movement to establish direct contact with African-Americans. Rai had initially visited in 1905 for three weeks. In 1915, now a political exile who could not return home, Rai arrived in the United States again, this time for a five-year stay. Lajpat Rai was an important link in a developing chain. He was convinced that "there is some analogy between the Negro problem in the United States of America and the problem of the depressed classes [Untouchables and members of tribal groups] in India." In his book *The United States of America: A Hindu's Impressions and Study,* Rai noted that he was prompted to pay a second visit to the United States by his desire to study at first hand the condition of black Americans. He was also interested to know for himself what measures the African-American community had taken to improve its education and economic condition. In the course of his stay in this country, Rai established personal contact with Du Bois and became his good friend. In addition, he sought out Booker T. Washington, founder of Tuskegee Institute, and John Hope, president of Morehouse College. Rai met the famous African-American scientist George Washington Carver (1860–1943) at Tuskegee, and visited Morehouse College. He also developed ties with white liberal leaders such as the journalist-writer Walter Lippmann, B. W. Huebsch, the owner of a publishing company, and the social activist Mary White Ovington, a friend and co-worker of Du Bois.[9]

During the course of his extended stay, Rai traveled through the length and breadth of the United States, actively working for the cause of Indian freedom. In the South, Booker T. Washington accompanied him on some of his travels to African-American communities and institutions. Rai wrote approvingly of the Tuskegee experimental self-help vocational program. He thought he saw in it an answer to an irrelevant British system of education. Through his contacts with the white liberal and African-American communities, Lajpat Rai sought to educate the American public about the independence struggle of his people and enlist their moral support for the Indian cause. According to Vijaya Joshi, editor of Lajpat Rai's *Autobiographical Writings*, Rai "carried on vigorous, but enlightened, propaganda for Indian independence throughout his stay in the United States and it met with considerable success, particularly among liberal circles." In 1917 Rai founded the Indian Home Rule League of America and the journal *Young India*. By then he was able to tell American audiences about the nationalist movement and the emergent leadership of Gandhi. "All these efforts were directed towards the sole object of creating a favourable opinion abroad towards India's aspirations," writes Joshi. Finally, in February 1920, Rai was given a passport to return home, but the seed had been sown in the African-American community.[10]

Meanwhile, after spending years in South Africa, where he first formulated and sharpened the concept of *satyagraha,* Gandhi returned home to India in 1915. He was forty-six years old. Before the decade was over, this British-trained lawyer turned revolutionary ascetic had taken control of the Indian National Congress—the pre-eminent organization of the national freedom struggle. Whatever their position on the causes he espoused and the motives he held, people in distant corners of the world had begun to take note of the nonviolent revolutionary from the East. His name had spread far and wide, partly because of his saintly personal qualities, partly because of his public espousal of the way of love and nonviolence, and certainly because he dared use such methods to challenge the world's most powerful imperial nation.

In response to the Gandhi-led nonviolent noncooperation actions

in the period from 1919 to 1921, British authorities in India imposed additional restrictions on the freedom of personal movement
and expression in the colony. This led other nationalist-minded
Indians to leave India, including a number who carried Gandhi's
message to the United States. Among those who made North America their base were Taraknath Das, Syud Hossain, and Haridas T.
Muzumdar. Using the public platform and the print media, they
explained the Indian situation to Americans. Chief among them
was Muzumdar, a Gandhi follower who later claimed he was "suf-
focated by the pervasive atmosphere of political oppression and
governmental terrorism in the wake of the 1919 Jallianwalla Bagh
Massacre." He reached the United States in February 1920, just as
Lajpat Rai was headed home, and unlike Lajpat Rai, who had not
yet entirely accepted the nonviolent way of Gandhi, Muzumdar
soon began "advocating non-violent revolution for freedom under
Mahatma Gandhi's leadership." He became another link in the
connecting chain.[11]

Muzumdar entered the mainstream of the African-American
struggle through his abiding interest in furthering the Gandhi-led
noncooperation movement. The African-American setting provided
him with an important platform and great visibility to explain the
immediate as well as the long-term goals of the Indian movement
to other oppressed people. In the course of his association with black
activists, he clearly helped to bring Gandhi and his nonviolent
philosophy into the consciousness of African-Americans. Signifi-
cantly, the initial opening for Muzumdar was provided by Marcus
Garvey, the flamboyant Caribbean leader who had originally organized the Universal Negro Improvement Association (UNIA) in
his native Jamaica in 1914 to campaign for freedom for Africa and
people of African descent.

In order to understand the setting for the connections which
Muzumdar represented, it is necessary to explore the important
context for Gandhi consciousness which Garvey provided. Solidarity
with other oppressed people was an especially important theme for
Garvey. He came to the United States in 1916, proud of his African
heritage, possessed with the vision of an Africa free of European
domination, and believing in the communality of the struggle of
oppressed people everywhere. The following year, aided by Hubert
Harrison, Garvey founded the UNIA in Harlem and quickly made

it into "the largest and most dramatic black mass movement ever to exist in America." Within three years, this organization claimed a worldwide following of over a million. Wherever possible Garvey made connections in his speeches and writings between the African-American struggle for freedom and justice and resistance movements in places like India, Ireland, and Egypt. Ireland had the maximum influence on Garvey; at the same time, India and Gandhi figured a great deal in his speeches.[12]

Garvey's international consciousness and message were similar to those of Du Bois and Harrison, but Garvey was building a constituency of followers and readers which for a time would far surpass the numbers reached by any other African-American leader. Through the hundreds of thousands of people who were active in UNIA and read the columns of *The Negro World,* Garvey reached a broad following with his message of the unity of the oppressed peoples of the world. The UNIA, which flourished from 1916 to 1927, had chapters in thirty-eight states. According to Randall Burkett, "no other twentieth-century protest movement in black America has achieved the wide currency enjoyed by the Universal Negro Improvement Association." On 1 August 1920, the UNIA held its first international convention in New York. In an address he gave to an estimated twenty-five thousand people at Madison Square Garden, Garvey pleaded for the solidarity of people of color.

> We have absolutely no apologies nor compromises to make where Negro rights and liberties are concerned. Just at this time, as we can see the world is reorganizing, the world is reconstructing itself, and in this reconstruction Ireland is striking out for freedom; Egypt is striking out for freedom; India is striking out for freedom; and the Negroes of the world shall do no less than strike out also for freedom.

Often Garvey emphasized that people of African descent would not give up until they had gained all that belonged to them. He believed that his was a fight for justice and equality for all people and that black people were in sympathy with the nationals of Egypt and India. Always the example of India was among the foremost models put forward to the masses who followed him.[13]

By the time Garvey and the UNIA had begun to make an impact on the political scene in the United States, dozens of Indian nationalists like Muzumdar had become active in the political arena in the United States. Garvey welcomed them to join him in the work of the UNIA. For example, according to a Bureau of Investigation report, in a meeting at New York city in October 1920 Garvey introduced a platform speaker from India and expressed the belief that the Indian people "were fighting for the same thing that he was fighting for hence they welcome them with open arms." The report added that the Indian nationalist stated that white people "should be fought tooth and nail" because they were enemies of humankind. Whatever be the basis of these sentiments, it is apparent that the theme of solidarity of people of color was reinforced from both directions, India as well as America.[14]

The Indian focus was continuous in Garvey's internationalism. In the summer of 1921, while the Gandhi-led challenge to British rule was at its height and a major UNIA convention was in session, Garvey sent a message to the Indian leader expressing solidarity with the Indian people and their struggle for independence. The message, which was signed "2nd International Convention of Negroes, Marcus Garvey, President," read, "Please accept best wishes of 400,000,000 Negroes through us their representatives, for the speedy emancipation of India from the thraldom of foreign oppression. You may depend on us for whatsoever help we can give."[15] Yet the powerlessness of Garvey and his beleaguered organization to provide material help to India must have been apparent to all. Despite its popularity, the UNIA had neither the necessary economic muscle nor the approval of major African-American leaders. Garvey was constantly ridiculed by Du Bois and the labor organizer A. Philip Randolph. In addition, the federal government kept up its own pressure through the Bureau of Investigation. At the same time, we cannot ignore the emotive power and the appeal of the sentiments expressed by Marcus Garvey for his audience.

Garvey followed the Indian struggle closely and encouraged his followers to do the same. For instance, he was aware of Gandhi's attempt to draw Muslims and Hindus together in a common cause for independence despite their mutual religious antipathies, which went back at least as far as raids into India by Mahmud of Ghazni in 997. At the August 1921 UNIA convention, Garvey alerted his audience to the Muslim uprising in India and declared that "racial kinship, religious kinship, is the cause of this new revolt in India."

Hoping the world might avoid a major conflagration along racial lines, he reminded his listeners that "three hundred and eighty million native Indians, on a matter of religion, on a matter of race, have revolted, in sympathy with the oppressed and defeated of their own race and of their own religion." Garvey knew that Muslim revolt in southern India was in the news. Sensing in that revolt the beginnings of a major national uprising against British rule, he declared,

> For centuries India has been kept apart; India has been crushed, through the caste syst[e]m of that country—religious differences of the people living in India; and because of their differences, because of their disunity, an alien race was able to take possession of their land, and oppressed them and kept them oppressed for decades. But today the worms of India are turning over, and simultaneously, when the real clash comes, 400,000,000 worms of Africa will turn over.

Applause followed. Continuing to teach the lessons which he saw for his people in other struggles, Garvey argued that "if it is possible for Hindus and Mohammedans to come together in India, it is possible for Negroes to come together everywhere." Again his audience responded with applause. Apparently the people were alive to these parallels and the possibilities they held.[16]

Garvey placed a great deal of emphasis on organization. Here again the Indian independence movement, along with others, provided an important model. In an address in Philadelphia in November 1921, he argued, "If you keep organized, as the Hindus are organizing, as the Indians are organizing, as the Egyptians are organizing, as the Irish are organizing, I tell you these heretofore oppressed groups will shake the foundations of the world." Early in the new year, Garvey, through the pages of *The Negro World*, encouraged its readers to recognize that he was willing to do what Gandhi was doing for India and Zagloul Pasha was doing for Egypt.[17]

All the evidence testifies to the fact that whether by itself or connected with other anticolonial struggles, the Indian movement was constantly being kept before the UNIA and thousands of other African-Americans by this powerful and highly influential spokesman. In "The Burden of a Weak Race," a speech Garvey gave early in January 1922 in New York, he said that the Hindus, the Egyptians, and the Irish had decided to become masters of their own destiny. "They are now determined that they shall utilize the intelligence that they have gained, which is similar to that of their masters to keep themselves, not slaves, but to become themselves masters." He reminded his audience that the Indians, under the leadership of Gandhi, were "now more determined than ever to work for an independent, free India." He noted that the Gandhian movement was supported by the poor and the rich alike, and pointedly mentioned that Gandhi was "held in the highest respect and regard by the people whom he leads." More importantly, Garvey continued to share his own conviction that India was headed for freedom. He predicted that all Indians would then "enjoy the benefits of their own country under a government of their own race."[18]

In January 1922, when he addressed a UNIA gathering in New York on the theme "The Rise of a Great Movement," Garvey invited an Indian nationalist and follower of Gandhi, Dr. Singh, to speak about the Indian freedom movement. Singh likened Garvey's contributions to Gandhi's and stressed the underlying unity of the struggles of Africans, African-Americans, and East Indians. Predictably, he drew applause when he stated, "We will never stand to fight against Africa." So long as the British had any say in the governance of India, Singh went on, there was the danger of colonized East Indians and colonized Africans coming into conflict. He considered Gandhi a key factor in moving Indians into action against oppressive British rule. In the end, Singh

> made a strong plea for unity, both of the East Indians to uphold the leadership of Mahatma Gandhi, and for the Negroes of the world to support Marcus Garvey, and each of the two peoples help shoulder the respective burdens of their great leaders; "for," said he, "if the 400,000,000 Negroes of the world come together and join hands with the 350,000,0000 East Indians of the same race, this great alliance of the two peoples will be so strong, so all powerful, that, unless justice be done to them, they can and will stop the world itself from turning on its axis, for they are determined that they shall be free."[19]

Two months later, Garvey again centered attention on Gandhi and India, noting Gandhi's arrest in March 1922 on the charge of sedition. Garvey told his audience, "You are well acquainted with the work of Gandhi," and went on to sum up the Indian leader's career of public service:

> For twenty-five years Gandhi has been agitating the cause of his countrymen. Within the last three years he became very active. He organized a movement that has swept the entire country of India— a movement that has united the different c[a]ste[s] of India that have been apart for centuries. The British people are now feeling the pressure of Gandhi's propaganda. It is customary for them to suppress the cause of liberty. It is customary of them to execute and imprison the leaders of the cause of liberty everywhere. Therefore Gandhi's arrest is nothing unexpected to those of us who understand what leadership means. Leadership means sacrifice; leadership means martyrdom. Hundreds of thousands of men as leaders have died in the past for the freedom of their country—the emancipation of their respective peoples—and we will expect nothing else from Gandhi but that self-sacrifice and martyrdom that will ultimately free his country and his countrymen.

Garvey regarded Gandhi as "one of the noblest characters of the day" and expressed his deep sympathy with the Indian leader and the anti-imperialist movement of India. He implored African-Americans to emulate the example of Gandhi, especially his self-sacrificing style of leadership. Accompanied by constant applause from the audience, the self-styled "Provisional President of Africa" pledged "the support of all the Negroes of the world" to the cause of Indian independence. Garvey also sent a telegram to the British prime minister, Lloyd George, protesting Gandhi's imprisonment. The continuing reinforcement of the bonds of connection between the Indian and African-American struggles, between the leadership of Gandhi and the leadership of Garvey was a persistent message from the UNIA and its spokesman to the actively listening UNIA constituency, which reached far beyond its official membership.[20]

This, then, was the internationalist setting in which Haridas T. Muzumdar and others like him found a relatively informed and appreciative African-American audience. Understandably, from the outset of his stay in the United States, Muzumdar maintained his association with the UNIA. "My concern to discover what Negro leaders were doing to rectify the situation led me to call on Marcus Garvey," Muzumdar later wrote. He observed that he had come to the United States "full of Gandhi and with plans to write a biography of the Mahatma; hence it was natural that I should talk to [Garvey] about Gandhi's ideas of non-violence and his 'constructive program' as an integral part of Satyagraha." It was not surprising that in 1922 Garvey invited Muzumdar to deliver a series of lectures at mass meetings in Harlem. Determined to make the appropriate connection between the struggles of the Indian people and those of African-Americans and to capture the hearts and minds of his audiences, Muzumdar highlighted their African roots and the achievements of their ancestors. He interspersed his stories about the glorious African past of black Americans with the news of Gandhi's nonviolent freedom movement. To underscore the relevance of Gandhi's example, Muzumdar also spoke about the Indian leader's "crusade in South Africa against racial injustice and discrimination against his people in that part of the world." He wrote that he himself "became interested (1921–22) in the plight of Negroes as second class citizens—especially after I read an account of a lynching in the South. After reading that account I could not eat for two days."[21]

Of course the UNIA, independent of Muzumdar, was already "full of Gandhi" and the Indian struggle. So it was only natural that *The Negro World* provided extensive coverage of Gandhi's arrest and trial. The text of Gandhi's statement in court was published in full in the 6 May 1922 edition of *The Negro World*. In the same issue, Muzumdar contributed an article on the Mahatma. On 3 May, Muzumdar spoke from Liberty Hall in New York on the theme "Gandhi and the Future of India." On 10 May 1922, he was scheduled to give an illustrated talk on India. Muzumdar took part in the August 1922 UNIA convention in New York, where he was introduced to the assembly as a member of Gandhi's noncooperation movement. In his remarks, addressed to the group dealing with Caribbean issues, Muzumdar praised the work of the UNIA and observed that "Indians were suffering in the same way as the Negroes of the West Indies."[22]

To summarize, in the closing years of the nineteenth century and the opening decades of the twentieth century, several influential African-American leaders pointed to the similarities between their movement in the United States and that of the Indian people against the British. Some immensely important ideological, historical, and personal links were established between the Indian struggle for independence and the African-American freedom movement. The nature of worldwide European and U.S. imperialism helped to bring together peoples of color. (In the Caribbean and Guyana, for instance, people of African descent and East Indians formed a common front against their common enemy. Initial contacts between them were established in the nineteenth century, and the two peoples worked together in labor associations.) The connections were initiated by such freedom-oriented intellectuals as W.E.B. Du Bois and Hubert Harrison. The contact which Lajpat Rai made with such diverse African-Americans as Du Bois, Booker T. Washington, and John Hope, on the one hand, and the working relation Muzumdar established with Marcus Garvey and his UNIA, on the other, also helped set the stage for much that happened in subsequent years. More important than all of these were the links which Garvey firmly established in his own thinking and in his teaching. Through his speeches across the country as well as in New York, and through the national circulation of *The Negro World,* hundreds of thousands of African-Americans were kept in continuous contact with Gandhi and the Indian movement. Through Garvey's approach they were challenged to see and feel the connections between the two freedom struggles.[23]

=2=

"Watch the Indian People"

As Indian visitors and African-American leaders opened the world of the Indian struggle to black America, there were clear signs of a rising discussion in the African-American community concerning the meaning, the message, and the methodology of Gandhi's nonviolence. The African-American press played a crucial role in this process. By 1918, less than a decade after its founding, Du Bois's *Crisis* was a widely read journal with a circulation of 100,000. As the official organ of the NAACP, *The Crisis* was its educational and organizational tool. According to the poet Langston Hughes, *"The Crisis* became America's leading publication devoted to the Negro, a position it held for well over a quarter of a century." Its significance in the life of the African-American community was best summed up by Hughes: "My earliest memories of written words are those of Du Bois and the Bible. My . . . grandmother . . . read to me as a child from both the Bible and The Crisis." The extent and the depth of the attention *The Crisis* gave to Gandhi and his movement is an indication of Gandhi's appeal to African-Americans.[1]

The immediate post–World War I years in India were crucial ones for the independence struggle there, and it was during these years that the African-American press's interest in that struggle escalated. Not only did the British government refuse to lift wartime restrictions on the civil liberties of Indians, but following the conclusion of the war, it also introduced the Rowlatt Bills, legislation designed to further curtail these civil liberties. The government sought powers to arrest, confine, or imprison anyone suspected of acts prejudicial to the security of the state. With the passing into law of these bills on 19 March 1919, Britain invited upon itself the wrath of the Indian National Congress. At Gandhi's initiative, six hundred men and women signed a *satyagraha* pledge to launch a nationwide civil disobedience campaign. This boycott campaign, which began with a day of prayer and fasting, was designed to cripple economic life in India's towns and cities. The city of Delhi observed the boycott on 30 March, the rest of the country followed suit on 6 April. Gandhi's opposition to the Rowlatt Act was the Mahatma's first political act in India.[2]

Two weeks after the start of the boycott, the situation in India's northern state of Punjab took an ugly turn. On 13 April 1919, the British massacred hundreds of unarmed demonstrators in the Sikh holy city of Amritsar. The massacre was a turning point for Gandhi. It undermined whatever remained of his faith in the possible goodness of British rule. In addition, the tragedy provided an avenue for him to establish his hold on the Indian Congress. From that point onward, Gandhi became the chief spokesperson and a living symbol of Indian discontent and determination. At its annual convention in December 1920, the Congress unanimously approved the decision to launch the noncooperation movement Gandhi had shaped and adopted *swaraj* (independence) as its goal. With the introduction of the noncooperation program, Gandhi demonstrated even more sharply than before his identification with the poor. Asceticism and voluntary poverty became central to his life and work. Thereafter he adopted the loincloth as his sole dress and pressed harder than ever before for the traditional Indian way of life as the best preparation for the way of independence.[3]

The noncooperation movement in 1921, when the mightiest empire of modern times was actively challenged by an unarmed people of color committed to nonviolence, touched the hearts and minds of African-Americans. From that time onward, African-American interest in Gandhi, his way of nonviolence, and the Indian challenge to British rule became markedly deep and intense. (Indeed, it was not until 1921 that the African-American press beyond *The Crisis* and *The Negro World* began to pay serious attention to Gandhi and the Indian struggle. However, the interest, once kindled, remained strong throughout the decade and in subsequent years.) The noncooperation movement caught the attention of African-American editors, and again it was *The Crisis* that took the lead. In the spring of 1921, a pro-India, interracial American group, the Friends of Freedom for India, held its national convention in New York. It charged that British rule had damaged India's economic, industrial, and social order. The May edition of Du Bois's journal reported these claims. British rule, it contended, served solely the interests of the empire and was "opposed to the welfare of all the Indian people." Moreover, said *The Crisis*, the Indian "industrial system has broken down and has almost wholly disappeared." Widespread illiteracy and the exploitation of women were additional accusations leveled against British imperial rule. In the light of their own experiences of oppression and the denial of fundamental freedoms in the United States, these accounts of the exploitation of the people of India evoked sympathy and moral outrage from many African-Americans.[4]

The July 1921 edition of *The Crisis* provided for its readership three perspectives on Gandhi and the noncooperation movement. The item in the regular column "The Looking Glass" was titled "India's Saint." There John Haynes Holmes, a white Unitarian minister and a member of the board of the NAACP, was reported to have said that "the greatest man in India today is Gandhi." Holmes also compared Gandhi to Jesus Christ. Quoting from an article in *Unity* by J. T. Sunderland, a friend and co-worker of the Indian nationalist Lajpat Rai, the journal informed its readers that India, which had decided to get rid of foreign rule, "prefers not to use force." Sunderland had argued that India "believes that in the end right is might. She has determined, therefore, upon a bloodless revolution." In addition, the journal reproduced for its readers an essay that Basanta Koomar Roy, an Indian scholar, had recently contributed to the *New York American*. Roy focused on the work the Mahatma had done in South Africa and noted that Tolstoy had much appreciated the Indian's work. He wrote of Gandhi's saintliness and gentleness of manner. *The Crisis* concluded that "it is this blameless life of his which has accomplished the incredible— that of bringing together the numerous sects of India. This one phenomenon ought to convey a warning to Great Britain." At an early stage in this encounter between India and Afro-America, then, Gandhi's saintliness and the religious grounding for his freedom movement were emphasized. The force of his personality and the power of his message had a particular appeal for a people who had already defined their own struggle for justice and humanity in religious terms.[5]

At the height of his noncooperation campaign, Gandhi wrote an open letter to every Briton in India in his journal, *Young India*. When *The Crisis* published the entire letter in August 1921, thousands of African-American readers had an opportunity to hear directly from Gandhi about his pilgrimage to noncooperation. The Indian leader explained how over a period of twenty-nine years of active public service, "in the face of circumstances that might well have turned any other man into a rebel," he had cooperated with the British government. The Amritsar massacre, he argued, had made him realize the essential oppressive nature of British rule. From then onwards, Gandhi's challenge to British rule was uncompromising. In a letter he sent to the viceroy announcing the return of all his official British medals, Gandhi had written, "I can retain neither respect nor affection for a government which has been moving from wrong to wrong in order to defend its immorality." *Crisis* readers learned that Gandhi had no illusions about India's capacity to overcome Britain militarily. At the same time, he was sure that there was another battleground—the soul of humanity—and he was determined to challenge his opponents on that high moral ground and invite them to rise to the best in the British tradition. "Bravery of the soul still remains open to us. I know you will respond to that also. I am engaged in evoking that bravery."[6]

The following month *The Crisis* borrowed more material from an article Basanta Roy had contributed to the magazine *Freeman*. "The Boycott in India" carefully explained the boycott programs of the noncooperation campaign. Boycott of British goods, courts, assemblies and elections, government schools and official functions, and the renunciation of titles were some of the key elements of Gandhi's program. Roy noted that "the formidable boycott of British goods in India is inflicting immeasurable injury upon British political prestige and financial power." He further observed that "the first condition of success, according to Gandhi and his followers, is the absolute abstinence from any act of violence. Even violent thoughts and words are to be studiously avoided." Roy was convinced that

non-cooperation is strengthening both the body and soul of India. It is more of a spiritual than a political movement. Whatever may be its outcome, the awakened people of India are at least giving the people of England ample warning that the time has come for a peaceful evacuation of the Indian motherland.

Basanta Roy argued that in the person of Gandhi the nationalist movement had at last found a saintly and public-spirited leader who could unite key elements for the cause of Indian independence. He pointed out that because of his "utter unselfishness of motives" millions of Indians had given this man their "unconditional obedience." Once again, the saintliness of Gandhi's personality and his public-spiritedness were underscored.[7]

The steady flow of information which *The Crisis* was putting forward was often matched in a powerful and moving fashion in the *A.M.E. Church Review*, a popular and respected organ of the African Methodist Episcopal Church, one of the African-American community's most socially conscious denominations. From 1912 to 1924, the journal was edited by the socialist bishop Reverdy C. Ransom (1861–1959). As a member of the Niagara movement, he had worked with Du Bois and others to counter the conservative politics of Booker T. Washington. He was well known for his militancy and his devotion to the removal of legal and social disabilities faced by his community. During his long and active career (he lived to the age of ninety-eight) Ransom exercised a strong influence on many African-Americans, including Paul Laurence Dunbar, Monroe N. Work, and Richard R. Wright, Jr. Placing the Indian leader in the context of religiously inspired social movements of the past, in 1921 Ransom published an editorial titled "Gandhi, Indian Messiah and Saint." It read in part:

From the ranks of the myriad millions of India has recently sprung a new messiah and saint. Gandhi, the new "Light of Asia," would deliver his countrymen from the rule of British imperialism, not by violent resistance, but through the peaceful method of non-cooperation. The Western nations, claiming to be Christian through the centuries, have rejected the doctrine of non-resistance as taught by Christ. Even to this day they are unable to think of concerted resistance save in terms of war. British statesmanship stands appalled at the power of Gandhi's peaceful methods to paralyze the British power in India. The spiritual weapon used by Gandhi is intensely practical.

Describing the noncooperation movement as an ordered spiritual and economic resistance, the editorial pleaded for "the sympathetic understanding of every man who waits for a new birth of freedom in every land." Anticipating the coming of another age, a peaceful age, when war as a means of resolving conflict would be a thing of the past, the editorial suggested that "if the triumph of India should mean the triumph of the spirit and method of Gandhi then indeed would a new day dawn for all mankind." For some race-conscious Christian churchmen like Ransom, such an outcome was even more attractive to consider when it offered the image of a brown man from India using the Christ-like weapon that the white West had rejected.[8]

Obviously, an important sector of "mankind" in search of "a new day" was located right in the United States, and the African-American press was quick to speculate on the meaning of "a new day" for their own oppressed people. This time it was the *Chicago Defender* which measured for its wide-ranging audience the historical possibilities and significance of the Mahatma for African-Americans. Founded in 1905 by the resourceful Robert Sengsttacke Abbott, it played an important role in that African-American community and beyond. Over time the *Chicago Defender* became so influential, both locally and nationally, that African-Americans began to view this Northern-based paper as "the black Bible." Its circulation was especially broad in the Midwest.

In December 1921, *Chicago Defender* columnist A. L. Jackson wrote that the noncooperation movement led by Gandhi was "going to worry somebody." Echoing Holmes's words, Jackson emphasized that "Gandhi is the greatest man in the world today." Recognizing the power and the relevance of the Gandhian method for the African-American struggle, he prophetically stated, "We believe that some empty Jim Crow cars will some day worry our street car magnates in Southern cities when we get around to walking rather than suffer insult and injury to our wives and children." Elaborating on the philosophy of Gandhian nonviolence, Jackson noted that Gandhi had rejected the doctrine of "tooth for a tooth and eye for an eye" and instead "is teaching his countrymen that their real strength lays [*sic*] in complete self-control and self-mastery." He added that the Mahatma "believes in the doctrine taught by the Christ and turns the other cheek twice and yet again if necessary," and that

Gandhi's political activities were based upon an "absolute obedience to a religious philosophy which is capable of very definite political application." Jackson was convinced that African-Americans, Africans, and Egyptians would benefit by giving the Gandhian movement thought and attention. He urged African-Americans to turn their eyes from the South and focus attention on the events in India. Jackson concluded his article with a plea on behalf of African-Americans: "Heaven send us prophets equal to the task." For churchgoing, God-fearing, Jesus-loving African-Americans, this was a familiar message—a religious command. That there was someone who was following the path laid down by Jesus, albeit in a distant land, and who was winning his battle against the mightiest of empires was religion at work. Indeed, it was the religion they had been taught, and in their own way had sought to live.[9]

The *Chicago Defender* was not alone in such observations. African-American opinion makers in a variety of settings encouraged their community to pay attention to the nonviolent Indian struggle. In an editorial in January 1922, *The Crisis* compared the freedom struggles of Ireland and India. While recognizing that the situation in India was "more complicated" than the situation in Ireland, the journal noted that "one party marches toward armed resistance with war on the horizon; another party proposes non-resistance and refusal to cooperate in any work or government with the British masters." The writer found the two struggles "marvellously interesting" and pleaded that "we should watch . . . every step."[10]

Two months later *The Crisis* carried a major article about the life and work of Mahatma Gandhi. The four-thousand-word essay, accompanied by a photograph of the Indian National Congress delegates who had endorsed the noncooperation movement, took up the majority of the journal's space. It provided a biographical statement describing Gandhi's birth, education, and work in South Africa, and his challenge to British rule in India. The anonymous author, whom we might guess to be Du Bois, drew heavily upon several sources, the most notable being Gilbert Murray, a British scholar and outspoken admirer of Gandhi. The essence and the power of Gandhi for the Indian people (and oppressed people everywhere) was forcefully communicated to readers. They were told that the people of India had lost faith in the British government and had turned instead to the exploration of Gandhian notions of noncooperation, nonviolence, and *swaraj*—which were described with sympathetic accuracy.[11]

Meanwhile, as civil disobedience spread in India, the British colonial government arrested hundreds of leading members of the Indian National Congress. Gandhi was arrested in March 1922 and, after a historic trial, was sentenced to six years in prison for his leadership of the nationwide civil disobedience campaign. By the end of the year twenty thousand persons were in jail for their part in the noncooperation movement. This crucial set of events was widely and quickly reported in African-American newspapers. In its 18 March 1922 edition, the *Norfolk Journal and Guide*, a popular African-American weekly which was read throughout the African-American communities of the Atlantic coastal region, addressed the questions of growing unrest in India and Gandhi's arrest eight days earlier. In its editorial, "Sedition Growing in India," the paper noted that in Gandhi the British had arrested a man "whom the Indian people worship for his wisdom and devotion to their interests." The writer noted the success of Gandhi's noncooperation movement and lauded his contribution to bringing about Hindu-Muslim unity. It also warned that "the arrest of Gandhi and other Indian leaders, charged with sedition, is bound to bring on a crisis, the end of which no man can foresee."[12]

The crisis the newspaper predicted never occurred. Before long Gandhi was jailed; he remained in jail until 1924, and India remained relatively peaceful, resigned to a quieter phase in the nation's march toward freedom. Nor did the Mahatma have as remarkable a success as the *Norfolk Journal and Guide* implied in its editorial. Nevertheless, the favorable, if somewhat inflated, assessment of Gandhi and the Indian scene must have left a positive impression with readers.

Two weeks later the *Norfolk Journal and Guide* deplored the arrest of Gandhi in an editorial captioned "The Mystic Ghandhi Imprisoned."* The paper made a strong and fascinating statement about African-American solidarity with the people of India:

> The readers of the *Journal and Guide* are interested in the millions of East Indians because they are an off-color people seeking a larger

---

*Gandhi's name was often misspelled in America during this period. However, the repeated use of *sic* has been avoided.

measure of self-determination and participation in their governmental affairs than the British Government allows them as a part
of the Empire . . . we are further interested in them because they are
in their basic race group descendants of Abraham through Keturah,
to whose six sons he gave gifts and sent them Eastward, in the East
country, their Buddhist and Barhminic [sic] sects denoting their
origin from Abraham.

Whatever the historical basis for the declaration that the people of
India were the descendants of Abraham may be, the claim suggested
another reason for taking the Indian cause to heart. The editorial
writer also noted the religious and social divisions of Indian society,
which had led to the loss of their independence to the British:
"Mohandhas [sic] K. Gandhi has done more than any other man to
harmonize the conflicting opinions of the people, who have come
to regard him as a prophet, a Mystic, one having supernatural
inspiration." The paper argued that the peaceful nature of his noncooperation movement "threatened the supremacy of the British
Government." The editorial announced Gandhi's arrest and concluded that "it is a difficult matter for tyrannical governments to
throttle the aspiration of the oppressed to be free." Clearly the
writer was alluding to more than India here.[13]

The extent and meaning of India's challenge to British rule was
also noted by *The Crisis*. In April 1922, an editorial in that journal
pointed out how Britain was giving in to pressure from the colonies,
"yielding to the darker races, not because it wants to but because
it must." The writer of the editorial also observed that the conces-
sions Britain had been forced to make to India were not enough.
In June 1922, *The Crisis* reproduced parts of two informative articles
from the mainstream press. Syud Hossain, Indian representative to
the 1920 Near East Peace Conference, made a strong case against
the British rule of India in an article he contributed to the *New
York Times*. He was convinced that India needed to

work out her own destiny, unfettered and uncoerced, and make her
own contribution, as in the past, to the culture and civilization of
the world. Not only India, but the world is the poorer for her
present compulsory emasculation and disorganization. The British
have fixed a stranglehold on her creative genius and national growth.
India must be free.

Freedom was the ultimate goal of Gandhi's movement, Hossain declared. He also observed that this fact "has at last begun to dawn even upon the British Government." The British may have realized that at heart the Gandhi-led Indian struggle was about freedom, but we know enough now to appreciate that Britain had no intention then, or for many years to come, of giving up control of India. Nevertheless, such assessments of British misrule and Indian determination to move forward were a source of encouragement to African-Americans fighting for their own freedom, and an invitation to explore seriously the alternatives offered by the Mahatma. In the same edition, *The Crisis* also reprinted a piece by Ralph Anderson of the *Boston Herald*, in which he emphasized that the response to Gandhi's noncooperation call had been encouraging. For instance, he noted, when the Prince of Wales landed in Calcutta, he found the streets deserted; business in the city had come to a standstill because Gandhi "had so commanded."[14]

The October 1922 edition of the *A.M.E. Church Review* carried an article by Lajpat Rai. Using Gandhi's own words, he explained that for Gandhi freedom meant self-reliance. In this article he gave his African-American readers a complete outline of the noncooperation program:

> (a) Rejection of all government titles, honors, and honorary offices, (b) abstention from drink, (c) withdrawal of all boys and girls from a system of education which has reconciled the best of Indians to slavery under foreign domination, without feeling the sting of it, and which has made of them parasites sucking the blood of the classes that produce and work, (d) establishment of such schools and colleges as will give a secondary place to the study of English and other European literature, reserving the first for the spoken languages of India and for manual training, (e) boycott of English forms of "justice," their courts and their lawyers, (f) boycott of foreign cloth and the rehabilitation of Swadeshi (i.e., Indian-made cloth), (g) withdrawal of Indians from the service of the British Government and from service in the British army and the British police, (h) nonpayment of taxes.[15]

This is likely to have provided much food for thought for at least some of the thousands of African-Americans who read it in their church journal.

Before Gandhi was imprisoned in March 1922, Gertrude Emerson, a white American sympathizer, visited India and interviewed the Mahatma. On her return to the United States she shared her observations through some of her writings. One of her articles was reprinted by the *Chicago Defender* in June 1922. "Gandhi in Prison Is Able Force, British Expect Silent Revolt in India by Non-Co-operators" the headline read. First published in the American journal *Asia*, Emerson's interview with the Mahatma raised several basic questions concerning his role in the nonviolent movement and the extent to which the population at large had accepted the way of nonviolence. She pointed out that Gandhi was convinced that "the people of India are receptive to the doctrine of nonviolence." Readers were told that even though Gandhi and several other nationalist leaders were in jail and the noncooperation movement had ended, opposition to British rule was not dead. By challenging British rule directly and openly, Gandhi had harmonized and strengthened nationalist forces. The message was direct and exciting: Indian nationalism had come of age. It was now a major factor in the Indo-British dialogue about the future of the Indian subcontinent.[16]

The change in the Indian-British equation did not go unnoticed by sympathetic black friends of the Indian independence movement. *The Crisis* continued to convey to its readers the uncompromising resolve of the Indian people to regain their freedom. In its May 1923 edition it recorded the observations of Blanche Watson, a well-known white American supporter of the Mahatma, who stated that "to-day, in India, this universal feeling of nationality has not only taken shape, but it is assuming enormous proportions."[17] A sense of cultural identity and the will to create a new nation was taking shape and coming into sharper focus than ever before in India under the leadership of Gandhi, and for African-Americans Gandhi had become the window to India and its struggle for freedom.

At the same time, not all African-Americans agreed on the meaning of the Gandhian movement. Much as many black Americans admired the Mahatma, approved of his method of nonviolence, and sympathized with him in his efforts to remove the British from power, at least some had serious reservations about the relevance of his way to their situation. In the course of the rising discussion, an early, significant voice which entertained doubts about the validity of nonviolence was that of E. Franklin Frazier, a highly respected African-American sociologist who taught at Howard University. In his lengthy piece in *The Crisis* in March 1924, he took issue with those who advocated what he called Christian humility as a method for bringing about change in the condition of African-Americans, and he challenged those who condemned blacks when they used force "in defending their firesides, on the ground that it is contrary to the example of non-resistance set by Jesus." He argued that it was not enough to remember that Jesus encouraged us to be meek. Placing the life and teachings of Jesus in a socio-political setting, he spoke of Jesus' "unrestrained denunciation of the injustice and hypocrisy of His day and His refusal to make any truce with wrong-doers." As for following the way of love, Frazier was firmly of the view that "a few choice souls may rise to a moral elevation where they can love those who oppress them," but that African-Americans needed justice and not love.

> Perhaps, in the distant future, men may love each other so that they will not need to define their rights and duties in society; but in the present stage of social evolution, we prefer to fight for the observance of the established principles of democratic political society. Where love has appeared of such dubious value, as in the South, we take our stand under the banner, *Fiat Justitia, ruat Amor* [Let justice be done, let love burst forth].[18]

Du Bois later reported that *The Crisis* had received "one or two letters protesting against the spirit of" Frazier's article, and it provided the author further space to reply in the editorial column in its June 1924 edition. Frazier made it clear that while he did not believe that African-Americans could gain their objectives through wholesale violence, he was convinced that "violent defense in local and specific instances has made white men hesitate to make wanton attacks upon Negroes." His primary concern was "in saving the Negro's self-respect." If it was possible to do so without hating the other person, that was fine, but, he wrote a person's "refusal to strike back is not always motivated by a belief in the superiority of moral force any more than retaliation is always inspired by courage." He believed that "it would be better for the Negro's soul to be seared with hate than dwarfed by self-abasement." Frazier said his "essay was directed against those Negro leaders who through cowardice and for favors deny that the Negro desires the same treatment as other men." Furthermore, the sociologist was disturbed that the advocates of nonresistance "are silent in the face of barbarous treatment of their people and would make us believe this is the Christian humility." He assured his critics that he was not opposed to those who believed "in the brotherhood of man and the superiority of moral force," yet he was firmly of the view that principles of nonviolent resistance were not practical for African-Americans.

> But suppose there should arise a Gandhi to lead Negroes without hate in their hearts to stop tilling the fields of the South under the peonage system; to cease paying taxes to States that keep their children in ignorance; and to ignore the iniquitous disfranchisment and Jim-Crow laws. I fear we would witness an unprecedented massacre of defenseless black men and women in the name of Law and Order and there would scarcely be enough Christian sentiment in America to stay the flood of blood.

At one level, Frazier's statements in *The Crisis* were in response to the experience of those who were actively working for justice; at another level, he was instrumental in pushing people to consider the question of method more seriously. Clearly, Frazier's reflections demonstrated that there was no unanimity over the application of nonviolence by African-Americans in their fight for freedom.[19]

Meanwhile, other issues raised by Gandhi's movement continued to concern African-Americans. For instance, according to Gandhi, economic freedom was an essential ingredient of self-rule. Towards that end, he initiated a major program of self-reliant nation building which included the production of homespun cloth. Gandhi even produced cloth himself; he did not want others to do what he himself was not practicing. Equally, he felt that the leadership of the Indian National Congress should participate in such an activity; the *Chicago Defender*, in its edition of 10 January 1925, noted that "Mohandas Gandhi who is president-elect of the annual Indian national congress has stipulated as a condition to retaining leadership that every member must spin 2,000 yards of yarn monthly." The paper also reported that Gandhi had won 200 out of the 212 delegates over to his side. The *Chicago Defender* informed its subscribers that the "boycott of foreign cloths [*sic*] and encouragement of home spinning" were among the objectives of the noncooperation movement of the Mahatma.[20]

Even though opinions varied, attention to India and Gandhi on the part of African-Americans and their journals never slackened. As the decade progressed, Indian nationalists pressed Britain for complete freedom. With a view toward weakening Indian determination to gain its freedom, the government in Westminster set up a body called the Simon Commission to consider the terms and conditions under which India might be granted greater freedom. Typically, Indians were excluded from this commission, and *The Crisis* noted the unfairness of the British decision in its January 1928 edition, sarcastically suggesting "England has convinced the world that it would be unfair, you know, to put Indians on a committee to investigate home-rule in *India*."[21]

In the same edition, *The Crisis* also drew attention to Mahatma Gandhi's *An Autobiography: The Story of My Experiments with Truth*, which was written in 1927 but not published in the United States until 1948. (John Haynes Holmes published the autobiography in installments in his Unitarian journal *Unity* from Chicago, 5 April 1926 to 25 November 1929.) The item focused on a white barber's refusal in South Africa to cut Gandhi's hair. "I certainly felt hurt," Gandhi recorded in his autobiography; then he noted that in India caste Hindus "do not allow our barbers to serve our untouchable brethren." African-Americans who read this item could not have failed to identify with Gandhi's sense of injury; readers must also have been impressed with the implied moral consistency of Gandhi's stand against untouchability, which made social outcasts of millions and excluded them from the political and economic processes of society. Considering that the plight of African-Americans was often compared to that of the Untouchables in India, it is likely that Gandhi's position on this question meant a great deal to the oppressed descendants of Africans.[22]

Before 1928 was over, India had lost Lajpat Rai. A courageous and committed man, he served the national cause for nearly three decades, until a police beating in India caused his untimely death. The news of his death moved his friend Du Bois to write that "every member of the 800,000,000 darker peoples of the world should stand with bowed heads in memory of Lajpat Rai, the great leader of India, who died of English violence because he dared persist in his fight for freedom." As noted above, Rai had focused special attention on the condition of African-Americans during his earlier visit to the United States, and he was known to *Crisis* readers. In

May 1929, *The Crisis* described him as a "martyr to British intolerance." Consistently, artfully, faithfully, Du Bois insisted that his readers face India, consider Gandhi and other leaders of his movement, and reflect on the meaning of that struggle in the North American setting.[23]

Other African-American journals did the same for their readers. In 1928, in the midst of his program of nation-building, the Mahatma inspired and instructed the farmers of Bardoli, Gujarat, to resist the government when it raised the taxes by as much as 20 percent. Led by Vallabhbhai Patel, the farmers organized a highly successful *satyagraha* against the government and held their ground, refusing to pay the tax hike. Soon the *Chicago Defender* carried an extensive comment about what could have been considered an obscure incident. Mary Church Terrell, a prominent educational leader who was also a writer and activist, wrote of the Bardoli campaign, "The peasants of India have beaten the British, but not with machine guns or gas." She described the firm resolve of the Indian farmers and also pointed out how the British found themselves ineffective in the face of the disciplined nonviolent resisters:

> The British officials found they could not cope with these peaceable, industrious people, because as soon as they would eject one peasant from his land, his neighbor would return, and before they had driven him out the first one was back again on his field. The revolt had become so great that the British had to do one of two things— either they had to imprison the whole population of 30,000,000 people, or they had to submit the case to a board of arbitration, as the farmers demanded. Naturally, they decided not to try to put 30,000,000 people in prison. . . . They [farmers] offered no physical violence whatsoever, though they themselves were often molested, their buffalo beaten to death and their property blown away like sawdust. The peasants were following instructions laid down by their leader, the great Mahatma Gandhi, who has assured them that they can eventually force the British to grant them home rule and accede to their other just demands by simply failing to cooperate with them, manufacture their own material and boycott the English goods.

This was a watershed event. The victory of the farmers of Bardoli, Terrell rightly suggested, "is a wonderful illustration of what an oppressed people can do who organize against injustice perpetrated upon them by the rich and powerful." In conclusion she wrote, "Just watch the people of India who have allowed the British to oppress them for years!" By now, this had become a persistent theme in black journals—"Watch the people of India." For many it was a deliberate and focused attention, a way to educate and embolden people to follow the Indian example.[24]

In 1929 *The Crisis* celebrated its twentieth anniversary. Du Bois invited Mohandas Karamchand Gandhi to contribute to the journal's special anniversary issue. In July 1929 Du Bois published, on the front page of *The Crisis*, "To the American Negro, A Message from Mahatma Gandhi." Du Bois provided a brief introductory biographical sketch of the Indian leader and his work in South Africa and India, and concluded his introduction with these words: "Agitation, non-violence, refusal to cooperate with the oppressor, became [Gandhi's] watchword and with it he is leading all India to freedom. . . . here and today he stretches out his hand in fellowship to his colored friends of the West." In his signed message, Gandhi wrote:

Let not the 12 million Negroes be ashamed of the fact that they are the grand children of the slaves. There is no dishonour in being slaves. There is dishonour in being slaveowners. But let us not think of honour or dishonour in connection with the past. Let us realise that the future is with those who would be truthful, pure and loving. For, as the old wise men have said, truth ever is, untruth never was. Love alone binds and truth and love accrue only to the truly humble.[25]

In the light of African-American interest in Gandhi and India, it was not surprising that the Mahatma's words quickly spread beyond *The Crisis*. For instance, the *New York Amsterdam News* informed its readers of Gandhi's message; on its Op-Ed page, the paper stated, "A message from Mahatma Gandhi, the great spiritual leader of the people of India to the American Negro, on the occasion of the twentieth anniversary of the National Association for the Advancement of the Colored People, is published in the Crisis Magazine for July."[26]

Throughout the third decade of the century, then, African-American journals and newspapers remained attentive to a number of crucial developments of the nonviolent Indian independence movement and kept that world open to their readers. At the same time, in the pages of some periodicals the major representatives of the community explored key elements of Gandhi's doctrine of non-violent resistance, such as boycott and noncooperation. The debate about the relevance of Gandhian nonviolence for black Americans—a debate which was to continue for many years—originated in this period.

Interestingly enough, from the outset African-American news-papers and journals gave considerable attention to the personal qualities and leadership style of the Mahatma. The notion that in Gandhi the world had a Christ-like figure had begun to take root among the opinion makers of the community. The power and mean-ing of such an insight for a people whose personal, social, and political existence was permeated by their religion is not difficult to understand, and Gandhi himself became a symbolic challenge not only to racism in the United States but also to "white" Chris-tianity. In 1922, in an editorial probably written by Du Bois, *The Crisis* made one of its most telling observations about the deeper meaning of the challenge of Gandhi for Christianity:

> White Christianity stood before Gandhi the other day and, let us all confess, it cut a sorry figure. This brown man looked into the eyes of the nervous white judge and said calmly, "It is your business to enforce the law and send me to jail; or if you do not believe that the law is right, it is your business to resign." Can you imagine such a judge resigning? Gandhi is in jail. So is English Christianity.[27]

African-Americans' continued interest in Gandhi, especially through their press, also helped to make the Indian leader accessible to and for their struggle in a psychological sense. In other words, "Watch the people of India" was precisely what many African-Americans did. The process continued to deepen and in subsequent years many African-Americans began to raise the call for the coming of "a Black Gandhi" among them.

=3=

"We Need a Gandhi"

BUILDING ON the attention given during the 1920s by the African-American press to Gandhi and the nonviolent Indian movement, the next stage of this connection was set to unfold as the next decade opened. Indeed, partly as a result of British miscalculations and intransigence, the entire world was soon to hear much more of the Mahatma and his inspired leadership. In the late 1920s the Simon Commission (after its chairman, Sir John Simon) had met without Indian participation to determine India's future relationship to "the mother country." The commission's refusal to take seriously nationalist calls for independence led the Indian National Congress to call for a major new campaign of civil disobedience in December 1929. Gandhi was given carte blanche to develop its specific elements.[1]

After a period of silence, searching, and meditation, Gandhi chose the apparently mundane but politically powerful issue of the British tax on the Indian manufacture of salt. The great Salt March of 1930 was the result. On 6 April 1930, the day after the conclusion of the 240-mile march (which took Gandhi and his colleagues twenty-four days and drew the attention of the whole of India and of the world), Gandhi, by symbolically taking a pinch of salt from the sea, broke the salt laws which gave the British government the monopoly over the manufacture and sale of salt in India. He appealed to the rest of the nation to follow suit. The people obeyed, filling up the jails by the thousands. Immediately African-Americans tuned into these epoch-making events. In its April 1930 edition *The Crisis* called out, "And now let the world sit and watch the most astonishing of the battles of peace which it has ever seen: The civil disobedience campaign in India, led by *Gandhi* and *Nehru* [original italics]." The following month the journal, in its "As the Crow Flies" column, declared, "*Gandhi* marches to the Sea!"[2]

Meanwhile, in a *Chicago Defender* article on "World Unrest," Julius J. Adams noted that European powers were aware of the discontent and dissension within their colonies. Concerning the situation in India, Adams perceptively observed that Gandhi was "seeking to have himself appointed dictator of 'civil disobedience,' a position created recently." As was his practice, the Mahatma ensured that he had the ultimate say in planning and executing the civil disobedience campaign which would finally break the British will to rule India. The Indian leader, Adams wrote, "has always been a power, and a thorn in the side of the British government." Gandhi, he suggested, was preparing to strike at the most opportune moment. The *Chicago Defender* invited a variety of writers to contribute to the column "Sidelights." In February 1930, its author was Frank R. Crosswaith, a key union organizer for the Brotherhood of Sleeping Car Porters who would become a co-worker of A. Philip Randolph in the World War II March on Washington Movement to end discrimination in the defense industries and the armed services. Crosswaith made a stirring plea to the international community, especially the League of Nations, to respond to legitimate demands for freedom from among the darker peoples of the world. He demanded that Euro-America "get off the backs of the darker races and allow these peoples, whose feet were the first to tread the path of civilization, an opportunity to enjoy the independence and liberty which are rightly theirs."[3]

Thoughtful observers in the African-American community recognized the basic connections between Gandhian nonviolence and the way of Jesus Christ. "Passive Resistance of Gandhi" was the title of an article the Howard University scholar and teacher Kelly Miller contributed to the *New York Amsterdam News* at the end of April. He contended that Gandhi was aware of the martial disadvantages as well as the helplessness of the Indian people, that "like his great master, the Christ, he [Gandhi] makes a virtue of necessity, and urges his people to gain the righteous end by passive resistance," and that Gandhi preached nonviolence because he did not have "the competitive power to throw off the British yoke." Miller believed prudence had dictated that Gandhi fall back "on the more subtle and powerful weapon of meekness and non-resistance." Regardless of the accuracy or inaccuracy of Miller's speculation, he came to the heart of matter when he compared the situation of African-Americans with that of the Indians, declaring that "Gandhi is now utilizing the most efficient weapon available to him."[4]

Miller also underscored the differences between their situations. African-Americans were vastly outnumbered and therefore did not stand a chance against the might of the dominant white forces. A violent struggle was also likely to delay the ultimate success of their cause, he argued. To "resist and die," which he suggested was the way of Denmark Vesey and Nat Turner, who led violent rebellions against slavery in the nineteenth century, was not a practical course of action. In his view, recourse to the legal system was the most appropriate avenue, and the NAACP was the appropriate agency to utilize this weapon. Defining "moral protest . . . [as] nothing but passive resistance," he pointed out that "the Negro's whole upward struggle has been on this basis." Given his concern for the moral factor in public affairs, Miller emphasized the importance of right means: "Nothing is settled that is not settled right. Any cause which is right will ultimately be rightly settled in harmony with the moral economy of the universe." He was sure that India would regain its freedom because dominion of one nation or race by another is against the moral order of the universe. Miller concluded that "the American Negro can learn valuable lessons from Mahatma Gandhi, who represents the best living embodiment of that mind which was also in Christ." Clearly Miller's advocacy of the Gandhian alternative was forceful and to the point. By hinging his argument to the religious dimension, especially the teachings of Jesus Christ, Miller made the concept of nonviolent resistance even more acceptable to his audience than it might otherwise have been.[5]

As the Indian freedom movement pressed for greater gains, African-American writers continued to draw parallels for their readers. In an obituary he wrote for Neval H. Thomas, a courageous and socially conscious teacher from Washington, D.C., Miller compared this African-American with Gandhi. Though he did not always agree with Thomas, Miller greatly admired this devoted and unstoppable fighter for the African-American cause. He pointed to the self-sacrifice of the Indian leader, how he had set aside the lucrative gains of a successful legal practice and adopted a loincloth to redeem the Indian people. In a like manner, Neval Thomas had renounced the comforts and successes of life to serve his community, he concluded. What Thomas meant to his community, there is no precise way of knowing. But Miller, by comparing him to Gandhi, helped to make the way and the life of Gandhi even more accessible to the lives of ordinary people.[6]

As in the 1920s, so also in this decade; not all voices were those of unrelieved praise. For instance, the *Pittsburgh Courier*, though favorably disposed to Gandhi and the Indian struggle, did carry occasional critical comments by George Schuyler, a noted writer and social analyst whose column "Views and Reviews" appeared regularly on the editorial page. In May of 1930, Schuyler raised serious doubts about the usefulness of Gandhi's nonviolent strategy in defeating the British: "Mahatma Gandhi is finding out what every sensible person ought to know, to wit, that you cannot over-throw [t]he government merely by non-co-operating non-resistance." He predicted violence, death, and suffering "whether it is desired or not." Without providing details, Schuyler noted that violence had spread in India and that Gandhi was unable to stop it. In contrast to Gandhi, whom he regarded as ineffective, Schuyler said he admired the "common sense" of the Bolsheviks, who recognized the necessity of using violence. Summing up his political and philosophical outlook, Schuyler declared that "government is established by force and violence and it can only be overturned in the same manner." He concluded his piece by chiding African-Americans for their advocacy of Gandhian nonviolence. Howard University's president, Mordecai Johnson, who was a great admirer of the Mahatma and his ways, came in for Schuyler's particular criticism: "Of course, Gandhism appeals to some of our superficial Negro thinkers like Mordecai Johnson because it seems to offer a chance to be revolutionary and secure at the same time which is never possible." No ordinary interpreter of the African-American scene, Schuyler not only stirred up much debate about a variety of subjects—racism, capitalism, socialism, Marxism, violence versus nonviolence, and imperialism—in the process of putting forth his extensive criticism and controversial views he also became an intellectual force which could not be ignored. By often articulating unpopular positions, Schuyler could be relied upon to keep a subject or a notion alive in the minds of his readers. From the time he began his writing career with A. Philip Randolph as a contributor to *The Messenger* until his death in 1977, Schuyler was a significant organizer and mobilizer of public opinion.[7]

The criticism of George Schuyler notwithstanding, by 1930 it was not uncommon for African-American journals and newspapers to present Gandhi to their readers as one of the foremost sages and seers of human history. Comparing Gandhi to the Buddha, Mohammed, and Jesus Christ and lauding the moral leadership in world affairs which Asia was taking, African-American writers, leaders, and spokespersons encouraged their people to learn from India. For instance, in July 1930 *The Crisis* declared that it was in India under the leadership of Gandhi, and not in the West, which professed faith in the Christian way, that "the cheek-turning ethics of Jesus Christ" were being tried out at a political level. "Today," the journal stated, "an attempt to conduct a great revolution, the object of which is the emancipation of several hundred millions of human beings, is being carried on by a program of passive resistance and civil disobedience."[8] It was no accident that one African-American interpreter after another continued to define Gandhi and his movement in Christian terms. The strategy made eminent practical sense. Over time, it also became a factor in making Gandhian nonviolence available to many who saw their lives and the African-American struggle rooted in the way of Jesus Christ.

In the same issue, *The Crisis* also claimed that the "mighty experiment" in India, along with the "effort of Russia to organize work and distribute income according to some rule of reason, are the greatest events of the modern world." Inviting African-Americans to keep abreast of developments, the writer made a plea that "the black folk of America should look upon the present birth-pains of the Indian nation with reverence, hope and applause."[9] In other words, the familiar message was repeated—"Watch the Indian people."

A few months later, the "Observations" column in the *Chicago Defender*, which was penned by O. R. Burns, a labor organizer, invited its readers to attend to the serious issues of their time. Until African-Americans changed their habits, Burns argued, people of color at home and abroad would continue to be oppressed. Finding the struggle in India an example worthy of emulation, he encouraged his readers to consider what was happening in that faraway land.

On your way home, perhaps, you have been reading of that 'wan spirit of a prisoned soul,' Ghandi, dramatically marching to the sea, or of his imprisonment and the brutal slaying of his people by brute British force and, perhaps, in some vague way you are asking yourself the question, "Why, oh why, must repression always and everywhere be the lot of fine souls housed within dark-colored bodies."

The answer, he suggested, "may be found in the oft-repeated question, 'How'd the Sox come out today?' " Expressing a concern about the victimization and brutalization of young people, he argued that African-Americans devoted their "energies to trifles" instead of to "a vigorous, sustained and concerted effort to secure decent treatment for our children." The writer challenged his readers to contrast their attitude with "that of the East Indian followers of the 'Mahatma.' " Burns was convinced that the people of India, though they had not yet won their case against the British, had demonstrated the power of nonviolent resistance. He further emphasized the "unreadiness" of his own people when he added,

> From present observations I conclude that if a Ghandi should arise here in Chicago on the South side and attempt to focus the attention of the world upon some grave injustice that was daily being given to our people, and to do this would attempt to lead a march to the lake, perhaps 5,000 would start with him, but he would lose 4,000 as he passed the first scoreboard and a large percentage of those remaining would fall out of line to phone somewhere to find out 'How'd the Sox come out today.'[10]

Although there is no precise way of determining how accurate Burns's critique of the people of his community was, he certainly communicated the potential power of Gandhi's example for African-Americans.

And Burns was not alone. By then there could be no doubt that in its coverage of the Indian struggle the African-American press had been relentless in its traditional task of informing its community of the perspective of the oppressed colored people of the world. For instance, mindful of the distorted view of events in India projected by British officials in the United States, who emphasized the achievements of the colonial administration and the gift of self-governing institutions which Britain had made to India, the August 1930 *Crisis* expressed the hope that African-Americans were "watching with bated breath the struggle in India." The writer, as others had done before, observed that the Indians were "succeeding to an unparalleled degree by the method of peaceful agitation." Convinced that "nothing like this has occurred in the history of the world," the journal suggested that the success of the Indian experiment "will revolutionize civilization." Commenting upon the Simon Commission's report, *The Crisis* pointed out that "twenty-five years ago it would have been a landmark and a beacon. Ten years ago it would have staved off revolution. Today, it is the last refuge of reaction."[11]

The call from the African-American press to watch Gandhi was, of course, being taken up by other forces in the society as well. In 1930, *satyagraha* was the focus of a major book. Richard B. Gregg, a white Quaker student of Gandhian nonviolence, published *The Power of Non-violence*, the result of a four-year study in India. As might be expected, the book was quickly brought to the attention of Du Bois's readers, and *The Crisis* claimed that Gregg's work was an effort to put Gandhian ideas "into Western terms in order to make it more understandable in America." Indeed, the author, who was deeply committed to Gandhi's way, made it clear that the Americans about whom he was most concerned were the African-Americans. He had written Du Bois, "I am sending the first copies that I have received, for I believe it is more important for Negroes . . . to understand this new method of handling conflict than for any other groups of the population." Gregg agreed with Gandhi "that once it [nonviolent resistance] is understood and used in disciplined, organized mass fashion, there will be an end to tyranny and oppression of all kinds." He wanted to help build connections between African-Americans and what he termed "the most momentous struggle anywhere in the world," and Du Bois was more than ready to continue to help.[12] Here, then, was another significant and deliberate attempt to bring Gandhi and his concept of nonviolent resistance to the attention of African-Americans in their struggle against racism and for fundamental human rights in the United States. And we now know that they took seriously the Gandhian method of resolving conflicts. Perhaps Gregg's encouragement helped to sow another seed which ultimately bore rich fruit in the 1950s and 1960s in the Southern nonviolent freedom movement.

The Mahatma was also the subject of attention from the African-American pulpit. Dr. H. H. Proctor, a noted preacher and lecturer of his time, focused on Gandhi in a sermon he gave in February 1931 at the Nazarene Congregational Church in New York. Reporting the event, the *Pittsburgh Courier* said that Proctor praised Gandhi and identified the Mahatma as "not only the greatest statesman in the east, but also the one public man most like Christ in spirit, purpose and method in the world today."[13]

The African-American press continued to express support for the Indian cause. In the "Postscript" column in the January edition of *The Crisis*, Du Bois wrote about "Magnificent India."

> First, there is a Gandhi, with his passive resistance, an apostle of Peace . . . [who] puts to shame the professional pacifist, who means less than nothing. . . . Finally, there is the splendor of India in London [at the Round Table Conference]. Prince and Untouchable, Muslim and Hindu, all standing shoulder to shoulder, when England counted upon disunion and mutual jealousies and hatreds to perpetuate her tyranny in India. . . . Magnificent India, to reveal to the world the inner rottenness of European imperialism. Such a country not only deserves to be free, it will be free.[14]

In the light of the realities of the Indian situation, Du Bois's statement smacked of romanticism. For by this time the Muslim League had emerged in India as a serious contender with the Indian National Congress for Muslim loyalty in certain regions, and a large body of Untouchables, under the gifted and inspiring leadership of Bhimjirao Ambedkar, had become disenchanted with Gandhi and the Congress. There was much jockeying for power. Nevertheless, Du Bois's romanticism is an important indicator of the deep desire that people like him had for the communication and development of a Gandhian spirit among African-Americans.

In an editorial on 7 February 1931, the *Norfolk Journal and Guide*, noting Gandhi's release from prison so that he might participate in parleys with the British government in London, pointed out that "Britain has at last recognized that Gandhi is the man in India to be reckoned with and the man who holds the key to the situation," and that "oppressed peoples throughout the world are watching Gandhi with sympathy in his aspirations for the Indian peoples. They realize that the success of his cause weakens the rod of oppression the world over." This key assumption of linkage permeated the African-American press.[15]

In a February 1931 editorial, "If We Had a Ghandi," the *Pittsburgh Courier* claimed that "the Negroes of the United States of America could learn a great lesson from the emaciated, quiet but resolute Ghandi," that his message of love, peace, and struggle based on nonviolent noncooperation offered a way and a hope. The editorial writer reminded the readers that Gandhi did not take arms nor did he invite his fellow Indians to take up arms, but instead "set about to build an army of public opinion against British rule by a simple sacrifice which has finally moved the entire population of India. . . . and the beautiful thing about his leadership is the complete and abiding faith of his people in the man." The paper suggested that the Indian example should encourage African-Americans to do likewise, that African-Americans might begin by supporting their leaders in the manner of the followers of Gandhi. Then, with sentiments bordering on despair, the editorial asked, "But where, oh where, in these United States of America is there a man who could win the plaudits and approval of his colored brethren?" The writer doubted if Gandhi-like leadership among African-Americans was likely to "enjoy half the confidence that Ghandi enjoys." With an eye on the larger community, the editorial ended with these words:

> If we had a Ghandi in this country—or, better yet, if we had the following of a Ghandi in this country—we might liberate ourselves from some of the ills of which we complain. The man who would undertake to be a Ghandi in this country would probably be called a fool.[16]

The possibility of raising up a Gandhi-like leader in the African-American community continued to provoke discussion in forums like the *Pittsburgh Courier*. Emphasizing the importance of the spiritual in the struggle for justice and humanity, it rightly argued that the African-American community's historical tradition was consistent with the search for a spiritual leader—an emphasis true to the courageous witness of a nineteenth-century mystic and rebel Nat Turner or A.M.E. Bishop Henry McNeil Turner. Gandhi, the carrier of soul force, was a familiar figure. Here was a spiritual leader who became a political force, a person who invested an apparent political struggle with profound religious meaning. This theme of the search for such a leader was never abandoned in African-American journals.

In his feature, "Between the Lines" in the *Norfolk Journal and Guide* of mid-March 1931, Gordon Hancock, a celebrated educator, clergyman, and journalist, made an eloquent plea for an African-American Gandhi. "Wanted: A Black Reformer" was the title of his essay. That the Mahatma had brought his people closer to their goal of freedom was most significant for Hancock, but even more important was the fact that the Indian leader, by opting for "the more excellent way" of nonviolence, "has set the world an example of soul greatness that must bear fruit through many ages." Spiritual power was more powerful than military power, Hancock believed. Making a vital religious connection, he noted that "not since Jesus was in the flesh upon earth has this world had such [a] vivid picture of the power that resides in a lofty ideal"; the secret of the Mahatma was his "love for India—for all mankind." Then Hancock pressed the most vital issue: "From Gandhi's love for India, the Negro race in this country has a most powerful suggestion and one which may be useful in the tribulations the race will come upon not many years hence." Without naming names, he attacked the "silly snobbery" of certain African-American leaders and challenged them to emulate the simple life-style of the Indian leader whom he found to be neither a snob nor a "high-hatter."

There must be a reformation within the Negro race! More and more we must turn our minds and hearts to spiritual values. In the last analysis there is more hope for the Negro in a loin-cloth with the spirit of a Gandhi than in a broadcloth with notions he has no way of satisfying. The reformation must first come in our leadership which is at present straining to maintain the material standards set by white men with world-wide dominion. IT CANNOT BE DONE! The Negro's slavish devotion to the white man's sumptuary standard will more and more become a detriment.

The sooner some black Gandhi comes with a reform program dedicated to revising our standards to conform to our economic opportunity, the better it is going to be for the Negro race. A tolerable existence does not necessarily mean abundance and luxury as we now suppose in too many cases. Life has a spiritual content that an oppressed and circumscribed people would do well to seek after! An abundant life does not mean material abundance and the Negro race needs some Black Reformers to drive that powerful truth! Wanted: A BLACK REFORMER![17]

In the person of Gandhi, the vision and the way came together. For their part, African-Americans had come to realize that the miracle which was afoot in India was desirable and possible in the United States. And in order for that to happen, it was necessary for the African-American community to put forward a black Gandhi.

An important debate was taking place. In the 12 September 1931 edition of the *Pittsburgh Courier*, George Schuyler again took a very different tack and published a scathing attack on Gandhi. In general, his criticisms and reservations were about the efficacy of nonviolence and the non-applicability of Gandhian simplicity among African-Americans. On this occasion, however, he criticized Gandhi as a person as well as his methodology of nonviolence. Schuyler argued that the Indian leader had "swayed scores of millions largely because his program is so mythical and so unsound." He wrote that "many of his disciples who yell loudest for the ousting of the British are merely eager to themselves climb on the backs of the horribly exploited Indian masses who are underpaid and oppressed chiefly by capitalists of their own color." About the outcome of the round table conference which had been called by the British to discuss the future of India, Gandhi had said that it all depended on God. These sentiments drew the maximum wrath from the *Pittsburgh Courier* columnist. In his typically cynical style, Schuyler added that "whenever a big leader begins talking about 'God' taking a hand, he is either insincere or ignorant."[18]

Given the pro-Gandhi editorial policy of the *Pittsburgh Courier*, it was not surprising to find in the next week's issue a letter answering Schuyler's criticisms. It was given a prominent place and a bold headline in the column "What the People Think." The headline read "Schuyler on Ghandi, Courier Reader Takes Slam at Noted Columnist Because of His Attitude on Ghandi." The correspondent, who used the pseudonym P.T.O., claimed that there was nothing mythical about "an active program headed by Ghandi," and added that "the entire British nation, including the Anglo-Saxon officials in India, will differ emphatically from this statement of Mr. Schuyler." Gandhi's economic boycott of British products,

said the writer, was aimed at encouraging the development of domestic industries. The Mahatma's active program, he continued,
had substantially damaged British trading interests in India and
was responsible for the growth of indigenous industries. Pointing
to the importance of Gandhi's methodology of nonviolent noncooperation, "P.T.O." wrote, "Mr. Ghandi has reduced the twentieth century imperialistic philosophy of force to an absurdity. The
most efficient colonial army in the British Empire is rendered powerless by the simple biblical advice of 'turning of the other
cheek.' "[19]

Schuyler's claim that Gandhi's talk of God's involvement smacked
of insincerity or ignorance was also questioned by the correspondent;
such an attempt to belittle Gandhi's stature was "blasphemous."
"P.T.O." further suggested that Schuyler's taking on Gandhi was
like "a poodle confronting a St. Bernard." Gandhi, the correspondent believed, "stands preeminently [as] the greatest figure in the
civilized world today." Indeed, the writer asked whether "anyone
during the past nineteen hundred years [had] given to the world a
more practical and successful interpretation of the Sermon on the
Mount." Gandhi's "belief in his 'God,' " the correspondent
concluded,

> with all the fanaticism and religiosity of the orthodox Hindu, should
> not and cannot be compared with similar professions of belief, let
> us say, by J. P. Morgan or Bishop [James] Cannon of the Methodist
> Church, Inc.—nay, not even of a prosperous Negro Baptist minister.
>
> This great man's entire life, his self-denial, his renunciation of
> all worldly goods, his love of truth, his martyrdom—all attest to
> the divinity within him, which may be, after all, the 'God' of which
> he speaks.
>
> Go slowly, Mr. Schuyler. Of the two greatest leaders in the colored
> world today, Ghandi and Garvey (whether the latter name is hurtful
> or not), both cannot be ignorant or insincere and at the same time
> command such stupendous following.[20]

In the fall of 1931, when Gandhi headed for London to participate
in the second round table conference, a conference forced on the
British government by the insistent power of the independence
movement, the African-American press kept up its watch. Du Bois

wrote, "Gandhi in a loin cloth with a quart of rice starts out to conquer Europe. David was a piker and Goliath the world's Easy-Mark compared with this." In an editorial in September 1931, the *Pittsburgh Courier* also reported on the progress of the conference. The paper noted that Gandhi "was an unusually brilliant man" because he refused "to bow to the conventions of European civilization." The writer said that the Indian leader warned the British that "if they don't get down to business he will leave the conference."[21]

The following month, the *Pittsburgh Courier* highlighted the Mahatma's use of the economic weapon of boycott in bringing the British down to its heels. "Gandhi is not a saint, but he is a clever politician who knows how to use showmanship, the spiritual appeal and economic pressure to gain freedom for his people," the paper noted in an editorial. It argued that as a result of Gandhi's boycott of British cloth hundreds of thousands of English workers were unemployed. There was a message in this for African-Americans:

> American Negroes can also gain a large measure of economic independence by use of the boycott. We spend two billion dollars annually for food and we can buy that food where we want to. We can favor the man who is fair to us, giving us employment, and we can pass up the man who is willing to sell us goods but unwilling to give us jobs. Or, we can purchase the necessities of life through consumers' co-operatives owned by Negro consumers. Either method will get us more jobs, better goods and more respect.

The writer was convinced that "the economic weapon is more powerful than the lethal weapon," and urged the African-American resistance to use it. Not altogether an original technique, the boycott played an important role in Gandhi's nonviolent struggle. African-Americans paid attention to this important instrument in Gandhi's concept of *satyagraha*, and in time put it to effective use in their own struggle.[22]

In October 1931, Du Bois contributed to the *New York Amsterdam News* three articles on India. In the first article, of 7 October, he gave an overview of India's religious, political, and cultural history and underscored the glorious heritage of that land. Reflecting on the importance of the growing nationalist opposition to British rule, Du Bois declared that "today India is occupying a front seat in the drama of the world." Forever in solidarity with the oppressed, Du Bois argued that "the great mass of them are brown people, with wavy hair, and allied more nearly to the peoples of Africa and of Asia than to those of Europe." Expressing how much India meant to him, Du Bois borrowed these words from his own novel, *Dark Princess*, to conclude the article:

> India! India! Out of black India the world was born. Into the black womb of India the world shall creep to die. All that the world has done, India did, and that more marvelously, more magnificently. The loftiest of mountains, the mightiest of rivers, the widest of plains, the broadest of oceans—these are India.[23]

Factual exaggerations apart, Du Bois hammered away at important themes of racial solidarity and the rich cultural heritage of the land of India. The psychological intention was clear. Du Bois wanted to affect his readers with the powerful impact of the Indian developments and of the African-American link to that drama.

The following week Du Bois offered another essay to the readers of the *New York Amsterdam News*. Here again the focus was on solidarity and the relevance of the Gandhian experiment for the people of color everywhere. First he outlined the impact of Europe on Indian political and economic institutions. He explained how Europeans had undermined India's small-scale industries and why Gandhi used a spinning wheel as a symbol of India's economic power. Du Bois recounted the proclamation in 1877 which made Queen Victoria the "Empress of India" and placed Whitehall more directly in control of Indian government. He reminded his readers that the birth of Mohandas Karamchand Gandhi eight years earlier "foreshadowed the end of the British rule of India." Then he summed up the meaning of those events for African-Americans.

> Of what interest is all this to the American Negroes, who are facing a winter of suffering and starvation? Why not talk about this situation in America rather than going half-way round the world for problems? Because the plight of no colored people is unimportant for us. If we are going to make our way in this modern world, we must know what the world has been doing to other colored folk and how it has done it, and what they are doing to achieve freedom and manhood. In the long run, this comprehensive knowledge is of more importance than our own narrow, provincial problem; and of more

importance, because our own problem depends upon the problems of the world for its solution.[24]

That fall the *Chicago Defender* continued its attention to the Indian situation with an essay on "That Little Man Gandhi" by the black teacher-historian Drusilla Dunjee Houston. The religious context was primary in her reflections. From the vantage point of African-American Christianity, she explored the meaning of Gandhi the man and his philosophy of nonviolence. Houston explained that nonresistance was the central teaching of Christianity and that the "little, bare, brown skeleton of a man, not professing Christ, but living His teachings, is the most powerful single individual in the universe." She noted that the Indian leader was "worshipped by the millions of India." Houston emphasized that Gandhi, who believed in the Christian doctrine of nonresistance, "has brought to his feet the powerful British empire upon which the sun never sets." She also lauded the self-control the Mahatma exercised in his daily life. Gandhi "is great because he literally follows the teachings of our Master, a thing that our Race might well note, for our leaders do not recognize the power of non-resistance," she suggested. One of the most significant aspects of Houston's essay was its illumination of the way many black Americans tied Gandhi's life and work to their own deepest religious convictions, especially their sense of connection to Jesus of Nazareth.

Gandhi has gained ascendancy over India and over us because he is a living embodiment of the command: "He that denieth not himself cannot be My disciple." When men see that we love humanity well enough to bear its hardships ourselves, to deny ourselves levity and indulgence, they are certain that we love them and that we have revelations from God. Thus they are constrained to follow such men as Gandhi. His views are authoritative to spiritual men. They are incomprehensible to men of undeveloped soul. England had Indian [*sic*] bound hand and foot, but the life of Gandhi, hateful as it may seem to the man of indulgence, has roused India and England to a sense of the wrongs being done 300,000,000 souls.

. . . Gandhi may seem to have failed, but ultimately he has in his life and present power proved the mightiness that comes from following the teachings of Christ. If a man would find true greatness and reach absolute power let him live those commands. They are but dark parables to the average man, but in their living is fame,

wealth and all of the things that men covet. Treasures hidden, saving
to those of understanding. Gandhi might have riches, earthly position; he spurns them. To him they are not success.[25]

This was a bold and challenging interpretation for the Christian-
minded readers of Houston's piece. By defining Gandhi and his
movement in Christian terms, she also made the Mahatma's Indian
experiment more readily translatable to the United States than if
she had interpreted Gandhi in secular or Hindu terms.

Despite the shared nature of their oppression, Gandhi and India
represented worlds which were in many ways different from the
reality of Afro-America. Therefore imagination and creativity were
needed to draw upon Gandhi and his work. In their discussion of
the applicability of Gandhi's way to their own difficult situation,
the black journals and newspapers, of course, recognized differences
between African-American and Indian mores. On 28 October 1931,
in his *New York Amsterdam News* column "The Wide, Wide World,"
Du Bois pointed out the problems African-Americans might have
in understanding and appreciating the style of leadership represented
by Gandhi.

> [Gandhi] has few of the characteristics that [black people] have
> been taught to associate with greatness. He is not a great orator
> but speaks slowly and in a low voice. He is not an impressive
> figure of a man but small and thin, weighing only about 100
> pounds. He describes himself as ugly and he dresses cheaply and
> quietly, after the manner of Indian peasants. He is an ascetic,
> eating little, playing little, and believing in peace and sacrifice,
> fasting and thought.[26]

These were some of the qualities which impressed Du Bois, and he
considered it especially significant that the Indian leader had chosen
to identify himself with the most oppressed at home and abroad.

The quality of the Mahatma's leadership and person apart, and
in spite of the hopes and perceptions of supporters like Du Bois
and Houston, the second round table conference (Gandhi did not
attend the first), which met from 7 September to 2 December
1931 in London to decide the future of India, did not go well
for Gandhi; he went away empty-handed. The British had successfully interjected the interreligious and caste factors to separate
various sectors of the Indian communities. "Gandhi says that he

is going home. London is too much for him," the *Chicago Defender* reported in November 1931. The writer noted that the Mahatma warned of "fiery days ahead" and declared that "NO PEOPLE EVER WON LIBERTY WITHOUT SUFFERING." Addressing the meaning of the Mahatma for blacks, the paper concluded that "[Gandhi] will win; not in the flesh, may be, but in the spirit long after he has gone. Follow him back to India. But the LIBERTY of which he spoke as coming through suffering is not yet yours. The truth is the light."[27]

Disillusioned and disheartened, Gandhi returned home. Meanwhile, the Conservatives had gained control in Ramsay MacDonald's coalition government. The new British leadership began to cut the ground from under the Indian National Congress. Emergency Powers Ordinances, designed to curtail the civil liberties of the people, were promulgated to deal with wide-ranging Indian discontent. On 4 January 1932, Gandhi was arrested again and taken to Yervada Jail in Poona. Relations between the British authorities and the Congress continued to deteriorate.[28]

As they had done for more than a decade, important sections of the African-American press kept their readers up to date, watching Gandhi. In the same month as the Mahatma's arrest, the *Chicago Defender* reported, "Latest news from India is that not only is Gandhi in jail, but that he doesn't care." The Mahatma's view that a person "had a right to refuse to pay taxes" was considered by the paper as "one of the greatest sayings." The paper argued that if hundreds of thousands of African-Americans who pay taxes were to say, "No, I'll pay no taxes unless I can be a citizen; VOTE, hold office," they would have "a different tale to tell."[29] A crucial lesson of Gandhi's concept of *satyagraha* was made available to the African-American community. A week later, the *Chicago Defender* shared an item—"The Imprisonment of Gandhi"—from the white-owned *Chicago Daily News*. "The arrest shocks persons who regard Gandhi as the greatest spiritual leader of the age," the *Chicago Defender* argued.[30]

Among blacks, debate about the relevance of Gandhian nonviolence to the United States situation continued unabated. In February William Pickens, a noted journalist, NAACP activist, educator, orator, and writer, raised serious questions about the workability of nonviolence in the United States. In his column

"Reflections" in the *New York Amsterdam News*, he rejected "Gandhi-ism and prayer as sufficient means of remedying the American Negro's societal ills." Referring to those who recommended the way of Gandhian nonviolence as persons of "a mystic bent of mind," he declared,

> Those who see in Gandhi's procedure a model method for the solution of the race problem in the United States are people who reason in shallow analogies; they think that a social formula which works at one time, in one place, within a given set of circumstances, can be made to work at all times, in all places, against all conditions.
>
> And those who 'think' that prayer alone will solve any social and economic problem whatsoever do not think at all. Such people have not carefully read their Christian Bibles where prayer is invariably coupled with 'work,' with suffering, sacrificing, paying with courage of performance. And as for Gandhi: the man who has organized and inspired the tremendous movement of 360 million people certainly knows that a leader and his people must not stop with praying in closets and 'sacred places,' but must go forth bravely into the avenues of struggle. We call it 'passive resistance,' but resistance is always active, if it be intellectual and social.[31]

Exactly which persons and arguments Pickens was critiquing is not obvious, but it is clear that he had put his finger on one of the key elements of Gandhian nonviolence, that of *active* public resistance, and he took to task those persons who equated "passive resistance" and prayer with inaction.

Turning to the differences between the two societies, Pickens first pointed out that unlike the Indians, African-Americans were greatly outnumbered by white people. Second, he argued that Gandhi and his compatriots were struggling against "foreigners," whereas African-Americans were pitted against fellow citizens. Therefore, recourse to "civil disobedience" or "boycott" was suicidal.

> If the Negro of Mississippi starts a boycott against working for and trading with white people, or against buying or employing any of the facilities owned and controlled by whites, the Negro race would be the very first to freeze and starve. White Mississippi would be crippled, but black Mississippi would be utterly ruined.
>
> Also, Gandhi's people may practice civil disobedience with at least some temporary and partial success—such as not paying taxes,

refusing to hold office, to vote or to obey the ordinary laws of the British-controlled government. Suppose the Negroes of America should try not paying taxes, not voting and declining to hold office, resigning as policemen, firemen, clerks—how beautifully they would deliver themselves into the hands of their worst enemies! Inside of twelve months all their property would be seized for taxes and all the leaders of their small minority would be in jail.

Whether the readers of the *New York Amsterdam News* agreed with him or not, Pickens's clear and forthright analysis is evidence of a lively debate taking place within the black community. Despite his deep reservations about African-American advocacy of Gandhian nonviolence for their struggle, he concluded that "the American Negro may learn much, in spirit and determination, from the Gandhi movement."[32]

Now, as always, the watch was not focused on Gandhi alone. In March 1932, Mrs. Sarojini Naidu, second in command to Gandhi, was arrested for disobeying prohibitive orders against attending the session of the Indian National Congress. The *New York Amsterdam News* devoted its lead editorial on 27 April 1932 to the Indian resistance movement and the arrest of this courageous and outspoken female colleague of the Mahatma. The editorial declared that the American colonies were never treated as barbarously as the East Indians were being treated, and yet the colonies had to resort to arms to effect their freedom from British rule—a rule built upon liberty for the white man and slavery for the darker races; the British, who lived by the sword "will some day die by the sword, even in India."[33]

Interestingly enough, there were times when the African-American watch on Gandhi and his people was mediated through other eyes. For instance, Du Bois was apparently very moved by one of Gandhi's earliest European biographers, Romain Rolland, and in May 1932 he presented his readers with one of the most perceptive appreciations of the meaning of Gandhi with the following quotation from Rolland:

From the universal point of view, I regard the present Indian crisis as going much beyond the question of a political conflict between the British Empire and India. In the eyes of millions who regard as intolerable the continuance of society as it is now organized and who have resolved to change it, Mr. Gandhi's Satyagraha experiment

is the sole chance now existing in the world of effecting this transformation of humanity without resort to violence. If this attempt
fails there will remain no other issue in human history but violence.
This is why all those who have at heart the social harmony and spirit
of peace should help India with all their strength.[34]

In these words Romain Rolland conveyed the essence of Gandhian
satyagraha. Freedom from British rule was only one part of Gandhi's
larger overall agenda. Recognizing the interconnections among all
spheres of human activity, he sought to create a nonviolent human
order. He refused to divide life into neat compartments, and he
sought new pathways to nonviolent economic, social, and political
structures. Freedom from British rule was essential, but it was also
essential for India to rid itself of internal contradictions and oppressive and cruel practices, Gandhi believed. For him the religiously
condoned practice of untouchability, which denied fundamental human rights of worship, education, employment, and social equality
to nearly a sixth of India's Hindus as outcastes, was one of the major
obstacles standing in the way of Indian freedom. Indeed, Gandhi's
very strong stand against untouchability was one of the key reasons
why so many African-Americans were drawn to him.

In his own way, Gandhi tackled the problem of untouchability
at various levels throughout his life. Early in his career in India,
while at the Satyagraha Ashram, Gandhi adopted an Untouchable
as his daughter. He also refused to go along with the usage of the
term *Untouchable*. Instead, he coined the word *Harijan*, meaning
"child of God," to describe outcaste Hindus. Gandhi did more than
that. Through the reorganization of the Indian National Congress,
he made it possible for the Untouchables to enter into the political
realm. He also made them members and full participants of his
ashram communities.[35]

A black community subjected to legal segregation was especially
sensitive to the issue of untouchability as an internal contradiction
of the Indian struggle. Certain sections of the African-American
press often chose to concentrate on the working of India's caste
system and the terrible conditions under which the Untouchables
were held by caste Hindus. They highlighted the similarities between the two situations—that of segregation in the United States
and that of untouchability in the Indian subcontinent. Repeatedly
the African-American press lauded Gandhi for his denunciation of

untouchability and for his attempts at bringing Harijans into the mainstream of political and social life of Indian society.[36]

While Gandhi was still in jail the British government moved to implement a new constitution. An important part of this measure was the creation of separate electorates for the country's sixty million outcastes. As early as March 1932, Gandhi had questioned the wisdom of the British plan in a letter to the British secretary of state for India, Sir Samuel Hoare. Ignoring Gandhi's stand on the subject, in August the British prime minister, Ramsay MacDonald, announced the formation of separate electorates for Untouchables and others. In September, unable to persuade the MacDonald government to change its mind through pleas and petitions, the Mahatma announced a fast unto death to force the British government to change its course. African-American journals and newspapers widely reported Gandhi's decision.

The *Atlanta Daily World*, started in 1928, was one such newspaper—a paper which enjoyed a monopoly on the African-American news market in Atlanta for the next thirty years. "Gandhi's Plan to Starve Self Not New As Political Weapon" is how the *Atlanta Daily World*, the only African-American daily of its time, broke the news of the fast in its 20 September 1932 edition. Next to a large photograph of the Mahatma were smaller photographs of MacDonald and the Irish leader Terrence MacSwiney. A lengthy caption explained why Gandhi was engaged in the fast and its parallel with the Irish struggle:

Courting death by starvation as a political weapon of the oppressed is not by any means new in history. Mahatma Gandhi, India's spiritual leader, in his determination to starve himself to death as a protest against the new British electoral plan for India, has seized upon a means of passive protest which dates back at least as far as the Spanish inquisition. Many of the oppressed in medieval Spain undertook voluntary starvation in protest against the tyranny that prevailed in those bygone days. More recently, the self-martyrdom of Lord Mayor Terrence MacSwiney of Cork attracted the attention and sympathy of the entire world to the Irish cause. MacSwiney, sentenced to a two-year prison sentence for sedition against the British crown, went on hunger strike and steadfastly refused to touch food until his death after 74 days of suffering in Brixton Prison, London. Gandhi plans to start his self-starvation program if Premier

Ramsay MacDonald does not rescind the electoral plan to which the Mahatma takes exception. However, MacDonald asserts that Gandhi would deprive the 60,000,000 'untouchables' he is supposed to champion of representation in the Indian Legislature and is determined to go ahead, regardless of the Mahatma's threats.[37]

Gandhi's vision of "the beloved community" and his alternative of nonviolent resistance were the focus of attention when an Illinois state representative, William E. King of the Republican party, compared the plight of Untouchables with that of African-Americans in the South. Early in October, the *Atlanta Daily World* reported King's remarks on the front page. The agelong oppression of the Untouchables in India was featured. At the same time, the news item noted the significance of the experiments Gandhi had been conducting in shaking the hold of untouchability on the Indian scene. King believed that "Gandhi's fasting has seriously disturbed this old persecution." The Republican representative went so far as to suggest that "it may be that the end of cruel caste prejudices in India is at hand and that the sixty millions of 'untouchables' will be accorded their human status." King suggested that "a six-day fast by the Indian 'holy man,' Gandhi," had the potential to "blast the centuries of prejudice and class feeling behind the caste system." While he saw prospects for radical change in the condition of India's oppressed and the workability there of nonviolent resistance, he had no such hopes for America. Coming to the point of the plight of the eight million people of African descent in the South, William King claimed that the Democratic white South would not allow the Gandhian miracle to work here. "No amount of fasting or penance would enable the American Negro 'untouchable' of the South to exercise his citizenship rights in the Democratic states of the south," he argued. "Robert R. Moton, John R. Hope, Will Alexander, Bishop R. E. Jones, Jesse O. Thomas, R. B. Eleazer and any one hundred of the foremost good-will racial leaders of the south might announce and begin 'a fast unto death' tomorrow without the slightest effect upon the Democratic Brahmins."[38]

William King was perhaps more right than he might have realized when he argued against the relevance of the instrument of fasting by African-Americans in their struggle against racism. After all, the tradition of holy men fasting for a social cause was missing in the cultural ethos of the United States. In the absence of cultural referrants such as fasting and tolerance of holy men, the warning from King was timely and appropriate. Here was another instance of lack of easy and universal agreement over the appropriateness of the Gandhian alternative in the United States.

When the Mahatma broke his fast later in 1932, the *Norfolk Journal and Guide* brought another perspective. The fast, which had touched Hindu hearts and led to a religious reformation of sorts, compelled Britain to give up its plan for a separate electorate for the Untouchables. An editorial, "Ghandi Staggers the Imagination," noted Gandhi's "tremendous influence and sure leadership" and observed how "merely by beginning and resolutely carrying out his threat to starve" he brought "the mighty British Government to its knees." The Mahatma "is so simple and sincere; yet he is a terribly mysterious character and influence. . . . Powerless in the sense that the great British Empire is powerful, he yet proves more powerful than it. Is it that he has truth and right on his side?"[39]

In an editorial on 1 October 1932, the *Pittsburgh Courier* also focused on Gandhi's fast for the sake of the Untouchables. The editorial noted how this "little old man without money and without armed force" had caused "nearly one-fourth of the human race to compose differences and co-operate for the common good of all and the repulsion of the invader." The inclusive dimension of the Gandhian notion of freedom was fully grasped when the writer stated that the Mahatma believed that "the Hindu . . . can with ill grace complain against the persecution and exploitation by the British overlords when he himself is more mercilessly exploiting and degrading one-sixth of his number, the Untouchables." The *Pittsburgh Courier* observed that the differences between orthodox Hindus and the Untouchable leader, B. M. Ambedkar, had been "ironed out" and that the occasion was "another victory in statesmanship and spiritually [*sic*] is chalked up for the astute little brown man behind the bars whom friends and enemies hail as Mahatma." And the paper asked, "When has there been his like before?"[40]

With the question of Hindu injustices against the outcastes in the news, George Schuyler contributed an article in the *Pittsburgh Courier* detailing graphically what it meant to be an Untouchable in India. He pointed out that the system, which had lasted for two thousand years, was based on the notion that Untouchables are "born wrong and can never be born right even unto the seventh generation." Not unlike others, Schuyler also suggested that the "social and economic positions [of African-Americans are] somewhat similar and in some respects identical" to that of the Untouchables in India. Encouraging black Americans to take a lesson from the experience of the Untouchables, Schuyler warned that they could ill afford to expect to have their conditions improved by the courtesy of white Americans. Organization was the key word. So as to gain their rights, Schuyler argued that African-Americans must organize, just as the sixty million Untouchables had, "under well-trained and courageous leadership to do for themselves what no one could or would do for them." "All human beings," the *Pittsburgh Courier* quoted Gandhi as saying in 1931, "are the children of God." Here was a powerful message, a message African-Americans had been given from slavery days by their elders and religious leaders. Gandhi, the writer continued, believed that so long as India treated its own people, the Untouchables, so cruelly, it forfeited its claim to independence. Gandhi was further reported as having said that "when the Indian deserves freedom he will get it." The problems which he faced from the right wing of the Indian National Congress, especially its leader, Madan Mohan Malaviya (1861–1946), were also reported by Schuyler. Gandhi's emphasis on the external and internal dimensions of the freedom struggle was reiterated, and he was presented to the readers as a principled leader. And this time Schuyler offered a more positive assessment of the Mahatma than he had done before.[41]

In an extremely perceptive article titled "Our Negro 'Untouchables,' " which he wrote for the *Norfolk Journal and Guide* in October 1932, Gordon Hancock declared that the mightiest empire of Great Britain "quails before Mahatma Gandhi, the little Indian, frail of body but robust of spirit!" He wrote that

> Gandhi's power is a tribute to the life and teachings of the lowly Nazarene that we conquer not so much by power and might as by a certain bent of spirit. . . . Gandhi knows that the limits to the rising Indians are set by those that are sinking, and that a race must be saved at the bottom as well as at the top.

Within the black community, Hancock found those who treated their fellow brothers and sisters as if they were Untouchables. Whether social and economic distinctions among African-Americans added up to Untouchability as in the Hindu setting, he did not explain. Of this Hancock was sure: that African-Americans suffered a "great handicap" from "the tendency for the 'caste' Negro to forget the Negro 'untouchable'—and there are many." The suggestion that the Untouchables were India's "Negroes" and that Gandhi was their ally was an encouraging message to African-Americans.[42]

Meanwhile, Du Bois was still at work. In November 1932 "As the Crow Flies" declared, "there is today in the world but one living maker of miracles, and that is Mahatma Gandhi. He stops eating, and three hundred million Indians, together with the British Empire, hold their breath until they can talk sense." Presumably referring to the low esteem in which the Indian leader was held in white America at large, Du Bois added, "all America sees in Gandhi is a joke, but the real joke is America." Elsewhere in the same issue *The Crisis* devoted a column to Gandhi and his fast to end separate electorates for Untouchables. The item, which had a full-length photograph of Gandhi, was titled *"Satyagraha."* The photograph's caption read "Karamchand Gandhi, *Brought an empire to heel."* The journal informed its readers that a "fortnight ago, Mahatma Gandhi broke his fast." The purpose of Gandhi's action was restated and the outcome was summed up thus:

> Purpose of his hunger strike: " '*to eat no food until His Majesty's Government reaches an agreement with Hindoos of all castes, terminating the decree of Raj that the higher caste should constitute an electorate separate from the Untouchables. . . .*' " An agreement that *will not* strengthen the caste barriers in India, and that should prevent (if anything could) outbreaks against the government by hundreds of millions of Untouchables [original italics].[43]

Here, as in scores of other reflections, African-Americans were watching Gandhi with thoughts of their own situation prominent in their minds. Thus it was of great importance to many that Gandhi offered an alternative for the path of social struggle. Time and again, African-American writers wrestled with the relevance and importance of his style of leadership for them in their setting. In a forthright editorial, the *Chicago Defender* asked, "Will a Gandhi Arise?" The Mahatma "is exerting a mystical 'soul force,' " the writer argued. To the *Chicago Defender*, Gandhi was a man of faith and peace who had "a determined belief in the effectuality of prayer." About the likely success of Gandhi and his movement the paper had no doubt, "because 'Truth crushed to earth shall rise again, eternal years of God are hers.' " The writer added that "India, like America, will outlive the oppressor, the murderer and the robber, and from the heathen altar of avarice, immorality and corruption will come a peaceful solution of both India's and America's problems."[44]

With an eye to the solution of problems at home, the editorial captured and projected the quality and meaning of Gandhi's leadership.

> What we need in America is a Gandhi who will fight the cause of the oppressed. One who, like Gandhi, can divorce himself from the greed for gold, one who can appreciate the misery of the oppressed and respond in spirit to their needs and requirements.
>
> We have fought a continuous battle largely under the baneful influence of artificial leadership. Men who have spoken for us have chosen their words in accordance with their personal gain.
>
> The name Gandhi is synonymous with the good intent of all who are struggling for a peaceful adjustment of spiritual differences. The observation can be safely made that the most essential thing needed by the world today is a better understanding of one's self. It is through this personal knowledge of ourselves that we are able to sense the value of our fellow man.[45]

As we know now, the call for a black Gandhi who would take the oppressed African-Americans to "the promised land" was not made in vain. The repeated plea for an unselfish leader with a vision of a nonviolent society helped to nurture a powerful dream. It was an important part of the preparation for the major post–World War II Southern nonviolent movement.

In the middle of 1933, as the United States felt the heavy weight of the Depression, the eloquent Gordon Hancock, in another of his articles in the *Norfolk Journal and Guide*, put before the people of his community one of the most powerful and concise assessments of the meaning of Gandhi when he wrote, "without doubt Gandhi is living upon the frontiers of a new world and is looking over the shoulders of a hundred generations." Hancock praised Gandhi for demonstrating that "things of the spirit are the real things." The answer to "our present woes," he said, lay in spiritual power, the kind possessed by both Jesus and Gandhi; he argued that "Gandhi's fasting . . . is not merely a plea for India's untouchables, but it is a plea for the possibilities of spiritual power; it is a plea for the realization of our better higher selves." He concluded that "the spirit is master and the body is servant. . . . The sooner the world learns the lesson the sooner will come the brotherhood of man and fatherhood of God."[46]

The issue of Gandhi's freedom struggle methodology was inseparable from discussions of his leadership, and this too continued to be examined in the African-American press. The September 1933 issue of the *Chicago Defender* gave considerable space to an article by Cleveland Allen about the appropriation of Gandhian methods by African-Americans in their struggle. The article was titled "Will Gandhi Movement Help Race?" and the subtitle read "Discussion of 'Passive Resistance' in India Give Rise to New Thought, Writer Sees Chance for Solution When Plan Is Tried Here." In the Indian movement Allen recognized "a direct application of the principles of the teachings of Jesus, and which makes an appeal to reason and a higher sense of justice rather than to emotion." African-Americans had been following such a path for a long time, he wrote, "They have tried to put in practice the program as advocated by Christ, which in short is 'love your enemy,' and apply the principles of the golden rule of 'doing unto others as you would have them do unto you.'" He was further convinced that "no race has shown a finer devotion to an ideal, and has followed more closely the Christ principle than our group." According to Allen, Booker T. Washington had preached this method "as the ultimate hope of the solution of the race issue." Washington was, in Allen's words, "the Gandhi of the Race." Allen also noted that African-American leaders in the South—for example, Robert Moton—"are preaching the doctrine of non-violence, good will and peace." He concluded that "the Race in America is in sympathy with the Gandhi experiment and will watch with interest its outcome." Finally, Allen declared that "the movement headed by Gandhi is the movement which must be adopted if the world is to be saved."[47] No matter how we view the accuracy (or inaccuracy) of Allen's comparisons, the significant point is that comparisons were being made, and powerful conclusions were being drawn.

As the Depression continued, interest in Gandhian methods of nonviolent resistance persisted. In his March 1934 address to the students of Virginia Union University, an African-American school, Dr. Kirby Page, the noted white pacifist, writer, and lecturer, advocated Gandhi's method of active nonviolent resistance as a way of overcoming "racial and economic injustices" in the United States. The *Norfolk Journal and Guide* reported the address the following week, informing its readers that Page had spoken about Gandhi's method of struggle based on resistance, right means, self-suffering, and love of the opponent. The reporter noted that "Ghandi's method is a challenge to the Negro," and listed what Page identified as the Mahatma's fourfold approach: "(1) Never lie down passively and accept oppression, (2) Never try to get rid of it by use of evil weapons, (3) Resist evil with life, (4) Be prepared to take the consequences and accept the penalties." In the same vein, a 1934 *Pittsburgh Courier* editorial touched on some of the internal dissensions of the Indian movement but emphasized that "we Negroes can learn from India that our worst enemy is often within ourselves." India had divisions around the issues of caste, religion, and language, whereas the writer encouraged African-Americans to consider that "here in America, Negroes are divided neither by religion nor caste. We are all more or less working people . . . [who] speak a common tongue, have common customs and common beliefs. There is every reason why unity should succeed with us, where it fails in India. Perhaps we need a Ghandi."[48] Steadily the early refrain of "watch Gandhi" or "watch the Indians" was developing into a repeated public reflection—"We need a Gandhi."

The connections continued to develop. By mid–1930, Ethiopia, an age-old symbol of independence and high civilization for black Americans, became still another active link in the binding chain. The Ethiopian question was important because African-Americans, all through their struggles, in and out of slavery, attached special significance to the soil and the nation of Ethiopia. "For many Biblically oriented blacks," Vincent Harding has noted, " . . . the word Ethiopian was synonymous with African."[49] It was also of great importance that Ethiopia had not been formally vanquished by European colonizers.

As the threat of military invasion of Ethiopia by Italy became a reality on the eve of World War II, African-Americans expressed serious and urgent concern for the safety of this ancient land. Others within the international community were similarly outraged by the machinations of Italy's fascist dictator, Mussolini. The people of India, even though they were under the military control of an alien power, offered their sympathy and support for Ethiopia. Perhaps the sincerest expression of Indian solidarity with Ethiopia came from Gandhi, and sections of the African-American press were quick to pick up his statements. For example, the 3 August 1935 edition of the *Pittsburgh Courier* carried the front page headline " 'India Cannot Ignore Mussolini's Threat Against The Colored People'— Gandhi." The paper noted that the Indian leader "appealed to the country to contribute money for an Indian Red Cross contingent for Ethiopia." On the same page there was a photograph of Gandhi. The *Pittsburgh Courier* correspondent in Calcutta argued that Gandhi's moral alignment with Ethiopia had "moved to swing India's 375,000,000 people to the support of ancient Ethiopia in its threatened war with Fascist Italy." Still under British control, India was hardly in a position to offer much material help to Ethiopia or any other country. Nevertheless, what mattered was the gesture of solidarity and the sense of justice. "Although India is under British rule," Gandhi pointed out, "she is a member of the League of Nations. She is fully entitled to assist another nation even in a noncombatant way."[50]

The 3 August issue of the *Pittsburgh Courier* also carried an article from the pen of George Schuyler. Drawn by the Ethiopian connection, he was able to praise Gandhi unhesitatingly. The Indian leader he had once criticized forcefully now became "a brilliant English-trained attorney . . . [who] had surrendered a lucrative practice to fight against the South African color bar which debased his people there." He was described as the political as well as the spiritual leader of his people. Schuyler argued that "Gandhi's moral alignment with Ethiopia in the present crisis may well halt Mussolini" and that "Gandhi is the colored man most feared by England." Schuyler said that "knowing his power [England] will undoubtedly redouble pressure on Italy to keep the peace." Although history did not bear out Schuyler's hopeful prediction, his reassessment of Gandhi, as well as the prominence the paper gave to Gandhi's statement, represented the African-American community's profound appreciation of India's alignment with the peoples of Ethiopia.[51]

The *Baltimore Afro-American* headlined the solidarity story from India as "Gandhi Urges India to Aid Ethiopia if War Begins." On 4 August the *Atlanta Daily World* gave major attention to the stand taken by the Mahatma—"Ghandi Backs Ethiopia" above a large photograph of the Indian leader, with a caption below reading "Mahatma Ghandi considered a 'savior' by the majority of 350,000,000 souls of teeming India, sounded a warning last week that Benito Mussolini's outburst against the darker races could not be ignored. He urged his countrymen to aid Ethiopia in her impending conflict with Italy." The *Atlanta Daily World* report from India was headlined "India Rallies To Ghandi's Summons." Gandhi was reported as having commanded his countrymen to "come to the aid of her darker brothers," and it was said that he "urged Indians to finance an Indian Red Cross unit in Ethiopia." The *Atlanta Daily World* stated that Indians "bitterly resented Mussolini's statement that whites must be supreme in Africa. They were aroused by his charges that the yellows and the blacks are united against white supremacy."[52]

Gandhi's strong stand against the invasion of Ethiopia in 1935 and his response to the condition of Untouchables in India provided two additional powerful points of attraction between him and African-Americans. Here, as with other connecting links, the African-American press was crucial in calling the attention of their hundreds of thousands—perhaps millions—of readers to the man, his ideas and actions, and their meaning for America.

On one level, this was not difficult to accomplish, for this brown-skinned saint's determined opposition to British rule, based on the doctrine of nonviolence, captured the imagination of countless African-Americans who longed for justice in this country and who believed in the life and teachings of Jesus. From the moment the Mahatma launched his noncooperation campaign, African-Americans began to explore at various levels the meaning of the man and his message. His Christ-like ways impressed a host of observers. His simple life-style and his self-effacing and self-sacrificing leadership style were greatly valued. Influential members of the black community believed that India and its leader were engaged in a struggle which was also theirs. As the challenge to British rule deepened, it became evident that nonviolence was working and that it was now a matter of time before the British would be forced to withdraw from India. The weapon of nonviolence made sound moral and practical sense to a good number of African-American students of the Indian scene. Finally, they recognized that the way of Gandhi, which was also the way of Jesus, needed to be explored in their own struggle for freedom and justice. In deepening those understandings, the African-American press continued to be an articulate and effective witness, but there were other witnesses at work as well.

=4=

Journey West, Journey East

FORTUNATELY African-American exposure to Gandhi and his movement before World War II was not entirely dependent on newspaper reports of events in India. Complementing these reports were personal contacts between the two communities. Following an earlier tradition, a number of Gandhi's English followers and Indian nationalists came to the United States in the late 1920s and 1930s. An important link was Charles Freer Andrews, a close friend of Gandhi and a supporter of the Indian freedom movement, who visited the United States in 1929. His encounters with African-Americans were a significant part of the story of mutual engagement.

Andrews, who began his career in India as an Anglican missionary in 1904, had early on found himself pulling away from his official role in the English-dominated Christian Church in India and drawing closer to the burgeoning nationalist struggles of the oppressed in that country and the rest of the British Empire. From the outset, Andrews defied conventions founded on racial exclusiveness. According to his biographers, within days of his arrival in India in 1904, Andrews "was brought face to face with the havoc wrought in human relationships by pride of race." Andrews's early experiences (in 1904 and 1905) turned him "into a passionate prophet of racial equality." Within a decade, he broke his relations with the white-dominated Indian Church. In 1914, at the encouragement of Gopal Krishna Gokhale, a leading nationalist leader and Gandhi's political mentor, Andrews also thoroughly immersed himself in Gandhi's *satyagraha* campaign in South Africa, first as a fund-raiser in India for the "passive resisters" and then in South

Africa, at Gandhi's side in the fight for dignity and equality for Indians in that country. By 1914 the Gandhi-led nonviolent resistance movement against the racist government in South Africa was at its peak. Thousands of Indians were in jail and many more from among the indentured laborers were on strike. The news of the struggle moved Andrews to donate all his money to Gandhi's movement. When Albert West, a key white co-worker of the Mahatma in South Africa, was also arrested, Gokhale sent Andrews to replace him.[1]

As they worked together, a personal bond developed between the two men which remained strong from that point on. Before Andrews's stay in that country was over, Andrews and Gandhi were on first-name terms; Andrews was "Charlie" to the Indian leader and the Mahatma was "Mohan." (Henry Polak, a leading co-worker of Gandhi in South Africa was the only other person who addressed him as Mohan.) Such was Gandhi's respect for the ex-missionary that when he started the Satyagraha Ashram in Ahmedabad, India Gandhi consulted Andrews before finalizing the Sabarmati Rule (ashram discipline), which became the organizing principle for Gandhi-led groups in India. For much of the twenty-six years that they were associated in the common causes of winning freedom for India, removing untouchability, and establishing racial justice, Andrews was Gandhi's voice to the West. He was an important interpreter of the Mahatma's life and thought, as well as of the vision and hope of the people of the Indian subcontinent. An inveterate traveler, Andrews carried Gandhi's message to distant parts of the world in person and through his books, which were available in the United States. These include *Letters to a Friend* (1928), *Thoughts from Tagore* (1928), *Mahatma Gandhi's Ideas* (1929), *Mahatma Gandhi, His Own Story* (1930), *Mahatma Gandhi at Work* (1931), and *What I Owe to Christ* (1932).[2]

While Andrews was on the journey which would soon lead him to the African-American community, Gandhi, who since his release from prison in 1924 had been focusing his energies on *khadi* (homespun cloth), Hindu-Muslim unity, and the removal of untouchability, was now getting ready to reenter national politics in India. Now his chief concerns were the regeneration of self and society. Among the practices Gandhi had adopted for his own inner growth was the observance of a day of silence once a week. Recognizing that if India were to be truly free it was necessary for the people to be self-reliant and live in religious harmony, he focused on women's rights, adoption of *khadi*, and Hindu-Muslim unity. He traveled extensively and raised funds for domestic reforms. Meanwhile, as the decade headed to a close, he was once again engaged in a regional *satyagraha* campaign, the campaign of the farmers of Bardoli, Gujarat (described in Chapter 2). From behind the scenes Gandhi guided this highly disciplined and immensely successful *satyagraha* campaign, one which hinted that the nation might be ready for an India-wide *satyagraha*.

As a part of his emissary work, Andrews landed in New York in January 1929. In a letter he wrote from there to his friend and first biographer, Benarsidas Chaturvedi, Andrews said that "he was determined to work against racism," which he defined as "the greatest menace of the present age." While in New York he was introduced to W. E. B. Du Bois and also met several African-American and white church leaders. According to his recent biographer, Hugh Tinker, "Andrews readily responded to the interest displayed by the Americans in his message." Since one of the tasks of his mission was to correct the erroneous impressions about India (its past and present) and Gandhi conveyed in Katherine Mayo's *Mother India* (1927), Andrews soon found opportunities to explain the Indian case as he saw it. Mayo's work was an indictment of Hindu India and of Gandhi. By focusing on themes such as child marriage, untouchability, poor sanitation, poverty, and disease, she portrayed Indian life in highly negative light. According to Mayo, Gandhi was a Tammany Hall politician who had no genuine interest in the welfare of the disadvantaged. Andrews also encouraged the Indian poet Rabindranath Tagore to go to the United States to answer the unfavorable impression created by Mayo's work. Though he did not participate in any resistance campaigns, Tagore supported nationalist leaders and the freedom movement. For his contribution to literature he was given a Nobel Prize in 1913. He had a large following at home and beyond India's borders.[3]

In February Andrews went south for "an eagerly-anticipated visit to Booker T. Washington's great institute of Negro education at Tuskegee." During the ten days he spent there, Andrews shared fully in the life of the school and made many contacts. In March

1929, the *Baltimore Afro-American* carried an impressive photograph of Andrews, with Robert Moton and other visitors from the East, at the Booker T. Washington memorial on the campus. Andrews described his time at Tuskegee as both "quite wonderful" and "peaceful." On 8 March he wrote to Gandhi, "The hearts of those Negroes there in Tuskagee [*sic*] are with you in every way that is indescribably real and deep. . . . It is a real asram, both of prayer and work." If Tuskegee warmed the heart of Andrews, he too left an unforgettable impression. The impact of his visit was recorded on 9 March 1929, in the *Tuskegee Messenger*:

> Tuskegee has had a messenger from the East. His spirit was a spirit of simplicity, of repose, of reflection and peace. He had a message, a plain unadorned story of the two greatest spirits in the world today, Tagore and Gandhi. Always there was the note of India's aspiration, of the self-denial of its leaders, and of the unity of their cause with the upward striving of all suppressed groups. He desired to establish bonds between Tuskegee in America and Santiniketan in India, which are dedicated in the same spirit to the same cause of emancipation. He was no recluse. He did not seem of another world; he was curiously practical. But as he lingered among us his face continuously reflected the joy of his inward spirit. One of the boys said it was just like Jesus himself talking to us.

Andrews helped to establish ties between Tuskegee Institute and Santiniketan, the university founded by the great Indian poet and spiritual leader Rabindranath Tagore. In subsequent years, several African-American students spent time at Tagore's school (which was later expanded and renamed Visva-Bharati). In this context, it is important to note that Howard University also showed interest in a visit from Charles Andrews. Alain Locke, a faculty member of Howard University, corresponded with Andrews and extended an invitation to him to spend time at the university, although that visit never materialized.[4]

Predictably, Andrews's presence received attention in the African-American press. Introducing him as an English friend of Gandhi and Tagore, *The Crisis*, in August 1929, reproduced an address Andrews had given at the quadrennial conference of the British Student Christian Federation. Andrews lamented the fact that "the Christian principle of racial equality, which was upheld by the greatest statesmen of last century has been virtually abandoned in the Twentieth Century." Citing historical evidence against racism, he provided a passionate case for the dismantling of the system and structure of racial injustice. Andrews ended his lengthy piece with these words from the Bible: "*In Him, there can be neither Jew, nor Greek, barbarian, Scythian, bond nor free, for all are one Man in Christ Jesus* [Andrews's italics]." Andrews also described how Gandhi could not attend a church service which Andrews led one Christmas in South Africa because he was Asian, and how Gandhi had several experiences of segregation with which all African-Americans could identify. By contrast, he claimed, "the Christian religion at its inception stood out boldly for racial equality." Here was a powerfully uplifting message from a white Christian colleague of Gandhi. Here was a message which was also the heart of Christianity as African-Americans understood it.[5]

Early in the fall of 1929, *The Crisis* published "A Message to the American Negro from Rabindranath Tagore," which appeared on the journal's cover in the poet's own handwriting. In it Tagore expressed his faith in the oneness of the human family. Du Bois wrote that he had secured the Indian poet's message "through the good offices of Mr. C. F. Andrews." In addition, the journal used the occasion to publicize acts of racial discrimination against Tagore during his trip to the United States earlier, in the spring of the year, and explained that the poet-educator was forced to cancel "his tour of American universities because he was oppressed by the air of suspicion and incivility toward Asiatics." Even though Tagore was inactive in the political arena, he was highly esteemed by African-Americans, who felt a special sense of pride in the fact that this man of color had won such worldwide literary distinction.[6]

His travels with Tagore on the poet's North American trip had taken Andrews to Canada. But when Tagore cancelled his lecture tour, Andrews left for British Guiana (later Guyana) to minister to the East Indian community. In March 1930, after spending several months there, he returned to the United States. Hampton Institute (now Hampton University), a leading African-American school founded for former slaves in 1868 by Union General Samuel Armstrong and the alma mater of Tuskegee's founder, Booker T. Washington, provided Andrews with another important contact with African-Americans. According to the *Hampton Script*, the Institute's student newspaper, Andrews spent a week in early March "studying and meditating in the hope, perchance, of taking additional ideas to his beloved home—India, to his adopted alma mater—Santi-Niketan [*sic*]." Highlighting Andrews's solidarity with the cause of Indian independence and his belief in Gandhian nonviolence, the *Script* introduced the distinguished visitor from India in this way:

> From the sacred walls of Santi-Niketan [*sic*], where India's youth sit at the feet of Tagore comes Dr. C. F. Andrews, friend of the Mahatma and associate of the Poet, with a message of good will to America and the West Indies. As a young English College graduate he left the banks of Cam for the Ganges, and there for fifty years he has dwelt among the great souls of India, interpreting and thinking, until he too has become, with Gandhi, a symbol of nonresistance and overpowering faith—a believer in Swadeshi, a sympathizer with the oppressed—one with India's mind.

How much opportunity he had to speak about Gandhi's leadership of the ongoing nonviolent struggle for Indian independence is not altogether clear. However, when we consider that Andrews spent a week there, we may surmise that he probably became the focus of some interest and brought further attention to his friend and leader.[7]

While at Tuskegee, Andrews had completed the manuscript of *Mahatma Gandhi's Ideas*. The book, an edited version of Gandhi's autobiography, was not an an exhaustive treatment of all of Gandhi's ideas, but it provided an important window to the mind and heart of the Indian leader. Andrews focused on subjects such as *satyagraha* in South Africa and India, Gandhi's position on the question of untouchability, and the religious roots of his private and public witness. He dedicated the book to Robert R. Moton and his staff at Tuskegee, who had assisted Andrews in preparing the book for the press—"Their love for Mahatma Gandhi is sincere and deep." Andrews believed that his work was likely to help introduce Gandhi's ideas to an American audience and pave the way for Gandhi to journey to Europe and North America. Gandhi, however, had no immediate plans to visit the United States, although several of his American well-wishers continued to press him to do so.[8]

Andrews certainly must have discussed the work with his hosts and audiences as he finished it, but how widely other African-Americans read the book or how well they received it there is no precise way of knowing, although it was on the reading list of books which Martin Luther King, Jr., consulted as he studied Gandhi. It is clear, however, that the book became a center of controversy in some parts of the African-American community. Certain passages on caste and interracial marriage in *Mahatma Gandhi's Ideas* gave the impression that the Mahatma was against marriages between African-Americans and whites. According to Andrews, Gandhi believed in the orthodox Hindu practice which prohibits "intermarriage and interdining." Problematic as this view might have appeared to African-Americans, Andrews's suggestion that Gandhi would also have been against his children marrying those of Charles Andrews's family must have appeared even more shocking to them. (The question, of course, was hypothetical, for Andrews had no children.) Andrews recalled a statement by Gandhi on the subject in these words: "Yes, I would never give my consent to such a marriage, because it would be contrary to my ideas of religion thus to transgress the boundaries wherein we were born. I would not personally agree to a marriage out of Caste."[9]

Though belatedly, it was these and related views, we might guess, which led the *Baltimore Afro-American* to take up the matter directly with Gandhi. In June 1934, the journal obtained an exclusive statement from the Mahatma, and provided its readers an opportunity to examine his views afresh. The report from Gandhi's ashram, which appeared on the front page, was adorned with the headlines "Gandhi Hits U.S. Bar, Gandhi Denies He Opposes Intermarriage, Indian Leader Brands Jim Crow as Negation of Civilization, Color Line No Worry To Him, This Isn't Reason He Does Not Visit U.S." In the text of the story, Gandhi was quoted as saying, "I fear that either the Rev. Mr. Andrews has misunderstood me or his writing has been misread." He also made clear his views on the Hindu caste system and reiterated that "caste as an offspring of untouchability is a most harmful institution. Either it has to go or Hinduism has to die." Gandhi strongly objected to restrictions on intercaste dining. Taking the debate to a higher level, he said that "inter-dining means much more than sharing a restaurant or hotel in common with others. Inter-dining that I have in mind means entry into one's kitchen." Gandhi's statement concluded with these words: "Prohibition against other people's eating in public restaurants and hotels and prohibition of marriage between colored people and white people I hold to be a negation of civilization." Gandhi's forthright stand against untouchability and against the prohibition of marriage across racial lines must have quelled the concerns of the *Baltimore Afro-American's* readers. The paper used some of the space in the story to inform its readers about the beginnings of Gandhi's public opposition to racial segregation in South Africa. It narrated Gandhi's personal encounters with racial segregation—first the occasion when he was thrown off a train in Natal, and later, when he was kicked into the gutter for walking on the sidewalk in Pretoria. Over the years, before and after issuing his statement to the *Baltimore Afro-American*, Gandhi had a great deal to say on the question of intermarriage and interdining. His speech of 20 April 1937 at the Gandhi Seva Sangh (a social service organization) meeting at Hubli, Karnataka, India, and his statement of 5 September 1937 on the duties of Gandhi Seva Sangh are worth noting. In both Gandhi made a strong plea for marriage and dining across caste and outside of caste lines. He was convinced that in order to remove untouchability, it was necessary to accept intermarriage and interdining between caste Hindus and Harijans.[10]

In spite of the seeming or real contradictions in his interpretation of Gandhi's position on the Indian caste system, there is no doubt that Andrews helped to keep African-American attention focused on Gandhi the man, his philosophy of life, and the method of nonviolent resistance. At the same time, Andrews's own clear commitment to a social order free of racism, which began early during his missionary tenure in India, must have strengthened his credentials as an emissary of Gandhi and his movement.

The first half of the decade of the 1930s brought two more of Gandhi's co-workers to the United States. As with other such visitors in the past, their itineraries moved them directly into the life of the African-American people. In the fall of 1932, Vithalbhai J. Patel, a close colleague of the Mahatma and the brother of Vallabhbhai Patel, the leader and organizer of the dynamic and highly successful *satyagraha* campaign of Bardoli in 1928, visited African-Americans in Memphis, Tennessee. On 27 October 1932, the *Atlanta Daily World* carried the announcement of Patel's November visit with the headline "Students To Hear Gandhi Follower." The Indian nationalist was invited at the initiative of Ira H. Latimer, a professor of history and sociology at a black Memphis college. Latimer was reported to have said that "no Hindu of greater importance has ever visited the United States as a leader." And, rather perceptively, he added that "Patel lacks the spiritual influence that the Mahatma has but he makes up for it in statecraft and diplomacy." The *Atlanta Daily World* further noted that "this follower of Gandhi will speak to the LeMoyne College [an African-American institution] audience at the Second Congregational Church in the latter part of November," when he "will give the Indian side of the Nationalist movement." Being an active participant in the nationalist struggle and an articulate spokesperson, Patel was eminently qualified to communicate the message of Gandhi and his leadership.[11]

About a year later, in January 1934, Manilal Parekh, an author and follower of Gandhi, visited Atlanta. The *Atlanta Daily World* reported that Parekh was "a friend" of the Mahatma whom "Dr. Stanley Jones [an American Methodist missionary friend of Gandhi] and other equally prominent religious leaders have commended" for his lectures. The following month, Parekh was in Atlanta for another lecture. His visit and the news of his proposed address at the First Congregational Church was announced in the *Atlanta Daily World*. The paper wrote on 24 February that "Atlantans who are interested in what their brown skinned brothers across the waters in India are doing will be able to obtain some important first hand information on that subject Sunday afternoon at four o'clock at the First Congregational Church." The following day (Sunday) the *Atlanta Daily World* carried Parekh's photograph with another announcement about the event on the front page. The paper noted that Parekh, "a personal friend of Mahatma Ganhi [*sic*], the aged, slender personage, who, frail in health, has defied the British government for years . . . will speak on 'Mahatma Gandhi and His Message for the World.' " The actual title of Parekh's talk was "Mahatma Gandhi and His Message to the West." The paper announced that the speaker would concentrate on the fight Gandhi was "waging against the British" and the action he was taking "to remedy the condition of the 'untouchables.' " According to the *Atlanta Daily World*, Parekh planned to "tell how Gandhi's 'passive resistance program' or war without arms is able to work so effectively against the powerful Englishmen that even imprisonment fails to halt his activities." In the absence of any follow-up about attendance in that paper, we cannot be certain about the response from the audience or the community at large, but it is clear that such Indian visits to black social, educational, and religious centers were well publicized and represented a persistent part of the connective relationships.[12]

Important as such emissaries as Andrews, Patel, and Parekh were in strengthening the links between African-Americans and the Mahatma, direct encounters between black Americans and the Indian leader did not take place until the mid–1930s. In the light of their people's constantly deepening interest in the example and the way of Gandhi, it was not surprising that a number of important African-American leaders from church and educational communities decided to gain firsthand knowledge of India, its struggle for freedom, and the Mahatma. During the years from 1935 to 1937, six well-known African-American leaders visited India and personally met with Gandhi.

In 1935 a delegation consisting of four African-Americans—the Reverend Edward G. Carroll, Mrs. Phenola Carroll, Dr. Howard Thurman, and Mrs. Sue Bailey Thurman—was invited on "a pilgrimage of friendship" as guests of the Student Christian Movement of India, Burma, and Ceylon (now Sri Lanka). In an important sense, the way for the delegation was opened by Juliette Derricotte and Frank T. Wilson. Derricotte and Wilson were the two African-American members of a six-member delegation from the United States who attended the General Committee of the World's Student Christian Conference at Mysore, India, in 1928. Initially, Thurman had reservations about the proposed trip. He agreed to participate only after the organizers assured him that the delegation would not be called upon to be "singing, soul-saving evangelists." In a later report he wrote that "when I was assured that I would be completely free to make any interpretation of the meaning of the religion of Jesus Christ as I, myself, had discovered that meaning, my course was clear."[13]

Thurman was then dean of Rankin Chapel at Howard University. At age thirty-five he had already gained a profound and powerful perspective on matters of the spirit as well as on the here-and-now concerns of the oppressed. Early in life he had learned the futility and unworkability of brute force. From his grandmother he had also learned the lesson that physical force is immoral. Morehouse College, where he did his undergraduate studies and initial teaching before going to Howard University in 1932, deepened his sense of self-worth and set him moving on "a long quest into my own past as the deep resource for finding my way into wholeness in the present." The time he had spent with the Quaker mystic Rufus Jones in the late 1920s provided Thurman with tools to further understand the power and meaning of the spirit. At Morehouse, Spelman, and Howard University, he had a central place within his community and he was already a popular lecturer and preacher. When he set sail for India, he was "ready" to meet the Mahatma.[14]

Thurman was prepared for the Indian trip in other ways. He had read many books about India, its history, religion, the state of the independence movement, and the life and work of Gandhi. He was particularly interested in the condition of the Untouchables and Gandhi's efforts to overcome their social and political stigmatization. In that regard, his exchange of letters in the weeks before leaving for India with a Gandhi sympathizer, Mabel E. Simpson of Ingomar, Montana, demonstrated his deepening understanding of the question of untouchability. In a letter he wrote Simpson in June 1935, Thurman expressed his appreciation of "your discussion of the Harijan peoples." He felt that as a black American he could "enter directly into informal understanding of the psychological climate" of the Untouchables and suggested that despite differences in the particular experiences of the two peoples, "they do not differ in principle and in inner pain."[15]

Sue Bailey Thurman, a graduate of Oberlin College, came from an influential Atlanta family. In her capacity as a staff member of the national Young Women's Christian Association (YWCA), she played an influential role in bringing to this body an African-American perspective. A social historian of African-American life, she was also a musician and a singer of exceptional gifts. In 1936 she became the first editor of the *Aframerican Woman's Journal*. Edward and Phenola Carroll, the other couple which made up the team, brought considerable strength to the delegation. Edward Carroll, who was the son of a Methodist clergyman, had studied at Morgan State College before going on to Yale Divinity School. According to Thurman, Carroll "had come through [the church] carefully nurtured by his father, a dedicated Christian minister, and a wise, sensitive mother." Phenola Carroll, a teacher in Virginia, had majored in education; she brought a special desire to explore the teaching methods of the Indian school system.[16]

The national councils of the YMCA and YWCA chose Howard Thurman to lead the delegation, and the particular gifts and talents of each member were fully utilized. In their planning for the journey it was decided that Edward Carroll would share the responsibility of preaching with Thurman and lead college and university chapel services. Given her background and knowledge of African-American life and history, Sue Bailey Thurman was allotted the task of addressing college gatherings and meeting with women's groups. Phenola Carroll was given the responsibility of visiting schools and speaking to young people's groups. The pilgrimage of friendship was financed jointly by the Student Christian Movements of the United States of America and of India.[17]

Once the trip was announced, some African-American newspapers covered its planning with great interest. In July 1934, more than a year before the departure, the *Norfolk Journal and Guide* carried the story, along with photographs of the Thurmans, on the front page. The members of the group were described by the reporter as the "products of prominent American institutions of higher learning," with "experience in social and religious work." The proposed visit was viewed by the paper "as distinctive and significant," as it was the first time that a group of African-American Christian leaders was invited to make such a representation. A photograph of Edward Carroll, with a brief biographical sketch, appeared in the *Norfolk Journal and Guide* on 4 August 1934. A week later, the *Pittsburgh Courier* provided details of the story. The July 1935 edition of *The Crisis* carried the news and provided attractive photographs of the African-American delegation. The article provided brief biographical sketches of the delegates and some information about their plans in India, including the statement, "It is also hoped that the group will be able to visit Tagore and Gandhi."[18]

While the arrangements for the African-American delegations to India were under way, Madeleine Slade (1892–1982), a British disciple and co-worker of Gandhi, visited the United States on a lecture tour. Slade, the daughter of a distinguished British admiral, had come to her guru (spiritual teacher) and to India in 1925 via Romain Rolland's biography of the Mahatma. When he learned of Slade's visit to the United States, Howard Thurman arranged to meet her. Thurman considered the meeting important for several reasons. As part of his own preparations for the impending trip, he wanted to get a sense from this disciple of Gandhi about the people of India and their struggle to overcome British domination, and firsthand information about Gandhi. He was also curious to find out how a person of Slade's upper-class English background had been "energized" to follow the way of Gandhi. At the same time, and perhaps more importantly, he felt the need to provide her with an "exposure, in a primary way, to American Negroes, in order that her reaction be shared with the Mahatma." He further added that "this would be a prelude to our journey and, however limited, it would be equivalent to firsthand information for Gandhi himself." Thurman's intuition and strategy would later be confirmed.[19]

In his capacity as dean of Rankin Chapel, Thurman invited Madeleine Slade to Howard University in October 1934. As the university's guest, she spoke to a large audience in the historic chapel. The *Baltimore Afro-American* shared the news of Slade's visit to this major African-American campus with its large East Coast readership. The story, which appeared on page two of the newspaper, was titled "Gandhi Praised by English Girl Before Audience in D.C." Slade, identified by the paper as a "wealthy English disciple of Mahatma Gandhi," likened Gandhi's ideals to those of the Sermon on the Mount and surely pleased her audience with the statement that "the greatest spiritual teachings of the world have all come from the darker races." Gandhi's program, she argued, had the support of the people, and through his program the Mahatma had given the Indian people the courage and the confidence to stand up to white people. Slade noted that "where 150 years ago, an Indian meeting a white man on the street got down in the ditch, he now passes him as an equal." She predicted that the movement led by Gandhi was likely to "have important repercussions all over the world." This, of course, was a message that had been rising in the African-American community for almost two decades.[20]

Madeleine Slade's visit to the United States was also covered by the *Atlanta Daily World* on 18 October 1934. Under the headline "Gandhi's British Assistant Touring U.S. to Laud Work of India's Humble 'Saint,' Madeline [*sic*] Slade, Who Renounced Wealthy Family for Mahatma, Seeks to Give True Story of Master," the paper provided a detailed biographical account of Slade along with photographs of her spinning, apparently clad in homespun clothes. A photograph of the Mahatma further underlined their connection. The article noted how "America is learning first-hand information on the life of Mahatma Gandhi, India's independence seeking saint" through Madeleine Slade, who "believes the Mahatma is a spiritual teacher of the highest order." Gandhi later acknowledged that her visit to the United States had been a success.[21]

Years later in his autobiography, Howard Thurman called attention to another important dimension of Slade's visit to Howard University. He recalled the impact of her speech on the students in terms of lifestyle and the imperative of their commitment to the poor. According to Thurman, the English Gandhian pressed her listeners to consider seriously that when so many the world over did not have their basic needs fulfilled, those in the audience had no right to consume or possess more than the bare essentials. Slade's remark that "he who has more than he needs for efficient work is a thief" stayed with the students. Her observation became a conversation point within the community. By focusing on this important working principle of Gandhi's philosophy, she challenged the students to redefine the meaning of the "good things of life." According to Thurman, though Slade's style of delivery was quiet and undramatic, "the intensity of her passion gathered us all into a single embrace, and for one timeless interval we were bound together with all the people of the earth."[22] Considering the fact that this African-American school had a politically vibrant and well informed community and a Gandhi-conscious president in Mordecai Johnson, its encounter with the Mahatma's English disciple must have been rich and full of significant ramifications; Thurman said that "its impact that night was sure!" Slade's visit to Howard University, and its coverage in the *Baltimore Afro-American*, forged another link between the two people and their nonviolent struggles.

In many ways, Howard University in the 1930s was an excellent setting for a visit from this disciple of the Mahatma. Within the world of African-American education, Howard held a preeminent position. It had a socially concerned and politically active community. (For example, in late April 1930, two of Howard's students, Martin Cotten and Vivian Coombs, engaged in nonviolent action of their own. The *Baltimore Afro-American* reported that while traveling on an interstate bus route between Philadelphia and Washington, D.C., they refused to go to the back of the bus. Considering that their acts of nonviolent resistance occurred within days of Gandhi's much-talked-about Salt Satyagraha, we might speculate

that the students had some knowledge of the Indian freedom movement.) There was also a large international student population. In
addition to representatives from Africa and the Caribbean, it had
students from India, China, Mexico, and South America. Later
Thurman would write of Howard that "there was a stirring in the
wind that we recognized."[23]

Perhaps the most important single force in that stirring was
Mordecai Johnson, Howard's dynamic preacher-president, who was
deeply impressed by the life and example of Gandhi. In an address
he gave in Washington, D.C., in March 1930, Johnson said, "Negro college graduates of today should don a special brand of cheapest
variety of homemade overalls to let the Negro farthest down know
that they are one with him." He declared that "Gandhi is conducting
today the most significant religious movement in the world, in his
endeavor to inject religion into questions of economics and politics."
Believing as he did that the economic situation of African-Americans
was akin to that of the Indian people, Johnson encouraged young
people to "study and understand Gandhi perfectly." The movement
led by Gandhi, and not communism, he argued, "is deserving of
the Negro's most careful consideration."[24]

Whatever the general significance of Slade's presence on the university campus, its effect on Thurman was important, for the meeting eventually opened the way for the African-American delegation's
meeting with the Mahatma. When Thurman shared plans of his
proposed visit to India with Slade, she told him, "You must see
Gandhiji while you are there. . . . He will want to visit with you
and will invite you to be the guests of the ashram. I'll talk with
him about it upon my return and you will hear from him." Sure
enough, even before their sojourn in India began, a postcard from
Gandhi inviting the African-American delegation to a meeting at
his ashram awaited their arrival in Colombo, Sri Lanka.[25]

It is important to note that in the middle of 1934 Howard
Thurman also met Muriel Lester, a British member of the pacifist
International Fellowship of Reconciliation (IFOR) and a well-known
activist for and on behalf of the poor of the East End of London.
Through her personal witness and writings, Lester had demonstrated
her solidarity with the darker peoples of the world. Lester came
into personal contact with Gandhi as early as 1926, when she stayed
in his ashram for a month. A bond of friendship was established

between the two, and from then onwards Muriel Lester became a faithful spokesperson of Gandhi and his movement in the West. Through her connections with the IFOR and her lecture tours in the United States, in her own way she kept the image of Gandhi and his way of nonviolence alive in the minds of many people. While on the west coast she invited Howard Thurman, through a mutual friend, to meet with her in Los Angeles. "The burden of her conversation," Howard Thurman recalled years later, "had to do with sharing her knowledge and feelings about Gandhi, [and] the Indian situation. . . . Above all else, she wanted to tell me about the students and the general mood of the Indian people as she knew them."[26]

In September 1935, the African-American delegation sailed for their six-month tour of colleges and universities in Burma, Ceylon, and India. On 5 October 1935, the *Baltimore Afro-American* carried the news of their trip under the headline "Thurmans, Carrolls Embark for India." While in India, the delegation kept a busy schedule, speaking before university and community audiences. Thurman searched to know the mind of the Indian people and to gain a sense of their view of the British, African-Americans, and the world. For Thurman the trip to Santiniketan to meet with Rabindranath Tagore was one of the high points. "It was important for us to see Tagore because he was a poet of India who soared above the political and social patterns of exclusiveness dividing mankind," he later reported. Thurman said the Indian poet "moved deep into the heart of his own spiritual idiom and came up inside all peoples, all cultures, and all faiths." In the company of Tagore he felt "as if we were there and being initiated into the secret working of a great mind and a giant spirit." It was with Gandhi, however, that he experienced a sense of fundamental identity.[27]

After they had been in India for several months, with a mere two weeks before the delegation was set to head home, Thurman and his party finally met Gandhi. In February 1936, Gandhi, on his way to the ashram at Wardha, invited the African-American delegation to meet with him at his camp near Bardoli. The note from the Mahatma read, "Bardoli is closer to Bombay than my ashram. But if you prefer, when your lectures are over, I will be back at the ashram and you can come there. If this is impossible I will come to see you." The Thurmans and Edward Carroll went to

Bardoli and were given a very warm welcome by the Mahatma. In a rare gesture, he came out of his tent to receive them; so impressed was Gandhi's secretary by the warmth of the Mahatma's welcome of the African-American delegates that he turned to Howard Thurman and said that in all his years with the Mahatma he had never seen him "greet a visitor so warmly." Their meeting lasted for three hours. Gandhi began by asking a number of questions of the visitors. "Never in my life have I been a part of that kind of examination: persistent, pragmatic questions about American Negroes, about the course of slavery, and how we had survived it," Thurman recorded in his autobiography.[28]

Before long the discussion focused on the issue of nonviolence. "Is non-violence, from your point of view, a form of direct action?" Thurman asked Gandhi. To this the Indian leader gave a detailed answer. "It is not one form, it is the only form." Not concerned with the limited technical meaning of "direct action," Gandhi made it clear that "without direct active expression of it, non-violence to my mind is meaningless." He regarded nonviolence as "the greatest and the activest force in the world." He failed to see how a person could be "passively nonviolent," for he considered nonviolence "a force which is more positive than electricity and more powerful than even ether." Gandhi was convinced that, "ahimsa means 'love' in the Pauline sense, and yet something more than 'love' defined by St. Paul, although I know St. Paul's beautiful definition is good enough for all practical purposes. Ahimsa includes the whole creation, and not only human." He concluded his lengthy response to the question with a statement of his conviction that "one person who can express ahimsa in life exercises a force superior to all the forces of brutality." Thurman pressed Gandhi and asked whether "one man can hold the whole violence at bay?" Gandhi believed that it was possible, and added that nonviolence, if expressed in its fullness, was bound to convert the heart of one's adversary.[29]

Apart from the theoretical questions pertaining to *satyagraha*, Howard Thurman wanted Gandhi to explain how to train individuals and communities in nonviolent resistance. Gandhi argued that constant practice in nonviolent living was essential and emphasized study, perseverance, "and a thorough cleansing of one's self of all the impurities." Sue Bailey Thurman asked an equally practical and pertinent question regarding individual responses to situations of violence—how was she to act if her own brother was lynched before her very eyes? True to his reputation as a religiously oriented non-violent resister and an experimenter in the way of truth, the Mahatma urged the need for faith. He began by redefining self-suffering.

> Supposing I was a Negro, and my sister was ravished by a white or lynched by a whole community, what would be my duty?—I ask myself. And the answer comes to me: I must not wish ill of these, but neither must I co-operate with them. It may be that ordinarily I depend on the lynching community for my livelihood. I refuse to co-operate with them, refuse even to touch the food that comes from them, and I refuse to co-operate with even my brother Negroes who tolerate the wrong. That is self-immolation, I mean. I have often in my life resorted to the plan. Of course, a mechanical act of starvation will mean nothing. One's faith must remain undimmed whilst life ebbs out, minute by minute. But I am a very poor specimen of the practice of non-violence, and my answer may not convince you. But I am striving very hard, and even if I do not succeed fully in this life, my faith will not diminish.[30]

Before their meeting was over, Gandhi requested that the delegation sing an African-American spiritual. Mrs. Thurman sang "Were You There When They Crucified My Lord?" and "We are Climbing Jacob's Ladder." The Mahatma and his friends, including Patel, "bowed their heads in prayer" as Sue Bailey Thurman sang and Howard Thurman and Edward Carroll joined. When the guests left, they invited the Mahatma to come to America. Mrs. Thurman reinforced the request with these words: "We want you not for White America, but for Negroes; we have many a problem that cries for solution, and we need you badly." Gandhi replied that he "must make good the message here, before I bring it to you. . . . You may be sure that the moment I feel the call within me, I shall not hesitate." Howard Thurman claimed that African-Americans were ready to receive the message of nonviolence. He said, "Much of the peculiar background of our own life in America is our own interpretation of the Christian religion. When one goes through the pages of the hundreds of Negro spirituals, striking things are brought to my mind which remind me of all that you have told us today." The exchange concluded with Gandhi's prophetic words: "Well, if it comes true, it may be through the Negroes that the unadulterated message of non-violence will be delivered to the world."[31]

The Bardoli encounter between the Thurmans, Carroll, and Gandhi was a deeply significant meeting of the hearts. At another level, it was also a culmination of the ongoing meeting of the two peoples and their freedom movements. The type of questions raised amply demonstrate that the Thurmans and Carroll were interested in the spiritual as well as the political dimension of the way of nonviolence, reflecting concerns which had long been present among African-Americans.

After their meeting with Gandhi, the delegation met with other Indian leaders. They made the acquaintance of Madame Vijaya Lakshmi Pandit, sister of Nehru and an important woman leader in the Indian independence struggle. They also met with Sarojini Naidu, a onetime president of the Indian National Congress and longtime colleague of Gandhi. She had taken a prominent role in the Salt Satyagraha, and after Gandhi's arrest the leadership of the campaign had fallen into her hands. The African-American press had given considerable attention to her role in the Indian struggle. A number of newspapers carried photographs and political accounts of her role during the critical phases of the Indian struggle for independence.[32]

Given the nature of the African-American community, with its sense of solidarity with the oppressed people of the world, and the special place the Thurmans and Carrolls held in their respective settings, it was only natural that upon their return they would seek out and create opportunities to share their experiences and that they would be welcomed by others. Howard Thurman was especially well suited to communicate the meaning of Gandhi to African-Americans. He did this through his position at Howard University as professor of social ethics and dean of Rankin Chapel. "Sunday morning service at Rankin Chapel," Thurman wrote years later, "became a watering place for a wide range of worshippers, not only from within the university community, but also from the District of Columbia." He was also an outstanding writer. At a profound level, he reinterpreted for his time the meaning of the religion of Jesus for his people in their struggle against cruel and inhuman structures. What he had seen and felt in India became a central part of that interpretation. Further, through church connections and lectures in various parts of the country, Thurman was able to reach a wide and varied audience with the word of Gandhi, India, and what they meant to African-Americans. The Carrolls also shared their experiences with church and related groups.[33]

On their return the Thurmans kept a busy routine. They gave a number of lectures and sermons throughout the country. In the spring of 1936, Howard Thurman was invited by the Reverend L. K. Williams of the Olivet Baptist Church in Chicago to deliver three lectures—"The Experiences of Christian Ambassador to India," "Viewing the Occident and Orient," and "The Contribution of Religion to Better Race Relations." In the *Chicago Defender* there was a notice of the coming lectures as well as an explanation of Thurman's reasons for going to India. Of course the Thurmans also shared some of their experiences in India with Howard University. For instance, a May 1936 *Norfolk Journal and Guide* reported the news of one of their exchanges with the university community. The report detailed some of the key elements of their Indian trip and noted that Thurman shared with his colleagues at Howard "how his visits and discussions with Mahatma Ghandi, great social religious leader, had revealed the striking similarity between the Indian and American Negro problems." The Thurmans also displayed an exhibit of some of the artifacts they had brought from India.[34]

In November Howard Thurman was invited to give several lectures at Morehouse College in Atlanta. In one of the school's Tuesday chapel services, he shared his Indian experiences with students and faculty. The *Atlanta Daily World*, as usual, gave prominent attention to the event. On 4 November 1936, the paper carried the story under a bold headline—"Lauds Gandhi In Stirring Chapel Talk"— on the front page. Thurman was reported to have highlighted the lives and thought of India's three leaders—Rabindranath Tagore, Jawaharlal Nehru, and Mahatma Gandhi.[35]

Early in 1937 Howard Thurman delivered a lecture, "What We May Expect of India," at the Race Street Forum in Philadelphia. The *Baltimore Afro-American* carried the story, reporting that the talk was based on what Thurman had "gleaned from a six-month sojourn in India." In the words of the writer, "Professor Thurman suggested complete exposure as a means of clearing up racial misunderstanding not only in India but also in America." A month later Sue Bailey Thurman lectured on the status of women in India to an estimated 650 students and faculty at Oberlin College in Ohio, her alma mater. The event had the twin purpose of informing the listeners and of raising money for an African-American exchange student to spend time at Tagore's international university, Visva-Bharati (formerly Santiniketan). It was covered by the influential *Baltimore Afro-American*. The newspaper noted that Sue Bailey Thurman informed her audience of the unfavorable light in which the British authorities in India portrayed African-Americans and that the exchange program was partly designed to overcome such impressions. In an interview after her lecture, Sue Thurman "suggested that colored Americans would do well to take an example from the Indians, who stand united in their fight against British domination." The paper further reported that Mrs. Thurman believed that the Indians, though lacking in business development, were more politicized than the African-Americans. After Oberlin, Sue Bailey Thurman went on to Chicago, continuing to spread the word. The Indian alternative was once again pushed in the black community, this time by one of its most respected artist-activists.[36]

At the level of person-to-person contact between the two peoples, one of the longer-lasting outcomes of the Indian trip was a scholarship fund for African-American exchange students to study in India, which Mrs. Thurman helped to establish in the spring of 1936. The following spring two students, Marian Martin and Anna Vivian Brown, took advantage of this scholarship. The *Norfolk Journal and Guide*, under the headnote "Ambassadors To India," printed their photographs. Later in the year, the *Norfolk Journal and Guide* once again brought into focus the meeting of the African-American delegation with the Mahatma when it carried a large photograph of Mrs. Thurman and Gandhi, under the banner "As American Educators Were Greeted By Ghandi." The paper reported that "Mahatma Ghandi is shown at the door of his home as he took leave of Mrs. Howard Thurman, who with her husband . . . and Mr. and Mrs. Edward G. Carroll of Morgan College toured India in 1936." The paper also reported Sue Bailey Thurman's "plans to resume her fall schedule of lecture-recital exhibits" to raise funds for women African-American students to study in India. The paper noted that the fund, which was "initiated last spring," was called the Juliette Derricotte Memorial Fund for Undergraduate Study in

India. A few months later, the *Chicago Defender* published the same photograph of Mrs. Thurman standing with Gandhi outside his home. Giving the photograph a prominent spot in the foreign news section, the paper provided the headnote "A Charming Visitor Draws India's Holy Man Out of Seclusion." The members of the African-American delegation who had visited India were listed and the photograph's caption drew attention to the fact that they were the "first of the Race to be received by India's Holy man." The *Chicago Defender* also made sure that its readers learned that the Mahatma "exhibited great interest in the plight of the American blacks and is familiar with their problems." It seemed the process of watching Gandhi had not only taken on a closer view, but also had become more reciprocal.[37]

In the summer of 1938, the *Atlanta Daily World* gave front page coverage to Sue Bailey Thurman's lecture-recital-exhibit at Atlanta University to benefit the Juliette Derricotte Memorial Fund. The exotic and rare artifacts, including a piece of cloth woven out of the yarn spun by Mahatma Gandhi, that had been selected for display at the exhibition were listed in detail. Through her special gifts in the arena of the arts, Mrs. Thurman continued to keep the focus on the rich and valuable offerings of India.[38]

In 1939, under the Juliette Derricotte program, two students, Betty McCree, a senior from Fisk University, and Margaret Bush of Talladega College, spent a year at Visva-Bharati. The *Atlanta Daily World* reported the news, with a photograph of McCree, on the front page on 5 May 1939. In a report McCree sent home, and which the *Baltimore Afro-American* published in November 1939, she communicated a sense of life in India. Before returning home, McCree expressed the desire to travel through the country and to meet Gandhi. Whether these students met the Mahatma or not, we do not know. Nor is it clear what kind of experiences they shared with their community. What is apparent is that there was in such a program another attempt at keeping alive a flow of information and person-to-person contacts between the two peoples.[39]

Not long after the trip the Thurmans and the Carrolls made to India, two other major African-American leaders followed in their footsteps. Towards the end of 1936, Benjamin E. Mays and Channing H. Tobias traveled to India to participate in the world conference of the YMCA at Mysore. At the time Mays (who later became one of Martin Luther King, Jr.'s mentors) was dean of Howard University's School of Religion and already a major African-American spokesperson in the realm of religion, politics, and education. His journey was that of a courtly rebel who challenged indignity and oppression throughout his life. In 1905 Tobias began his career at Paine College in Savannah, Georgia, as a twenty-three-year-old teacher. After a six-year stay there, he became the secretary of the national council of the YMCA, a position he held until 1923. From 1923 to 1946, he held the post of senior secretary of the "Colored Department" of the national council. His YMCA work has been described by the historians Rayford Logan and Michael Winston as "one of the most significant activities of his career." It was in that role that he was asked to attend the world conference. They also argue that Gandhi "greatly influenced [Tobias's] religious beliefs."[40]

The YMCA world conference met at Mysore in January 1937. Thirty-five nations were represented by more than two hundred official delegates. Mays and Tobias were a part of the thirteen-member American delegation. The headnote "Sails for India," with a photograph of Mays below it, began *Chicago Defender's* report on 7 November 1936. It pointed out that Mays and Tobias were "Race" members. A week later the *Baltimore Afro-American* shared the news with a photograph of Tobias and a caption, giving brief information about their proposed India trip. As Mays planned to attend the annual session of the Indian National Congress and to meet with Gandhi, he reached Bombay on Christmas Eve 1936, several days before the start of the conference. He was aware of the revolutionary role Gandhi was playing in transforming Indian society as well as in ridding the country of alien rule. Decades later, Mays recalled in his autobiography, *Born to Rebel*, his thoughts on the significance of Mahatma Gandhi:

> For a very long time I had wished to see and talk with this ninety-pound brown man who had done so much to make Indians proud of their history and culture; who had identified himself with fifty million untouchables, determined to lift them to a place of dignity and respectability in the life of India; and who had started a movement for India's independence.[41]

Before the conference began, Mays obtained an interview with Gandhi at the latter's ashram in Wardha. Tobias was also present at the meeting. In the ninety minutes they had with Gandhi, Mays asked the Mahatma to define the meaning of nonviolence and to explain why the Indian leader had not rid Indian society of the caste system and untouchability. As Gandhi had done a year earlier with the Thurmans and Edward Carroll, so also this time with Mays and Tobias; he differentiated between passive resistance, nonviolent resistance, and violent resistance. The Mahatma was convinced that it is through constant practice that nonviolence is made "more effective and inexhaustible." The miracle of nonviolence, like all miracles, he believed, is "due to the silent and effective working of invisible forces. Non-violence is the most invisible and the most effective." Gandhi added, "a violent man's activity is most visible while it lasts. But it is always transitory."[42]

Mays agreed with Gandhi about the superiority of nonviolence but expressed doubts about its applicability on a large scale. Reflecting on the experiences of the Indian movement, especially the noncooperation movement, Gandhi suggested that the only way to be effective is through training and practice; "Non-violence cannot be preached. It has to be practiced." He continued, "Non-violence, when it becomes active, travels with extraordinary velocity, and then it becomes a miracle." He elaborated his theme thus: "So the mass mind is affected first unconsciously, then consciously. When it becomes consciously affected there is demonstrable victory."[43]

Above all, Gandhi's acceptance of nonviolence was a matter of faith, and his faith in the way of truth and love was growing stronger. He was convinced that "non-violence to be worth anything has to work in the face of hostile forces." To Mays's question, "How is a minority to act against an overwhelming majority?" Gandhi answered, "I would say that a minority can do much more in the way of non-violence than a majority." Recalling his *satyagraha* struggles in Africa, he revealed, "I had less diffidence in handling my minority in South Africa than I had here in handling a majority." Fully aware of his limitations and the experimental nature of his work, Gandhi said that he was not the final authority on nonviolence. At the same time, he insisted that the use of nonviolence "is not restricted to individuals merely but it can be practised on a mass scale." It was a powerful message for Mays to take back to the African-American communities.[44]

Mays returned home early in March 1937. On 6 March the *Baltimore Afro-American* reported his return and noted the contributions of Tobias and Mays to the work of the YMCA world council. "Mays Back from YMCA Conference" was the headline of the story. Mays felt the need to share his observations with African-Americans. Starting on 8 May 1937, he wrote a series of six articles about his Indian experience for the *Norfolk Journal and Guide*. The first two articles dealt with the political crisis in India. "Gandhi And Non-violence" came next. In it, Mays explained the meaning of Gandhian nonviolence. His article, he informed the readers, was based on "reading on the subject of non-violence and from an interview on the subject which the writer had with Mr. Ghandi." The profundity of his grasp of the concept of Gandhian nonviolence soon became apparent. At the outset, Mays emphasized the active nature of nonviolence, as opposed to the passive, less active forms. He went on to develop the four cardinal principles of nonviolence: *ahimsa*, love, fearlessness, and truth. Gandhi's doctrine of nonviolence was traced to Jesus, Tolstoy, and the Hindu scriptures. Mays concluded this highly informative essay by stating that the Indian leader "is the first man to try the non-violent method on the mass level."[45]

"Gandhi Rekindled Spirit of Race Pride In India, Dr. Mays Finds," and "Has Always Stood Up For Depressed Group, Dean's Contention" were the headlines of another article, in which Mays assessed Gandhi's contribution to India, drawing heavily upon his reading of Gandhi's writings, personal observations, and "primarily upon what the Indian people themselves have to say about their hero." Mays wrote that Gandhi "has gone a long way towards making the Indian people proud of their race and proud of their great history." He noted that this newfound sense of race and cultural pride was manifested, for example, in the adoption of the native dress and local language. As for the quality of Gandhi's leadership, he argued that "a leader who teaches his people to love their native culture and who teaches them not to be ashamed of their heritage will take his place among the immortals." Mays was convinced that Gandhi had helped Indians to become fearless. (In support of his thesis, he quoted at length from a recent article he had written about the Mahatma in the *Journal of Negro Education*, which I will discuss below.) Mays also elaborated on the program Gandhi had initiated for the amelioration of the condition of the Untouchables.[46]

In another article, Mays highlighted the differences between the socialist Nehru and Gandhi on questions of the role of religion in public life, the relevance of nonviolence as means of struggle against the British, and the place of village industries in the improvement of the living standard of the Indian people. Implicit in all this was the suggestion that Gandhi was not the sole leader of the Indian freedom struggle. Whatever the nature of the internal debate within the Indian struggle, Mays had no doubt that African-Americans could learn a great deal from the Indian experiment. "The Negro people," he wrote,

> have much to learn from the Indians. The Indians have learned what we have not learned. They have learned how to sacrifice for a principle. They have learned how to sacrifice position, prestige, economic security and even life itself for what they consider a righteous and respectable cause. Thousands of them in recent times have gone to jail for their cause. Thousands of them have died for their cause.[47]

Mays's articles were an event, a high point in the continuing tradition of African-American attention to and reflection on Gandhi and the Indian struggle. The significance of his contributions was noted by the *Norfolk Journal and Guide* in a variety of ways. A June 1937 editorial drew attention to Mays's plea that there was much the African-American people could learn from the Indians when it came to sacrificing position, prestige, and economic gain for a righteous cause. "Death, intense suffering, self-denial, imprisonment—these hold no terror for the little brown man of Asia," the paper noted. Somewhat exaggeratedly, their readers were told that Gandhi's "spirit is lord of his universe, where values are weighed in the scale of a community of interest rather than in the light of fleeting materialism." Somewhat unfairly, the *Norfolk Journal and Guide* bemoaned the fact that there were "no real Negro leaders in jail, none in exile, none upon whose head there is a price, none suffering martyrdom." Having pointed to the lack of such exemplary qualities in African-American leadership, however unfairly, the paper ended the piece with the following exhortation:

> People who have not learned how to suffer, how to subordinate self, how to be humble and charitable, can not appraise spiritual values, can not walk and talk with God and commune with his fellowmen and serve humanity. Until then, such people are doomed to oppression and poverty and servitude.[48]

In the spring of 1937 Mays contributed a lengthy essay to Howard University's *Journal of Negro Education* on "The Color Line Around the World." Though the essay was based on Mays's personal experiences during his trip to India, he also drew upon C. F. Andrews's *India and Britain*, and Jawaharlal Nehru's *Autobiography*. Despite its focus on white attitudes toward people of color, Mays's essay again turned the attention of his readers to Gandhi's leadership of the Indian freedom struggle.

> Just a word about Mahatma Gandhi. The world is too close to him to appraise him adequately. Certainly my knowledge of him is too meager for me to speak of his influence with finality. But I believe that future historians will record among his contributions to India something like the following: "He did more than any other man to dispel fear from the Indian mind and more than any other to make Indians proud to be Indians." That the non-violence campaign was a failure, no one has a right to say. All the evidence is not yet in. Time alone will write the final verdict. But the fact that Gandhi and his non-violent campaign have given the Indian masses a new conception of courage, no man can honestly deny. To discipline people to face death, to die, to go to jail for the cause without fear and without resorting to violence is an achievement of the first magnitude. And when an oppressed race ceases to be afraid, it is free.

It is apparent that Mays had a genuine interest in and knowledge of the Indian struggle and its Gandhian concepts of nonviolence, and the ability to communicate it to his fellow African-American women and men in struggle. Repeating some of the major themes of the continuing African-American appraisal of Gandhi, he wrote,

> The cardinal principles of non-violence are love and fearlessness. A leading Indian woman told me that before Gandhi came on the scene, the average Indian was very much afraid of a Britisher. Many Indians would run and hide when a British officer appeared. She thinks this is hardly true now. They face him and talk to him as man to man. She gives Gandhi credit for this change of attitude. It is the conviction of a missionary that Gandhi has made the Indian masses proud of their language, has created in them a respect for their culture and has instilled in them a feeling that, 'It's great to be an Indian!' If these observations are true, they will go a long way to gain greater respect for the Indians in the minds of the British and the world.[49]

As already noted, Channing H. Tobias, a major church figure of twentieth century Afro-America, accompanied Mays to the Mahatma's ashram. During his India trip, in addition to the meeting with Gandhi in Wardha, Tobias also spent time with the Mahatma while the Indian leader was on his way to Travancore to direct a temple entry protest for Untouchables. Before Tobias left India, the Maharaja of Travancore made a decision which permitted Untouchables to worship freely in Hindu temples.[50]

From India, Tobias sent a brief account of his Indian visit and meeting with Gandhi to the *Chicago Defender*. On 6 March 1937 the paper published his report. The correspondence gave the readers a clear sense of Indian determination to win freedom, the importance of the Indian National Congress as a major voice of the national struggle, and the differences between Gandhi and Nehru over the extent to which nonviolent means might be utilized in ridding the nation of alien rule. Tobias also reported on Gandhi's continued insistence upon the method of nonviolent resistance, and his call for Hindu-Muslim unity and an end to untouchability.

> Mahatma Gandhi is still the proponent of the philosophy of nonviolence, believing that if caste and religious lines are modified to the extent that political unity is realized, and the masses are taught to develop simple home industries for sustenance, political freedom can be won without bloodshed. . . . Regardless of the fact that he has for the past two years taken no active part in politics, Gandhi is still the idol of the masses of India. He is now living in an aschram [*sic*] or hut in a village of outcasts [*sic*] in order to set the example for high caste Indians to abolish caste.[51]

As Thurman and Mays had done earlier, Tobias probed Gandhi on the philosophy of nonviolence and its relevance for African-Americans. The two and a half hours he spent with Gandhi led to a rich dialogue. Tobias was so moved by his experience that he decided to contribute another article to the *Chicago Defender*, but there is no known record that their conversation was published in the African-American press. The most complete available version, from the *Collected Works of Mahatma Gandhi*, runs as follows:

> *Dr. Tobias*: Your doctrine of non-violence has profoundly influenced my life. Do you believe in it as strongly as ever?

Gandhiji: I do indeed. My faith in it is growing.

[*Tobias*]:   Negroes in U.S.A.—12 million—are struggling to ob-
                tain such fundamental rights as freedom from mob vi-
                olence, unrestricted use of the ballot, freedom from
                segregation, etc. Have you, out of your struggle in
                India, a word of advice and encouragement to give us?

[*Gandhi*]:   I had to contend against some such thing, though on
                a smaller scale, in South Africa. The difficulties are not
                yet over. All I can say is that there is no other way than
                the way of non-violence, a way, however, not of the
                weak and ignorant but of the strong and wise.

[*Tobias*]:   Travancore indicates that your full identification with
                the untouchables is bearing fruit. Do you think Tra-
                vancore's example will be followed by other States in
                the near future?

[*Gandhi*]:   I shall be surprised if it is not.

[*Tobias*]:   What word shall I give my Negro brethren as to the
                outlook for the future?

[*Gandhi*]:   With right which is on their side and the choice of
                non-violence as their only weapon, if they will make it
                such, a bright future is assured.[52]

This was quite a promise for African-Americans, and within less
than two decades they would go far toward wresting its great hope
out of the tragedy of their peculiar situation. They had begun to
create their own bright future with a movement which eventually
showed many signs that they had not been watching the Indian
people in vain and that their call for a black Gandhi was not merely
a dream.

≡5≡

Exploring
Gandhian Techniques
of Nonviolent
Direct Action

THE COMING of World War II opened a new stage in the ongoing connections between African-Americans and the Gandhian movement. Indeed, by the time the war was over, some of the major bearers of Gandhian ideals had positioned themselves at the heart of the black freedom struggle. In an important sense, their interest in the methods of Gandhian nonviolence deepened in the early 1940s. Dissent and disagreement over nonviolence notwithstanding, they gave form to the practice of Gandhian nonviolence in the United States. Significant institutional attempts were made to apply Gandhian techniques to the American struggle.

Worsening economic conditions during the post-Depression years and the continuance of racial oppression accentuated African-American discontent. As the European war spread, the United States rapidly expanded its wartime production capacities, but the armament industry, which was federally controlled and privately managed, barred black Americans from the war industries. As a result of blatant racism, African-Americans had difficulty in getting even unskilled jobs. Meanwhile, black servicemen faced harsh discrimination and even physical attacks, especially on and near military bases in the South. In September 1940, moved by the gravity of the plight of their community and the intensity of discrimination, African-American leaders began to press President Franklin Roosevelt to act. Several, including Walter White of the NAACP and A. Philip Randolph, head of the Brotherhood of Sleeping Car Porters, met the president to complain about discrimination in the armed forces. The meeting brought no fruitful results.[1]

Disappointed, yet eager to end discrimination in the war industries and in the military services, Randolph sought to force the hand of the president. Perhaps no one understood the meaning of power and the factors which made politicians respond better than Randolph. Out of his labor-organizing experience and his socialist studies, he also understood the power of the masses. He recognized that new anti-segregation tactics were needed, that African-Americans needed to move beyond writing letters, sending telegrams, and submitting petitions. Neither the picketing in which the NAACP engaged nor the radio appeals of the Urban League would be adequate. Building on this knowledge, Randolph, one of the most notable and visible leaders of the African-American community, called on his people to resist oppression. Beginning in 1941, he organized a mass protest movement, the March on Washington Movement (MOWM), to overcome segregation in the war industries. At the height of his leadership of the MOWM he consciously turned to Gandhian methods for confronting injustice.[2]

The idea of the March on Washington came to Randolph in December 1940 on a journey through the South with Milton Webster, vice president of the Brotherhood of Sleeping Car Porters. Randolph turned to Webster and said, "I think we ought to get 10,000 Negroes and march down Pennsylvania Avenue asking for jobs in defense plants and integration of the armed forces. It would shake up Washington." Randolph publicly broached the subject at a meeting in Savannah, Georgia. In subsequent days and weeks, he discussed the idea with others, including Walter White of the NAACP, Frank R. Crosswaith of the Negro Labor Committee, Channing Tobias of the YMCA, and Lester Granger of the National Urban League. In January 1941 Randolph proposed a march on Washington of ten thousand African-Americans. The immediate goal would be to bring to an end racial discrimination in war industries. Nothing like this had been tried before, but Randolph believed that power resided with the people: "Only the voice of the masses will be heard and heeded—Negro America has never yet spoken as a mass, an organized mass." He urged the people to "speak" with ten thousand in the nation's capital "singing 'John Brown's Body Lies a Mouldering in the Grave,' and 'Before I'll be a Slave, I'll be Buried in My Grave and Go Home to My Father and Be Saved.'" He did not want "white friends" to participate in the struggle: "There are some things Negroes must do alone. This is our fight and we must see it through." At the same time, he did not want any communists in the movement. A national MOWM committee, with Randolph as its director, was formed. Regional committees, supported by the organizers of the Brotherhood of Sleeping Car Porters, were started throughout the country. In addition to the national and regional committees, the MOWM constituted a sponsoring committee which included such people as White, Granger, and the Reverend Adam Clayton Powell, Jr., the fiery religious and political leader from Harlem.[3]

As for Randolph, he kept unrelenting pressure on the federal government with mammoth mass meetings in different parts of the United States. He mobilized people into action all across the country. "Why does not the President who is unquestionably a great humanitarian, with definite and high ideals, issue such an order in the interest of national unity and national defense?" he boldly asked in the *Norfolk Journal and Guide*, referring to the executive power of the commander in chief.[4] At the same time, he called upon his people to develop the techniques of organized mass protest which he had perfected as a labor leader. Even though there was no specific reference yet, the people who had been watching India were now developing their own Gandhian-type resources.

Meanwhile, President Roosevelt and his advisors were watching Randolph and the MOWM. As the white power structure woke up to the implications of the march, it sought to pressure Randolph into canceling it. Intermediaries—New York's Mayor Fiorello La Guardia and Mrs. Eleanor Roosevelt—were sent to convince Randolph to drop the march for national security reasons. Recognizing the firm resolve of African-American leaders and fearful of the consequences the march might have on the national war effort, Roosevelt met with Randolph and White in the middle of June. On 25 June, the president signed Executive Order No. 8802, designed to correct certain abuses which were practiced against African-Americans by government departments as well as by the contracting agencies of the government. The executive order also set up a committee on fair employment in the Office of Production Management.[5]

Randolph agreed to postpone the march on the nation's capital and instead called a mammoth mass meeting at the Lincoln Memorial. Following the executive order, on 28 June, Randolph, in a nationwide radio broadcast, explained the reasons for calling off the march. Even though the presidential order did "not meet the vital and serious issue of discrimination against persons on a basis of race, color, creed and national origin in various departments of the Federal Government," Randolph and the MOWM felt that because it was now government policy not to "countenance discrimination" it was "unnecessary [to hold the march] at this time." Randolph also expressed the hope that the president might follow up the executive order with a second order, "complementing and supplementing this one, that will strike down for all times discrimination . . . in all departments of the Federal Government." In conclusion, he advised the various committees of the MOWM to "remain intact and watch and check the industries in their communities to determine the extent to which they are observing the executive order of the President." Randolph had not given up the option of having a march in the future.[6]

As a result of these developments, Randolph emerged as the most favored of African-American leaders. According to his biographer, Jervis Anderson, "Randolph now became, and would remain for almost a decade, the most popular and sought-after black political figure in America." He was seen as a man with the honesty of purpose and the ability to lead. Here was a leader who had shunned personal honor and glory, who had risked and sacrificed his personal well-being. Noting the significance of Randolph's rise to a preeminent position of leadership, the *New York Amsterdam News* concluded an editorial with these words:

> Other organizations and other leaders have done some good work, but because their support has not come from the masses, and because they have rushed to get jobs for themselves at every opportunity, their leadership has been weak and ineffectual. It's an old saying, 'He Who Pays the Fiddler Calls the Tune.'
>
> For many years the Negro has been groping for a leadership that could be trusted. It seems, now, that that leadership is being ushered in. We regard A. Philip Randolph as the man of the hour. His

sacrifices in the past, which were made in times of stress and want, would seem to indicate he cannot be bought. On his record we heartily endorse his program and commend him to the Negroes of America who look for and hope for a better day.

Here was a clear sign that Randolph's leadership was a critical factor in the struggle. From his position of great influence he emphasized the importance of organizing the masses and using nonviolent methods during those critical years, actions which led the media to call him "the American Gandhi."[7]

In April 1942, a specific plea for Gandhian methods of resistance came from the general ranks of the African-American community. This was sparked by an editorial, "Color Call to America," in the *New York Amsterdam News*. Inspired by deep concern for both the wartime security of the nation and the welfare of the African-American community, the editorial demanded that the nation guarantee fundamental constitutional rights, including free access to employment in the nation's defense industries. Several readers wrote to the paper in response. One of these, Thomas E. Wilson, encouraged the nation to grant the legitimate demands of African-Americans. A delay, Wilson argued, was bound to make matters worse for those in leadership. He hoped that the United States might learn from British mistakes in India. Indo-British relations continued to deteriorate. Neither Gandhi nor any of the key nationalist leaders were prepared to join the Allied war effort as long as the British were in charge of Indian affairs. It seemed that the two nations were pulling apart with no genuine compromise in sight. By early 1942 the ground had been prepared for the British to quit India. "If England had only listened to Gandhi and Nehru years ago, it would not have to be on its knees now to them," Wilson contended, and he added that "unless America grants its loyal millions of colored citizens full opportunity and equality now, in 10 years from now, Uncle Sam will be pleading with them to save his soul." Another reader, Rebecca West, suggested,

Why don't you take a full page and tell the Government just why in detail our attitude is one of passive resistance? England has at last got its lesson from India. 'Independence or nothing,' says Mahatma Ghandi. There are no colored leaders in this country who

have the courage and love of people, as well as patriotism, to tell
America that it cannot win unless it gets on God's side and practices
today what it has always preached—equal chance in life. Keep up
the good work.

Apparently, West did not view Randolph as a Gandhi-like leader.
Nevertheless, she made an important observation about the relevance of the quality of Gandhi's leadership.[8]

Meanwhile, aware of the necessity of keeping up the pressure on
the government, Randolph advocated a series of large mass meetings
to protest discrimination against African-Americans. Working-class
and poor urban blacks responded in large numbers. Early in July
1942, the MOWM committee organized a mammoth mass meeting
in Chicago, with twelve thousand persons from the community
filling the coliseum. According to Herbert Garfinkel, the "spon-
taneous involvement of large masses of Negroes in a political protest
without the collaboration of whites" was a new factor. Randolph
had gone into the heart of his community and had begun to mobilize
African-Americans as had not been done since Garvey galvanized
them immediately following World War I. In a speech (which was
un-Gandhian in spirit) at the Chicago mass meeting, Randolph told
the crowd that "if the President does not issue a war proclamation
to abolish jim-crow in Washington, the District of Columbia and
all government departments and the armed forces, Negroes are going
to march and we don't give a damn what happens." He would
rather that African-Americans "die standing on our feet fighting
for our rights than to exist upon our knees begging for life." Randolph's thesis was simple: people in power respond to the coun-
terforce of protest and resistance; this was the case with labor,
business, and farming communities. The president, he told the
people, will "respond to protest from an aroused Negro public."
He promised to fight with all the energy he had to regain independent status for the Fair Employment Practices Commission
(FEPC).[9]

In the meantime, connections between the African-American
struggle and worldwide anticolonial movements were becoming
even more well-defined and visible. By the fall of 1942, Randolph
had begun to make concrete references to the similarities between
the method he was using and that of Gandhi. The *Chicago Defender*
of 26 September devoted considerable space in its magazine section
to a number of essays on the meaning of the worldwide struggle

for African-Americans, with a special focus on India. Randolph contributed one of the articles. He emphasized that African-Americans, along with the peoples of India, Africa, China, were leading the world to "democracy and freedom, justice and decency, peace and love, today," by following the "old medieval doctrine of salvation through suffering and sacrifice." For example, he saw no basic difference between the problems facing Gandhi's India and those of African-Americans. Nor did he differentiate between the methods and strategies employed in the two struggles.

> Both countries are greatly influenced by the doctrines of racism. Both countries have highly developed forms of monopoly capitalism. . . . Both the Indian people and the Negro people are subject people, lacking the constitutional civil and political rights of a free people. The Indian and Negro people are immensely important to the winning of this war against totalitarian tyranny. But, the Indian and Negro people insist upon their right to fight for democracy in the true spirit of democracy, namely, as a free people. . . .
>
> To secure it, the Indian people have been forced to declare and conduct a social, political and economic program of civil disobedience. And in America, to secure their rights as American citizens, the Negro people have been compelled to threaten to March On Washington. Both of these challenges won some concessions from British [sic] and America. In India, the movement of civil disobedience hurried Sir Stafford Cripps from England with a belated proposal for dominion status. . . .
>
> In America, the March on Washington Movement secured from the President the Executive Order 8802.[10]

In the same article Randolph forcefully articulated that African-Americans were fighting for freedom on two fronts, one out in Europe and Asia, and the other at home in the United States. Recognizing the indivisibility of freedom and justice, he argued that the fact "that this is so, is a blessing to the Negro and the world today." He said he was also convinced that it was the people of India, China, and Africa, and not the imperialist nations of Europe or the United States, with their racist structures, who were leading the world to "freedom, peace and plenty." At the same time, Randolph had no illusions that an Allied victory over the Axis powers was going to bring liberty and justice to the colored peoples of the world. "All imperialisms," he thundered, "are oppressive, exploitive and do not only serve to rob the darker races

of their land and labor but . . . humiliate and insult the very souls
of the natives." Euro-America, he argued, could not be trusted
because it had no intention of giving up control of lands overseas
and gave no thought to "the hundreds of millions of brown, yellow,
and black peoples who are under the yoke of despotism of the United
Nations [meaning the Western allies]." Randolph said that because
Euro-America could not be relied upon, "India and the Negro people
of America call for freedom now." Possessed of a universalist vision
of humanity and fully appreciative of the redemptive quality of
struggles of human liberation, he concluded that "the Negro and
Indian people are not fighting for freedom now for themselves alone,
but for the moral and spiritual salvation of America and England,
if not of western civilization."[11] After more than two decades, a
movement seemed to be arising in the African-American community
which progressed from watching India to experimenting consciously
with its own versions of Gandhian methodologies and goals.

Meanwhile, Randolph was under pressure to continue preparing
for an actual march on Washington. To answer his critics and to
keep the pressure on the government, in January 1943 he announced
the plans for a national conference around the theme "I Am An
American Too." Initially scheduled to take place in May at Chicago,
this would be the first formal national convention designed to sym-
bolize wartime protest of the entire African-American community.
In preparation for the national convention, a full-time national
executive secretary was appointed. With a view to energizing his
followers, Randolph spoke at several meetings all over the country
and the MOWM organized branches in twenty-four cities. In anticipating the conference and its goals, the *Chicago Defender's* headline announced, "Randolph to Adopt Gandhi Technique, Nonviolent Disobedience May Be Used." The paper reported that "the
technique of non-violent civil disobedience popularized and used
effectively by Mahatma Gandhi in India will be adopted by the
March on Washington movement at its May conference if the wishes
of A. Philip Randolph founder of the movement prevail." The
announcement outlined a five-point program to be observed nationally during the week of the conference. "The civil non-violent
disobedience proposal is point number one on his agenda for the
week," the *Chicago Defender* noted. For the duration of the convention, African-Americans were urged to boycott Jim Crow cars and

waiting rooms in the South and advised to sit in the main sections of the cars and use normal waiting rooms. The *Chicago Defender* reported that Randolph advised that the participants in the program "not fight back," but instead refuse "to enter jim-crow cars and waiting rooms, in an orderly, peaceful and quiet manner." The other four points of the "I Am An American Too" convention called upon African-Americans throughout the country to march on city halls to petition mayors and city councils; to send letters and telegrams, and make long distance telephone calls to the president and the secretaries of various federal departments; to send telegrams, letters, and make long distance telephone calls to the presidents and personnel managers of every southern railroad company; and to request preachers and newspapers to preach sermons and write editorials on "I Am An American Too."[12]

Continuing to encourage African-Americans to challenge segregated structures, Randolph used the black-controlled newspapers to explain further his position on civil disobedience. In the article he wrote for the *Baltimore Afro-American* in February of 1943, Randolph declared that the MOWM was against Hitlerism at home and abroad, and as such was not opposed to the national war effort. He argued that Hitlerism expressed itself in the United States "in all forms of discrimination, segregation and jim crow." He defined his program as "a form of social protest and revolt against unjust, unfair, and undemocratic laws that violate the basic moral and human citizenship rights of the colored people." It is likely that he felt obliged to make this pro-war-effort statement repeatedly because of the significant sentiment within his community that questioned the logic of supporting the war efforts of colonizing and segregating nations like the United States, France, and Great Britain. (It must also be noted that during the course of World War II, Gandhi came under much criticism in the African-American press for his conditional support of the Allied war effort.) Convinced that only powerful pressure would force the government into action, Randolph called for the boycott of Jim Crow cars and schools in the South. Such an action, he believed, was "certain to have a profound spiritual and moral influence upon the whole social thinking of America."[13]

Randolph's call for civil disobedience and noncooperation drew mixed comments about both the appropriateness of the method and its timing. Du Bois was ready with his observations. Although deeply interested in the cause of the Indian people and supportive of Gandhi's nonviolent struggle against the British, Du Bois wrote in the columns of the *New York Amsterdam News* to argue against "launching a broad national program based on non-violent civil disobedience and no-cooperation [*sic*], modeled along the lines of the campaigns of Mohandas K. Ghandi"; given the fact that African-Americans constituted a mere fifteenth of the work force, as against the Indians, who made up "practically the whole working class of India," a call for a strike "would be playing into the hands of our enemies." Challenge to existing laws, he believed, "is a serious thing to be entered upon only in great extremity and after careful thought and will to sacrifice." Du Bois had no illusions about the condition of African-Americans. Yet he felt that "our case in America is not happy, but also it is far from desperate." He declared that "compared with the laboring masses of the world our progress in the last seventy-five years has been rapid and our outlook is hopeful." Even more important, fasting, prayer, sacrifice, and self-torture, he argued, had been "bred into the very bone of India for more than three thousand years." Du Bois could not imagine a similar approach succeeding in the United States—on the contrary, it "would be regarded as a joke or a bit of insanity"—and he went on to caution his readers that African-Americans "cannot then blindly copy methods without thought and consideration." He had no doubt that African-Americans resented the color bar, that they were willing to contribute resources for agitation and publicity, and finally, that they were even less willing than before to "submit to arbitrary and illegal discrimination," but he noted that all this should not lead to the conclusion that African-Americans were "ready for systematic lawbreaking."

> My own feeling is distinctly that Agitation and Publicity are still our trump cards, and that their possibilities, within bounds of law and order, are by no means exhausted; especially, Publicity. Why not publish [Judge William H.] Hastie's explanation of his resignation as a full-page advertisement in the New York Times?[14]

Du Bois, the master publicist, was not yet ready for the possibilities of a new form of public discourse and democratic "agitation" carried out through the physical presence of thousands of men, women, and children. (Hastie was the first African-American civilian appointed to assist the Secretary of War; because of his strong stand against discrimination in the armed forces, he resigned his position.)

The newspaper debate was picked up that spring by a *New York Amsterdam News* reader, Ralph T. Templin, a white Methodist missionary colleague of J. Holmes Smith of Harlem Ashram—a community based on the Gandhian principles of living. Templin, who was the director of the School of Living, in New York, took issue with Du Bois and claimed that the African-American leader and others like him did not understand the full meaning of Gandhian nonviolence. People in this country had "presented to them only its [Gandhi's plan] most superficial, the political and negative, aspects," Templin suggested. The full meaning of the Indian movement, he added, could only be understood as the product of "the rugged fearlessness of self-help and interdependence." Next Templin went on to show the links between Thoreau, Tolstoy, and the Gandhian approach. Gandhi, he was sure, had "borrowed his idea of non-violent civil resistance from the early Abolutionists [*sic*] of the United States" and "Thoreau remains still the great theorist of this movement"; nonviolence was "the all-sided sword" and Gandhi "its latest prophet." Grasping the essence of Jesus' way of love, Templin ended his letter with a powerful plea for the way of nonviolence. He observed, "To accept injustice is the way of a slave. But to resist with violence is to enslave oneself and one's opponent. To suffer with steadfast courage for a conviction which leads one to refuse to accept injustice, is the way of men both wise and free."[15] Templin's analysis of the religious and theoretical dimensions of nonviolence could not be faulted. Nor could one ignore the cautionary note Du Bois sounded about recourse to civil disobedience. In any case, Randolph was well aware of the problems of uncritically re-planting Gandhi's concept of *satyagraha*. It is with at least that concern in mind that he emphasized the "good will" aspect of his own approach. Nevertheless, the debate sparked by Du Bois's essay raised some valuable questions for all who cared to watch the developments which had been unfolding in India.

Meanwhile, Randolph carried his message of nonviolent resistance with missionary zeal to different parts of the United States. In the spring of 1943, in a lecture he gave to an audience of some fifteen hundred persons in St. Louis, Randolph explained his civil disobedience project. He assured his listeners that if African-Americans wished to gain their basic rights and privileges, they could depend on neither Republicans nor Democrats. He also "warned against alignment with the Communists." Randolph emphasized that the evil of racism can best be overcome "by 'non-violent, good-will direct action.' " He insisted that African-Americans actively protest against "every law, custom, and practice violative of the citizenship rights of the colored people." He encouraged Southern-based African-Americans to refuse to ride segregated street cars or send their children to segregated schools. Northern African-Americans were invited to collaborate with sympathetic white people to challenge discrimination in restaurants and hotels. Gandhian "non-violent, good-will direct action" was the only way of destroying Jim Crowism, he contested.[16]

Beginning on 12 June 1943, to coincide with the "We Are Americans Too" convention, Randolph contributed a series of six articles to the *Chicago Defender*. He used the opportunity to answer criticisms in detail and to explain thoroughly his program. This time he made even more clear the connections he saw between Gandhian concepts of nonviolence and the concepts he was developing and trying to put to use in America. In the first article he pointed out how parleys with the policy makers had never worked and why he had to resort to the method of nonviolent, good-will direct action which "is a modified expression of the principle of non-violent civil disobedience and non-cooperation set forth by Gandhi in India." He argued that there was "no difference between Hitler of Germany and [Governor Eugene] Talmadge of Georgia or Tojo of Japan and [Senator Theodore] Bilbo of Mississippi." Randolph explained that it was out of desperation that people like him resorted to mass action. About the positive results of the MOWM he had no doubt: "In the March on Washington Movement, the voiceless and helpless 'little men' became articulate," he observed.

> Though jobless, for the first time they experienced a thrill from a sense of their importance and worthwhileness. In meeting after meeting, the 'forgotten black man' could rise and tell an eager and earnest crowd about jobs he sought but never got, about the business agent of the union giving him the brush-off, how he had gone to the gates of defense plants only to be kept out while white workers walked in, how he cooled his heels in an office and finally was told

with a cold stare, 'no more workers wanted' or how the government employment services would not permit him to enroll as a skilled worker but only as a porter or janitor or how he was denied entrance into certain government training courses for skilled defense jobs.

In very truth, the March On Washington, little men can tell their story their own way.[17]

In the second article (19 June 1943) he outlined the philosophy of the MOWM as well as its central objective which was total equality for all Americans in all areas of life. According to Randolph, revolutionary times demanded revolutionary methodology and technique so as to place "the cause of a minority into the mainstream of national and international public opinion."[18]

Throughout the summer, Randolph continued his major teaching and consciousness raising campaign through the pages of the *Chicago Defender*. In an article accompanied by a photograph of Mahatma Gandhi, the MOWM leader explained the technique of civil disobedience. Gandhi was identified with the words "Indian National Congress leader whose tactics are being studied by the March on Washington." Randolph stated that the forthcoming conference would "thoroughly" explore Gandhian strategies of nonviolent civil disobedience and noncooperation. He disagreed with those who "condemned and denounced" this technique because it was developed in a "foreign and oriental situation," and he reminded his critics that Jesus Christ too was born in the Eastern world.[19]

Randolph went on to clarify the differences between his concept and the one practiced in India by the Mahatma, defining the MOWM program as "constitutional obedience or non-violent goodwill direct action." Insofar as his program sought to uphold rather than break down civil government, it differed from the Gandhian concept of civil disobedience. "The objective" of the Indian people, he explained, "is to effect a transition of governmental power from the hands of the British imperialists into the hands of the Indian people." He recognized that the logic of such a position must necessarily lead to "the breaking down of British Civil government and the establishment of an Indian Civil government," but the purposes of African-Americans, Randolph felt, were different. He said that they had "no desire to see the collapse of American civil government," and added that they were "not seeking independence as a racial unit." Finally, he argued that the MOWM was against calling on "the Negroes in the armed forces or defense industries to disobey commands or stop work at any time."[20]

As he continued his education campaign, Randolph wrote on 3 July 1943 about the necessity of putting pressure on all levels of government to abolish Jim Crowism in the United States and to bridge the gap between educated and uneducated African-Americans. Before a change of this magnitude could happen, he was convinced, masses of people would have to be mobilized. Randolph kept open his options about the inauguration of such an action. The timing of action based on "non-violent mass activity and disciplined non-violent demonstration," he argued, would depend upon the readiness of the people. Finally, he stated that "the people must not only be ready but they must be prepared and disciplined to march on Washington. . . . But a March on Washington must be the Negro's last resort."[21] Randolph had succeeded in integrating into the MOWM the core principles of Gandhian nonviolence. These principles were most dramatically and astutely utilized by him in galvanizing African-Americans all over the country. Hence the march on the capital city of the nation had become only one ingredient, albeit an important ingredient, of Randolph's overall strategy.

Meanwhile, the MOWM organized its "We Are Americans Too" conference to impress upon the nation that African-Americans were determined to press for the removal of all legal and social disabilities faced by them. The conference, which took place in July 1943 in Chicago, was the first such formal gathering of a predominantly African-American group whose purpose was to take the Gandhian principles, add them to traditions of their struggle, and use them as a way of attacking segregation in the United States. A total of 109 delegates from fourteen states and the District of Columbia participated in the "We Are Americans Too" convention. To continue to educate and energize its supporters in the nation, the leadership planned to send organizers to states not represented at the convention. Randolph addressed the final mass meeting, which was attended by two thousand persons. The convention authorized the executive committee to prepare plans for organizing the proposed march on Washington. At the concluding session of "the fiery five-day convention," Randolph reminded the "wildly enthusiastic" crowd which jammed Chicago's DuSable High School auditorium that the callous disregard for the legitimate and just rights of African-Americans by the Democratic and Republican parties was responsible for the recent wave of rioting. He challenged the government yet again to "stop the jim-crow treatment of Negro citizens and begin to integrate them into the government and war and peace time industry on a basis of equality."[22]

James Farmer and Bayard Rustin, co-secretaries of the race relations department of the nonsectarian, pacifist Fellowship of Reconciliation (FOR), and E. Stanley Jones, a well-known white American Methodist missionary to India and a friend of Gandhi, were among those who addressed the convention. To what extent they tied their movement to the Indian experiences is not altogether clear from the newspaper reports. Platform speakers emphasized the necessity of disobeying unjust laws. Rustin detailed the various elements of nonviolent direct action and the importance of training. He argued that the MOWM campaign was "designed to overcome jim crow by changing attitudes of people." Jones highlighted one of the essential Gandhian principles concerning nonviolent resistance; echoing Gandhi on the need for stern discipline by nonviolent activists, he said that the practitioner of this way believes, "I don't hate you but I won't obey you. This law or order is wrong and unjust. Do what you may, I won't strike back and I won't obey." Jay Holmes Smith, a white American former Methodist missionary to India, stated that his most embarrassing moment in India was "when Indians asked me why do you com[e] out here to tell us about Christianity when in your country they lynch colored people." In the resolutions which they passed, the delegates gave "unqualified support . . . [to] the non-violent, goodwill direct action non-cooperation technique to secure equal rights." The MOWM resolved to "awaken, teach, organize, mobilize, direct and lead masses of colored people to fight and struggle for their own liberation from racial discrimination, segregation and jim-crowism." The convention recognized the need to set up regional institutes to train people in the technique of nonviolent resistance. The delegates dedicated themselves "to help to build a free world without regard to race, color, creed or national origin." Hoping to empower African-Americans and fearful of communist infiltration, the convention decided to restrict membership to blacks only. The week-long proceedings were covered in the African-American press.[23]

From within the African-American community there was continued opposition to the idea of a march on Washington. For example, the Christian Methodist Episcopal Bishop, C. L. Russell of Washington, D.C., said that the proposed march "would be a dangerous undertaking at the present time," leading to loss of life and property, and he warned that it was also likely to "handicap interracial good will." Russell said he did not doubt the intentions of the organizers but felt strongly that "the crowd itself would look like a crowd of rioters in the eyes of some of the members of the white race who take pride in participating in riots with colored people." The MOWM raised questions of another kind in the minds of some critics. The *Chicago Defender* columnist, John Robert Badger, while recognizing the exceptional qualities of Randolph's leadership, concluded that Randolph's was a "faulty program" which was bound to result in "the isolation and persecution of his people." Isolationism in this context was defined by Badger as Randolph's insistence on African-Americans relying on their own resources and denying the necessity of "Negro-white unity."[24]

For a variety of reasons, the MOWM failed to execute specific acts of civil disobedience or noncooperation. Thirty-four people (twenty-five of them African-Americans) died in the mid–1943 race riots in Detroit, days before the "We Are Americans Too" conference. The riots, set off by a rapid increase in black migration from the South and worsening economic and social conditions, were an immediate blow to the MOWM's plans for civil disobedience. By 1944 the FEPC had lost its earlier status and that directly weakened the movement. Meanwhile, the NAACP had begun to distance itself from the MOWM. Furthermore, wartime conditions were not conducive to the execution of civil disobedience campaigns. Though the MOWM continued to maintain its official existence until 1947, its initial impetus, once lost, was never regained.[25]

Despite his failure to execute a national program of civil disobedience, Randolph kept alive African-American interest in revolutionary nonviolence through his speeches, articles, rallies, and protest meetings. In a direct way, as never before, blacks were encouraged to consider the way of Gandhi. On a personal level Randolph's activities led to significant valuable collaborative connections with a number of black activists, some of whom were to play key roles at the height of the modern African-American freedom movement. Perhaps the most important among them were E. D. Nixon, James Farmer, and Bayard Rustin. Nixon, based in Montgomery, Alabama, was a union organizer and one of Randolph's lieutenants. His later support of Rosa Parks's acts of resistance and his contribution to the formation of the Montgomery Improvement Association, led by Martin Luther King, Jr., are widely acknowledged. Farmer was a pioneer in the application of nonviolent direct action. It was as a result of his initiative that the Congress of Racial Equality was constituted in 1942. Farmer also worked closely with Randolph in the exploration of Gandhian techniques of nonviolent resistance during the heyday of the MOWM. Rustin's association with Randolph began with the MOWM in June 1941. He was a lifelong believer in and a practitioner of nonviolent direct action. As he acted and deepened his knowledge of the Gandhian methodology of nonviolence during the decade of the 1940s, Rustin became a vital link between the pre–1955 years and the freedom movement of the 1950s and 1960s.[26]

Randolph's leadership and the focus he placed on mass organization and resistance also helped to link the struggle of the 1940s with that of the 1950s and 1960s. As Lerone Bennett writes, "despite the opposition and/or silence of many Negro men of power, Randolph raised, almost singlehandedly, a new issue; and he focused the Negro's mind on a new technique and a new vision." Despite the fact that the march never took place, the MOWM created circumstances whereby the idea of nonviolent direct action on a mass scale was institutionalized for the first time in the United States and the upholders of the status quo, an unjust social and economic order, were put on the defensive. Perhaps the most important facet of Randolph's contribution was the manner in which he combined the way of Gandhi with the armor of resistance developed and used by the labor movement. In so doing he built on a strong, ongoing tradition. The energy and the power that he thereby unlocked and thrust on to the political scene in the United States became a major factor in furthering the goals of the freedom movement of the 1950s and 1960s. Indeed, Randolph provided a critical generational link which went a long way toward making the black-led nonviolent revolution a reality.[27]

Randolph was no Gandhi. While the important role of religion and spirituality in Gandhi's personal and political campaigns is generally acknowledged, this was not so with Randolph. Neither his language nor his style of working was that of the ascetic, saintly, Hindu leader. His social analysis was more Marxian than religious. Nor was Randolph a Gandhian pacifist. What is important is that Randolph had the desire and the capacity to open the possibility of applying Gandhi's technique. He adopted the Gandhian philosophy of nonviolence and put it to creative use as a powerful consciousness-raising method in serving the objectives of the African-American struggle. He was a great publicist and used the African-American mass media to bring his views into the heart of the community. According to Bayard Rustin, such was Randolph's genius that he offered his people a modified version of Gandhi's *satyagraha*: "non-violent goodwill direct action" as a political technique. Rustin was convinced that Randolph's ideas "sprang directly from those of Gandhi. . . . [Randolph] was a follower of Gandhi's philosophy but he was no blind follower of his tactics." Furthermore, the MOWM placed Randolph at center stage in the struggle during the decade of the 1940s—so much so, it is said, that the offices of the Brotherhood of Sleeping Car Porters became the "political headquarters of black America."[28]

Meanwhile, several other persons from the "We Are Americans Too" conference continued to carry the black connection with Gandhian nonviolence to another level. By the end of World War II, these activists, along with Randolph and E. D. Nixon, had helped to deepen the connection between African-Americans and the Gandhian movement and prepare the way for manifestations that none of them could have dreamed of in the 1940s.[29]

While the MOWM was gathering momentum, Gandhian nonviolence was explored on a much smaller scale by a group of social activists based in Chicago. Early in 1942, a Gandhi-inspired interracial pacifist group made up of James Farmer, Bernice Fisher, and George Houser, among others, formed the Congress of Racial Equality (CORE) and launched nonviolent direct action campaigns in that city. First they pressed the University of Chicago to desegregate campus housing. Subsequently, CORE members tested Gandhian tactics against other segregated facilities in the city of Chicago. Here was another experiment in Gandhian nonviolence, focused on the elimination of racism, and the role of its African-American center, James Farmer, was crucial. Through him, the connections with an earlier generation of African-American Gandhi-watchers and the advocates of Gandhian nonviolence came alive. In this CORE was also well served by Bayard Rustin.[30]

The initiative for the founding of CORE had originally come from Farmer. In 1939 he was a student at the Howard University's School of Religion. While there he was introduced to the work of Gandhi by Howard Thurman. He "began studying Gandhi, Gandhi's program, his work in India in nonviolence." Two years later, his studies over, Farmer decided against ordination in a segregated Methodist Church and instead elected to work to "destroy segregation." To his father, who wanted to know what he was going to do, Farmer said, "I'm not sure yet, but it'll have something to do with mass mobilization in the use of the Gandhi technique." As he wrote years later,

> Segregation will go on as long as we permit it to. Words are not enough; there must be action. We must withhold our support and participation from the institution of segregation in every area of American life—not an individual witness to purity of conscience, as Thoreau used it, but a coordinated movement of mass noncooperation as with Gandhi. And civil disobedience when laws are involved. And jail where necessary. More than the elegant cadre of generals we now have, we also must have an army of ground troops. Like Gandhi's army, it must be nonviolent. Guns would be suicidal for us. Yes, Gandhi has the key for me to unlock the door to the American dream.

Furthermore, he urged that "we must demand of all who believe—whites, too—that they must, as a matter of conscience, as well as strategy, withdraw from participation in racist practices."[31]

Thanks to the helpful intervention of Howard Thurman and John Swomley, an FOR staff member, Farmer became a full-time staff member of the mostly white pacifist organization. Concerned as he was about racism in America, Farmer encouraged FOR to adopt "a distinctive radical approach" and initiate a program of action to eradicate racism. He turned to Gandhi's concept of *satyagraha*. Farmer argued that a plan which would draw upon a Gandhian mode of resistance was needed in the United States. He argued for the creation of "an organization which would seek to use Gandhi-like techniques of nonviolent resistance—including civil disobedience, noncooperation, and the whole bit—in the battle against segregation." Possessed with this vision, he wrote a memorandum entitled "Provisional Plans for Brotherhood Mobilization" to A. J. Muste, the executive secretary of FOR, in which he argued the imperative for ridding the country of racism, root and all. He called for a movement which

> must strive . . . not to make housing in ghettos more tolerable, but to destroy residential segregation; not to make Jim Crow facilities the equal of others, but to abolish Jim Crow; not to make racial discrimination more bearable, but to wipe it out. . . . We must effectively repudiate every form of racism. We must forge the instrumentalities through which that nationwide repudiation can be affected. We must not stop until racial brotherhood is established in the United States as a fact, as well as an ideal.

As Farmer saw it, this was the vision and work to which the Congress of Racial Equality would dedicate its life. With the promise of help from FOR, CORE was constituted in 1942. Yet action by the Chicago-based student pacifist group predated the formation of CORE. "While I was drafting a memo, they had already begun formulating action projects," Farmer later recalled; when the authorization came from Muste, "we had only to stretch out our hands to one another, and a movement was created."[32]

Meanwhile, Krishnalal Shridharani, a keen student of Gandhian nonviolence, arrived in the United States in 1934 for graduate studies. A graduate of Tagore's international university, Shridharani was one of the 67 satyagrahis who walked with the Mahatma on the epic 240-mile march from Sabarmati Ashram to Dandi by the sea in 1930, to join in the civil disobedience campaign against Britain's imposition of salt taxes. His dissertation at Columbia University, which focused on Gandhian nonviolence, was published in 1939 as War Without Violence: A Study of Gandhi's Method and Its Accomplishments. In this work, Shridharani defined the key characteristics of satyagraha and explored the applicability of Gandhian principles in building a nonviolent world. War Without Violence helped him to reach a wide range of American people.[33]

While in the United States in the 1930s and 1940s, Shridharani kept close contact with pacifists and pacifist organizations. He addressed scores of student, religious, and peace activist groups. As a result of the discussions he had with sociologists, political scientists, and peace movement communities, he modified his views about the application of Gandhian nonviolence in the West. Writing in the introduction to *War Without Violence*, he explained his position in the following words:

> My contact with the Western world has led me to think that, contrary to popular belief, satyagraha, once consciously and deliberately adopted, has more fertile fields in which to grow and flourish in the West than in the Orient. Like war, satyagraha demands public spirit, self-sacrifice, organization, endurance and discipline for its successful operation, and I have found these qualities displayed in Western communities more than in my own. Perhaps the best craftsmen in the art of violence may still be the most effective wielders of non-violent direct action.

The Gandhian way of resistance was to become a reality in the West sooner than Shridharani might have imagined, for he and his book came to play a singularly important role in bridging the gap between Gandhian concepts and their creative application in the United States. That fulfillment emerged through the founding of CORE, as Shridharani's book became a guide to Farmer's group in its campaigns in Chicago. The process was further aided when the FOR published an abridged version of the book for peace groups and gave it much publicity in its organ, *Fellowship*.[34]

For Farmer and his colleagues, who were "anxious to change the world, or at least our corner of it," Shridharani presented the Gandhian approach as a viable and principled method of change. Farmer wrote, "Gandhi, whose assumptions about the power of love and righteousness resembled those of Jesus in the Sermon on the Mount, had nevertheless superimposed upon them a specific and viable program of action. This was what appealed to us, and we adopted it, at least in the beginning, to the letter." Step by step, using Shridharani's work and their knowledge of Gandhi, the CORE group tested techniques of nonviolent resistance. Shridharani's book, recalled Farmer,

> caught our imagination because that was precisely what we were aimed at. It was not acquiescence, as most people at that time, when they heard of nonviolence, assumed that it was . . . in this book Shridharani had outlined Gandhi's steps of investigation, ne-

gotiation, publicity, and then demonstration. And we adopted those steps as our method of action.

It was not surprising that *War Without Violence* became a guide, "rule book and Bible," to CORE in its campaigns in Chicago. As the Chicago CORE group was getting ready to launch their sit-in at the White City Roller Rink, they met and consulted with Shridharani. How methodically CORE followed Gandhian methods is evident from the group's campaign to eliminate segregation at Stoner's, a popular Chicago restaurant. It was only when negotiations failed that the activists resorted to agitation. Their theoretical understanding was such that in one of the CORE newsletters it was noted that

> we are an action group, and within the month the investigation will grow into the demanding of justice from any restaurant with such undemocratic policies yet unremedied. Remember technique! . . . Gather facts. Negotiate. Rouse public opinion, and then, if absolutely necessary, and only as a last resort, Take Direct Action.

As Meier and Rudwick rightly point out, "the strategy developed by Chicago CORE was an adaptation of Gandhian techniques to the American scene." Thus the first experiments in sit-ins in this country were started in Chicago. And before the 1940s were over, CORE had led "freedom rides" also.[35]

Partly because of its racially mixed, urban-educated, middle-class composition and partly because of the nature of its campaigns, which did not connect nonviolence to the essential inner needs of African-Americans, CORE failed to elicit much positive response. By and large its activities were ignored in the press. Even the influential sections of the African-American press were not impressed by this experiment. The local African-American newspaper, the *Chicago Defender*, which had over the years provided excellent coverage of Gandhi and his movement in India, did not pay much attention to the activities of CORE. In the words of Farmer:

> They [the African-American press] were not really interested because this was a rather bizarre technique to them. . . . 'They hit you and you are not going to hit them back. . . . What is this nonviolent crap?' They had not warmed up to it, and we had discussions then with a number of the Negro leaders of the time, and they simply

could not see nonviolence: "No, no, that is just unrealistic. If they hit you, you've got to do something. Hit them back. It just won't work."[36]

Although CORE did pioneering work with nonviolent direct action, it did not then emerge as a major force. It encouraged many persons to learn and experiment with the methodology of Gandhian nonviolence, but CORE remained more of an elitist organization in the 1940s than its members might have wished. The nation had to wait until the start of the Montgomery bus boycott and the rise of King (and the rise of television) in 1955 for nonviolent resistance to grip the imagination of ordinary African-Americans and energize them into action. According to Farmer, CORE failed to become a mass movement partly because it was secular in its composition and outlook. He added that it was not till King brought nonviolence into the heart of the religious community through the church that black Americans applied a Gandhian methodology of resistance on a mass scale. Speaking of the situation in the 1940s, Farmer observed that "nonviolence was still an unknown technique and the word caused adverse reaction."[37] But CORE held fast to its convictions and its actions, and by the early 1960s it was ready for a second coming, this time firmly embedded in the life of the mass freedom movement of the African-American people.

≡6≡

African-American Solidarity and the Post–World War II Encounters with Gandhi

THE END of World War II marked a dramatic rise of anticolonial energies and the assertion of the rights of peoples of color across the globe. India, as it drew nearer to its long-sought goal of independence, became a major focal point for such activity. At the same time the African-American community entered a new phase of its own centuries-long freedom movement. Within a decade after the close of the war, some of the major insights, energies, and traditions of the two movements were joined.

All through the early postwar period, the African-American press continued to play a significant role. Indeed, one of the most direct, grass-roots links between the struggles of the two peoples was provided by the African-American war correspondents stationed in India to report on the contribution of black soldiers (mostly in road building and/or engineering regiments) in the India-Burma theater. Such was their concern that in addition to resident correspondents, the African-American press invited important black community leaders who traveled there to report on the conditions of soldiers. In 1944, Walter White, executive secretary of the NAACP, joined the teams of war correspondents assigned to the United States army in Europe and elsewhere. "Walter White To Interview . . . Gandhi," the *Chicago Defender* announced on 29 January 1944. The report stated that while in India White hoped to meet with other nationalist leaders and to visit jailed Indians. It is not certain, however, whether White got an interview with Gandhi.[1]

All through the war years these correspondents educated African-American readers about Gandhi and his movement through the columns of some of the black community's leading newspapers. For instance, not long before the end of the war the readers of the *Chicago Defender* were told, "Defender Reporter Visits Gandhi." In a front-page story, Deton J. Brooks, Jr., the newspaper's war correspondent, told his readers that the Indian leader had "keen sympathy and understanding of the American Negro's problems." Reporting the now-familiar theme, Brooks wrote that the freedom of India "was closely identified with [the] welfare of all other under-privileged peoples." The correspondent stated that when he was asked to send a message to Americans, Gandhi said that his "life is its own message" and that "if it is not, then nothing I can now write will fulfill the purpose." Brooks also told his readers that Gandhi "still feels that the best weapon for use of under-privileged peoples is non-violence." Anticipating the post–World War II decolonization movements, Gandhi added that "the freedom of India will demonstrate to all exploited races of the earth that their freedom is very near and that in no case will they be exploited." Quite apart from predicting the collapse of European empires, Gandhi's words were a tonic to a people who were putting up a brave fight against racism in the United States.[2]

Brooks was not the only African-American correspondent sending word home from India. Frank Bolden of the National Negro Press Association was also present, and in the summer of 1945 he sent back important observations concerning the rise of Muslim nationalism and the dangers it held for Gandhi's vision of a united India. Before leaving India for his return to the United States, he met with Gandhi, who, despite the immediate pressures of the independence movement, found the time to talk with his African-American guests. Back in the United States the headline read "I Talk to Gandhi." The interview vividly indicated again how Gandhi wanted to communicate his goals clearly to Bolden's readers. He emphasized that the goal of the Indian independence movement was complete freedom from British controls, therefore the Cripps Mission's offer of Dominion Status was unacceptable. "We have not the same relation to Britain as the dominions [Australia, Canada, and New Zealand] which are white and settled, for the most part, by emigrants from Britain or their descendants," Gandhi declared.

"We did not and do not wish any status conferred on us. If a status is so conferred, it means that we are not free."[3]

By this time, the Muslim League's demand for a separate Muslim state (eventually Pakistan) had gained even greater momentum, and in the interview Gandhi repeated his opposition to the division of India on the basis of religion. The Mahatma also said he feared that Hindu-Muslim disunity was bound to work to the advantage of Britain. He wanted African-Americans to know that he rejected the notion that India was incapable of managing its affairs, adding, "If there should be chaos, God will work it out." He attributed disharmony between religious communities to outside interference. Gandhi said he believed that once the people were left alone, they were bound to settle their differences.[4]

Then the earlier message for Afro-America was repeated—Gandhi reiterated his faith in the method of nonviolence. Underscoring the philosophical as well as practical aspects of nonviolence, he told Bolden that "non-violence is the best way of fighting the enemy within the city's gates, especially when you are too weak physically and economically to exert physical force or violence." The Mahatma doubted that the Allied nations would help to create a better world were they to come through victorious in the war. Laying faith in the emergent world order, he contended that the future held promise only if the democracies adhered strictly to the Charter of the United Nations. As was his way with African-American visitors, Gandhi inquired about their condition in the United States. He wanted to know what gains they had made and showed much interest in the interview. Bolden observed that "all during our discourse, I noticed the great Mahatma's face registering first sorrow, then disgust, then agreement; followed by humor, and ending with pleasure." Before he was finished, Bolden returned to the familiar African-American fascination with the power of Gandhi's leadership and the sources of that power. The fact that Gandhi devoted his life to the people of India was significant for African-Americans. Bolden also underscored the point that the Mahatma lived like his people and shared in their material hardships and poverty. He concluded that Gandhi had no money and no property—"He wants only one thing—a free India. And since so many Indians desire the same thing, Gandhi has become the symbol of a nation's yearning. . . . This is the man, Gandhi, and the sum and substance of his creed and personality."[5]

As war correspondents and soldiers returned to the American soil, the anticolonial struggles of the world's colored peoples, and especially Indian opposition to British rule, had gathered fresh impetus. Meanwhile, following the conclusion of World War II, just as they had done when World War I ended, the victor nations initiated moves to establish a world organization to assist in the process of establishing world peace and preventing new hostilities. Indian leaders expressed their views on the conditions necessary for peace in the post–World War II era in clear and forthright terms. In a statement he submitted to the United Nations charter conference in San Francisco, Gandhi expressed the belief that "there will be no peace for the Allies or the world unless they shed belief in the efficacy of war and its accompanying terrible deceptions and fraud, and are determined to hammer out a real peace based on universal freedom and equality of colored races and nations." The *Chicago Defender*, in the spring of 1945, headlined the news of Gandhi's statement to the conference on its front page with the words "Gandhi Urges Justice For Colored Peoples." George Padmore, the *Chicago Defender*'s radical, London-based correspondent, noted that the Indian leader had voiced "the aspirations of the darker races" when he said that "imperialistic exploitation and domination by Europeans and Americans over Asia and Africa can have no place in a postwar world striving for lasting peace." Gandhi was also reported to have denounced Britain's assumption that it had the right to appoint Indian representatives to the newly constituted world body.[6]

In the fall of 1945, Mrs. Vijaya Lakshmi Pandit, Jawaharlal Nehru's sister, attended the conference in San Francisco and quickly gained celebrity status. She made clear her own and her nation's position on world affairs, particularly on the situation of oppressed people everywhere, and set the stage for the things to come with the memorandum she submitted to the secretary-general of the newly created world body. In her memorandum, she was speaking for India and all "those countries, which like India, cannot speak for themselves." Reaching out and making links with the politically and economically oppressed, echoing Gandhi's words, she warned that "the voice of six hundred million of the enslaved people of Asia may not be officially heard at this conference . . . but there will be no real peace on earth so long as they are denied justice."[7]

For their part, African-Americans, sensing new possibilities opened up by the United Nations, fought for the provision of fundamental human rights in the United States and colonial territories. In their capacity as consultants to the official United States delegation to the conference at San Francisco, such outstanding African-Americans as the educator and activist Mary McLeod Bethune, the internationalist Du Bois, and Walter White of the NAACP took major initiatives in challenging Euro-American positions on human rights. Their activities were closely monitored in the African-American press. For instance, in a report he did for his paper, Metz T. P. Lochard, the editor in chief of the *Chicago Defender*, reported that Bethune, Du Bois, and White found the official United States stand on the human rights situation "wholly inadequate." Lochard noted that African-Americans must not be taken in by Jan Smuts, the prime minister of South Africa, because he stood only for the preservation and maintenance of those rights which are "applicable to the white race without consideration for status of the black world." In an article entitled "Du Bois, White Run From Photo With India Stooges," Du Bois concentrated on the continuing need for cooperation among the people of color. To illustrate the point, he wrote at some length about his and White's refusal to be photographed with pro-British Indians at the UN conference. Always seizing opportunities to educate, he then provided background information about British misrule of India.[8]

Meanwhile, early in 1946 general elections were held in India. The Indian National Congress, headed by Nehru, did well and formed an interim government. In the fall, when the interim government in India appointed her to head the Indian delegation to the UN General Assembly, Vijaya Lakshmi Pandit was back again in the United States. Indian spokespersons expressed their nation's solidarity with the people of color and their deep concern for the welfare of "all colonial and dependent peoples and their full right to self-determination." Such expressions of solidarity not only deepened the bond between African-Americans and Indians, but also brought key leaders of the two communities together. Indeed, concern for the welfare of African-Americans was shared by ordinary Indians through the media in that country. According to White, "the Indian newsmen appeared to possess encyclopedic knowledge of lynching, disfranchisement, segregation, Senate filibusters against such civil-rights legislation as Fair Employment Practices Committee bills, and the anti-Negro speeches of Americans such as [Theodore] Bilbo, [John] Rankin, [Eugene] Talmadge, and [James] Byrnes." In their expressions of solidarity with African-Americans, some Indian journalists went so far as to call America's treatment of its people of color "barbarous."[9]

Thanks to her inclusive perspective on world affairs and India's anticolonial and antiracist policies, Pandit soon became a point of attention for the African-American press. Earlier they had been fascinated by Gandhi; now items about Pandit's radical role in the UN in the service of people of color began appearing regularly. One of the first full-length articles about her appeared on the Op-Ed page of the *Chicago Defender*. Walter White, the NAACP leader, provided her portrait in his column "People, Politics and Places" on 30 June 1945. He noted Pandit's gifts of personal beauty and intellect, and her sacrifices for Indian freedom. Affirming her stature as a world leader, White underscored Pandit's solidarity with the struggles of peoples of color when he declared that "she sees the flow of history of all people and countries and thus understands the relation of the fight for freedom of Indians to that of other oppressed people." Getting to the heart of the matter, he added that "when it was suggested to Mme. Pandit on her arrival in the United States that she would injure India's cause if she identified it with the Negro's struggle for freedom, she indignantly exclaimed, 'What do you mean—I am colored myself and so are my people!' " Du Bois also wrote about Mrs. Pandit in his *Chicago Defender* column, "The Winds of Time." He described her as a person of "unusual beauty, out of whose eyes the sorrow of life never quite drains," and pointed out that Jawaharlal Nehru, her brother, who had been imprisoned for his part in the Quit India movement in 1942, was "rotting in an Indian jail lest his words and writing disturb the British Empire."[10]

As the UN began to develop its life, the African-American press continued to help their readers "watch the Indians," especially as their representatives boldly took on South Africa and that nation's colonial actions against Southwest Africa (now Namibia). For instance, the *New York Amsterdam News* ran a large picture of Gandhi ("Fighting Since 1893" the caption read) as a part of its story on India's strong UN stance against South Africa's discriminatory practices against people of color. "India," the article argued, "struck a mighty blow at race prejudice and discrimination this week" when it forced the South African representative at the UN "to explain and defend its racial policies." Thus, in the post–World War II years, Gandhi, nonviolence, and India came into focus over the future of South Africa and the formation of the UN. India's forceful stand against racism in the world body became another crucial link between black America and Gandhi's nonviolent movement.[11]

From the floor of the world assembly, Mrs. Pandit took up cudgels against South Africa for its ill-treatment of Indians. "India, South Africa Set for Color Bar Test in UN, Jan Smuts, Supreme Racist, Madam Pandit, India's 'Joan of Arc,' Chief Antagonists," was the banner headline of an item in the *Baltimore Afro-American* of 2 November 1946. Pandit declared that the Indian delegation to the UN must "claim for Indians in South Africa the removal of all restrictions imposed on them on the grounds of race and color, and ensure to them fundamental freedoms to which they are entitled." "India," she said, "stands for equality among the peoples and for the independence of all colonial areas." Segregation in South Africa was, in essence, an issue of human rights, she argued. With words which must have been music to African-American ears, Pandit warned that "the colored man is on the march, and will not tolerate domination by the white because of color." She reiterated "that enduring peace cannot be achieved so long as there is discrimination against one race by another."[12]

India's challenge to South Africa's treatment of Indians continued. The *New York Amsterdam News*, on 14 December 1946, published a moving editorial lauding the efforts of India's Pandit in the fight she was conducting. The writer stated that racism was against the spirit and Preamble of the United Nations Charter and added that the world body, by a vote of thirty-two to fifteen, censured South Africa for its discriminatory policies against Indians. The paper pointed out that Pandit, who "has broadly identified herself with the struggle of all colored peoples against discrimination, won" despite "the full battery of American arrogance, English chicanery, and their bootlicking stooges." The *New York Amsterdam News* viewed the approval of the Indian resolution as a victory for the high idealism of the United Nations, and Pandit was saluted for putting Field Marshall Smuts, prime minister of South Africa, in his place. "Also, Mrs. Pandit taught colored nations something," the writer declared. In contrast to nations such as Liberia, Ethiopia, Cuba, Haiti, China, who had sided with Western nations, the *New York Amsterdam News* observed that Pandit had "closely identified herself with the struggle of American Negroes for justice and equality." Finally, the editorial noted that "the victory which demanded that the Union of South Africa . . . give satisfaction on the charge of jim crow is historic. It now remains for us, and for all who believe in 'One World,' to work that first step out to its fuller conclusion of justice for all men everywhere." The paper also carried a large cartoon on the editorial page showing Pandit as the new David conquering the Goliath of world racism. India's solidarity with African-Americans was underscored by *The Crisis*. In its February 1947 edition *The Crisis* put Pandit on its cover with the caption "VICTOR OVER SMUTS AT UN." The journal shared some background information about Pandit and reported that she opposed racial discrimination "because it is against the principles and purposes of the United Nations Charter, and because it is bound to sow the seeds of future conflict." Mrs. Pandit was also reported as having said that "the discriminatory laws we oppose affect not only Indians but also Negroes as well." Such sentiments from key official spokespersons from India were bound to bring the two peoples closer together. An intellectual bond which had been developing in the previous decades was now getting newfound momentum and strength over the issue of worldwide racism.[13]

Mrs. Pandit continued to draw attention in the African-American press. With the words "Slave States Join India, Condemn Racism in S. A., Mrs. Pandit Warns UN that Final Decision on Indian Problem in S. A. May be Fateful," the *Baltimore Afro-American* broke the story to its readers early in December. According to the *Baltimore Afro-American*, India reminded member states that segregation against Indians in Southwest Africa was "a denial of human rights, a basic guarantee of the United Nations." India kept pressing for UN action against South Africa. The *Baltimore Afro-American*, on 14 December, calling Pandit a "militant chairman of the Indian delegation," reported on her insistence that South African policies constituted "a denial of human rights and fundamental freedoms." She reminded the members that "while the matter is being decided people go to jail," then, in a tone full of sarcasm, added, "What does it matter if black people go; they have no feelings?"[14]

In mid-December, the *New York Amsterdam News* reported that the world body "saved itself from dismal failure and ended its eight-week sessions on a high note of achievement, when the majority of the delegates of fifty-one nations condemned" racism in South Africa. The creation of the Trusteeship Council, the paper noted, was another important achievement of the session which had just ended, and it singled out India and the Philippines for their moral leadership. "The United Nations, as a world forum, has served its purpose well so far as its 1946 sessions are concerned," the writer concluded. Constantly making the connection between colonialism in Africa and Asia and racism at home, the *New York Amsterdam News*, in an editorial later that month, declared,

> The United Nations limped, stuttered, sputtered, and gagged. Then just when cynicism was highest, the colored nations of the world twisted the tail of the British Empire and voted a censure of South Africa's jim crow laws. Local folks are working to make Uncle Sam next to get a world black eye.[15]

A piece about Mrs. Pandit appeared in the *Baltimore Afro-American* in early 1947 under the headline "Head of Indian Delegation to U.N. Is Colored Too." Pandit, who pleaded for better understanding between the two peoples, also suggested that, indirectly, the Indian freedom movement could help African-Americans. She told the reporter, Michael Carter, that "Indians knew about the Detroit and Philadelphia race riots and felt a kinship for American colored people." When questioned about the applicability of nonviolence in the African-American struggle, she gave an unexpected answer; Pandit said she believed "that it is an Indian method and that it has to do with the soul of a people," adding, "I think it worked to some extent in India only because it appealed to the conscience of the English people." Another reason why nonviolence worked in India, she said, was because India had Gandhi, "and as yet you have no Gandhi." She lauded Gandhi's attack on untouchability, but it was clear that Mrs. Pandit was not only talking about India when she said that "no country can deny freedom to a part of its nationals and still call itself a democracy." Like a number of Indians before her, Pandit revealed that she had personally experienced American-style prejudice, and this simply strengthened the ties that bound her and her nation to African-Americans.[16]

Meanwhile, the first postwar general election in Britain brought the socialists back to power. Clement Attlee, the leader of the Labour party, defeated the Conservative party's Winston Churchill, the nation's wartime leader and a staunch upholder of the white supremacist empire. Attlee was committed to Indian independence, and in March 1947 he announced Britain's decision to withdraw from India. By the middle of the year, a date was fixed. Ralph Matthews of the *Baltimore Afro-American* observed that the proposed British plan to partition India was "one of the greatest of all human dramas being enacted in India." He suggested that Britain had the hidden motive of prolonging its control there and in the rest of Asia. The *Baltimore Afro-American* welcomed the fact that India was at last getting out from under British domination. Emphasizing racial kinship, the article stated that, "as one-fifth of the world's population, we are naturally interested in seeing India relieved from subjugation and domination by white exploiters." Matthews paid tribute to Gandhi, his spirituality and the method of civil disobedience, and noted that new leadership had emerged. He lauded the decision of the constituent assembly in New Delhi to abolish untouchability. Matthews also acknowledged India's contribution to human rights when he stated that "the voice of India in the United Nations has been the loudest and most profound calling for human rights for people of all colors and creeds."[17]

As India's independence drew near and as the rift between Hindus and Muslims deepened and became more violent, Gandhi left for Bengal in the hope of bringing peace between the warring communities. He walked through Noakhali, one of the worst affected parts of the region, bringing the message of peace, harmony, and love. In this very painful time he was still being watched by African-Americans. Commenting on Gandhi's travels, the *Baltimore Afro-American* noted that "the world witnessed the remarkable spectacle last week of 100-pound Mohandas K. Gandhi, 77-year-old Indian leader, walking across the country in India trying to bring about peace between the Hindus and Mohammedans."[18]

Soon black America had a representative to walk at Gandhi's side. With the progressive deterioration of relations between Hindus and Muslims in Bengal and the worsening famine conditions, Quakers in Britain and the United States sent a team to work in the strife-torn area. The Friends Service Unit (constituted by Quakers in 1943 in the aftermath of the Bengal famine) was called upon "to deal with some of the chronic ills of Indian social life in small ways which can be adopted and expanded." The overall mission of the Quaker team was "to heal and reconcile in the name and under the guidance of the God of all." At a practical level, the team, which was made up of British as well as American members, distributed food, provided relief, ran a rehabilitation program, organized a fisherman's cooperative, and loaned personnel to Indian agencies, including the Red Cross. Gandhi's presence in Noakhali encouraged the Quaker team to base itself there so that it might work alongside the Mahatma. William Stuart Nelson, a leading African-American educator and church leader, was invited to join the team in his capacity as a senior member of the American Friends Service Committee (AFSC).[19]

When he accepted the invitation to go to India, Nelson was dean and vice president of Howard University, thus he continued the tradition of Howard University connections with India established by Mordecai Johnson, Howard Thurman, and Sue Bailey Thurman. Like them, Nelson said he "found the Indians keenly interested in America and particularly the problems of 'underprivileged Americans' such as the Negro groups." Midway through his stay, Nelson was chosen to head the AFSC unit, and he remained on for a year in India. During his stay, Nelson met and held "unusually intimate and searching conversations with Mr. Gandhi." He studied the principles of Gandhian nonviolence and their meaning for America, and in the course of the next ten years he visited India on two other occasions. Through his writings and speeches he became another embodiment of the decades-old connection between the two peoples and their struggles. (Nearly twenty years later, he joined King on the Selma to Montgomery march.) In 1960, Nelson introduced a course entitled "The Philosophy and Methods of Non-Violence" at Howard University, probably the first academic course of its kind.[20]

"Our first step upon arriving was to seek the advice of Gandhi," Nelson recalled years later. In January 1947, he and three other members of the team called on Gandhi at Srirampur, Noakhali, to "find out how Quakers may help the Indian people" in the riot-torn area. Gandhi encouraged the delegation to provide relief and not advice. "When men are without food or clothing or shelter, they are not amenable to an appeal to the spirit until these needs are satisfied at least to a degree." In an item headlined "Gandhi

Interprets God to Dr. Nelson, Hungry Men Need Food, Not Advice, Sage Says," the *Baltimore Afro-American* shared the story of Nelson's visit with the Mahatma in its edition of 1 February 1947. Encouraged by Gandhi, the Friends' unit initiated a program of relief and rehabilitation, and provided support for the riot victims. Thus the methodology of nonviolence and the vision of a just community were brought together and shared as a potent force for social change.[21]

Consultations with Gandhi over, the delegation joined the Mahatma in a prayer meeting. The Indian leader asked the Americans to sing a hymn. Nelson and his group sang Isaac Watts's "O God Our Help in Ages Past," which pleased Gandhi. The profound simplicity of the occasion did not escape the visitors. According to Nelson, "what had been anticipated as a visit in search of counsel on the practical matters of relief and reconciliation developed into a spiritual experience of great significance to all of us." Nelson was deeply affected by his meeting with the Mahatma. In a report he submitted to the American Friends Service Committee in March 1947, he wrote that the meeting with Gandhi

> has proved one of my very great moments in India. The two hours in his retreat were packed with an inspiration which will abide with me for a very long time. This, I realize, can be accounted for in part by the fact that I was meeting for the first time one of the very great men of the earth. I am equally convinced that the impression which I bore away from the conference derived from the extraordinary spiritual and intellectual qualities which he revealed even in so short a time. A mere glance at the scene was proof sufficient that Mr. Gandhi has a complete mastery over the material demands upon his life. His pure white home spun garment covered but a portion of his body, the food which he ate as we talked with him was simple and of such secondary concern that neither he nor we were distracted by his eating, and the room could scarcely have been plainer. His mind met our problems most directly and constructively and in the light, I felt, of a total view of life which makes easy his answers to most questions.

About the moments spent at the prayer meeting, Nelson observed that "in retrospect the event takes on great importance, and I suppose the farther it recedes into the past the more the story will be embroidered and the greater the significance it will have for

me." As a consequence of his encounter with Gandhi, Nelson became an important figure in the transmission of Gandhian nonviolence to America. He was impressed by the healing power of the
Mahatma's nonviolent witness in strife-ridden Bengal, and the relevance of the spiritually grounded concept of *satyagraha* for the
African-American struggle struck him even more powerfully than
before.[22]

In the midst of the preparations for the birth of the new nation,
on 10 August 1947, Gandhi found the time to bid farewell to
Nelson prior to his departure for the United States. Moved by horror
of the violence which accompanied the partition of India, Nelson
asked the Mahatma why "Indians who had more or less successfully
gained independence through peaceful means were now unable to
check the tide of civil war between Hindus and Muslims." Gandhi
argued that "the long struggle by Indians for independence had not
been one . . . of nonviolence but of passive resistance, a weapon of
the weak." Gandhi further believed that "Indians had harbored ill
will and anger against their erstwhile rulers while pretending to
resist them nonviolently. Their resistance, therefore, had been inspired by violence and not by regard for the man in the British,
whom they should convert through satyagraha." Gandhi thus emphasized one of the cardinal principles of *satyagraha*: the imperative
of converting the opponent through love and truth. The lesson was
not lost on Nelson.[23]

In the months after his return from India, Nelson gave scores of
addresses in a wide range of places, including Howard University,
Lincoln University, Hampton Institute, Talladega College, and
North Carolina Agriculture and Technical College (Greensboro).
As usual, the African-American press kept the bridge alive. He
published *Bases of World Understanding*, based on his Indian lectures,
in 1950. Alain Locke reviewed the book for Howard University's
Journal of Religious Thought, noting that "an interesting incidental
feature of Dr. Nelson's discussion is his speculation in passing on
the possible potentials of non-cooperative protest techniques on the
part of the American Negro to bring about pacific but powerful
pressures for the fuller realization of civil rights and social equities."
However, Locke also noted the author's skepticism about the prac-
ticability of "the present leadership resources for mass movements
on such a basis."[24]

The following month, Nelson gave three addresses and met with smaller groups at Hampton Institute. He was confident about the future of India and expressed the view that its government could be depended upon "to stand by those who are suppressed in the world." India had begun to exert "its influence to protect Asia against foreign exploitation" and the people there were "showing interest in the problems of the Negro in America," a *Norfolk Journal and Guide* reporter noted. Indians, Nelson observed, were horrified "at the story of our sufferings and were delighted at the story of our advances." They were curious "to know more about Negro people and their life here." Nelson reported that his Indian audiences were particularly interested in learning about the efforts African-Americans were making to "bring discrimination to an end in America."[25]

Nelson returned to India twice, once in 1950, and again in 1958. However, his undying interest in Gandhian nonviolence sprang from his stay there in 1946 and 1947, when he came to know the Mahatma and "see at first hand his transforming effect upon that country." He believed that Gandhian principles needed adaptation for African-Americans, and he would later argue during the modern freedom struggle that "it is important that American citizens come to a deeper understanding of the principles and methods of Mr. Gandhi and their continuing effect." He was convinced that wider application of the Gandhian method would "effect swiftly a vital change in our present situation." In conclusion, he added that he hoped "to contribute vitally to the use of this method."[26]

While Nelson was in India exploring the way of Gandhi, Bayard Rustin, a theoretician-activist of the discipline of nonviolence, was preparing to apply Gandhian methods against racism in the United States. By the late 1940s, he was a seasoned practitioner of and a steadfast adherent to the Gandhian principles of nonviolence. This gifted black organizer began his opposition to war and his career of resistance early. In 1938, at the age of twenty-one, he became an organizer of the Young Communist League. He was a conscientious objector in World War II, for which he served a little over two years in prison. As a race relations secretary of the FOR, he worked with James Farmer to further the work of CORE. After the war he helped to organize the Free India Committee, a group committed to the independence of India. In his support of the cause of Indian freedom, he conducted several sit-ins at the British embassy in Washington, D.C., which led to a number of arrests.

In 1947, Rustin, acting on behalf of FOR, and George Houser, acting for CORE, organized what was called the Journey of Reconciliation. This was really the first Freedom Ride, intended to test the implementation of the Supreme Court decision of June 1946—the Irene Morgan case—which had banned segregation on interstate transportation. According to Rustin, through such acts of resistance, the organizers "also wished to learn the reaction of bus drivers, passengers, and police to those who nonviolently and persistently challenge Jim Crow in interstate travel." He argued that "the Journey of Reconciliation was organized not only to devise techniques for eliminating Jim Crow in travel, but also as a training ground for similar peaceful projects against discrimination in such major areas as employment and in the armed services."[27]

From 9 April to 23 April 1947, a party consisting of eight African-Americans and eight whites traveled by train and buses to fifteen cities in Virginia, North Carolina, Tennessee, and Kentucky. "During the two weeks of the trip, twenty-six tests of company policies were made. Arrests occurred on six occasions, with a total of twelve men arrested," writes Rustin in *Down the Line*. A number of those arrested spent time on chain gangs in Southern and border states. The news of their experience was followed by the African-American press. For instance, on 26 April 1947, the *Baltimore Afro-American* gave a detailed account of the arrests of the Journey of Reconciliation activists on its front page. In another section of the paper, a correspondent assigned to cover the story reported that "much information on techniques of combating segregation was gained." This item was headlined "Journey of Reconciliation Knocks Props From Under Weak J.C. System, History Made." In September, James Peck, one of the white members of the group, also shared his observations about the journey in a lengthy article he wrote for *The Crisis*.[28]

For his part in the Journey of Reconciliation, Rustin himself served twenty-three days on a chain gang in North Carolina. His commitment to Gandhian nonviolence was made abundantly clear in an address he gave before the Council Against Intolerance in America in April 1948, where he received a Thomas Jefferson Award "for the advancement of democracy." Years later, he recalled,

As a follower of the principles of Mahatma Gandhi, I am an opponent of war and of war preparations and an opponent of universal military training and conscription; but entirely apart from that issue, I hold that segregation in any part of the body politic is an act of slavery and an act of war. Democrats will agree that such acts are to be resisted, and more and more leaders of the oppressed are responsibly proposing nonviolent civil disobedience and noncooperation as the means.

In the light of that commitment, it is important to note how deeply Rustin later became involved in the post–1955 freedom movement, especially as an advisor to Martin Luther King, Jr. Indeed, he became one of the major carriers to bring the Gandhian tradition to the heart of the modern African-American freedom struggle.[29]

Meanwhile, the all-powerful British Empire did more than totter. It collapsed. On 15 August 1947, less than thirty years after Gandhi launched the first national noncooperation campaign against the British, India won its freedom. The fifteenth of August was a magnificent moment for the people of the subcontinent of India. They were free at last of alien rule. Yet, there was deep tragedy mixed into the setting. The event was marred by mutual mass killings by Hindus and Muslims. For the nationalists, Gandhi in particular, it was a sad day because India was partitioned into two nations—India and Pakistan—one based on the acceptance of the rich diversity of different faiths and the other based on a single religion, Islam. As might have been expected, African-American newspapers gave much more attention to Indian independence than the failure of Hindu-Muslim unity. They allotted significant space and importance to the emergence of India as a free nation.

Du Bois, who had not written for *The Crisis* for more than a decade, was brought back by the NAACP to write about this momentous event. His article took note of the greatness of India's past and traditions as well as the events leading up to freedom. Du Bois wrote, in October 1947, that the freedom of India was important because it offered prospects of independence to oppressed people everywhere. Indeed, he hailed 15 August 1947 as "the greatest historical date of the nineteenth and twentieth centuries," greater even than the dates of the Emancipation Proclamation in this country or the Russian Revolution. He stressed the fact that the British did not give freedom to India, the people in that subcontinent had had to work for their independence and ultimately to seize it. "It was not a gift or an act of grace. It was forced from the British Empire by determination of the Indians themselves."[30]

"Great things happened in India last week when two independent governments, one Mohammedan and one Hindu, were born, and British rule in India ended," is how the *Baltimore Afro-American* shared the news of Indian independence. Referring to Indians as "400 million colored East Indians," the writer stated that the people of that land were now masters of their own destiny. The story noted with approval that India had begun renaming the streets, that the For Europeans Only signs were coming down, and the sacred Ganga river was no longer "the Ganges." The editorial also suggested that "there will be a lot of other changes made by Indians giving free reign to their newly-won freedom."[31]

The government in New Delhi was beset with a great many problems, the chief among them being the religious rift between Hindus and Muslims. Gordon Hancock, in his column in the *Norfolk Journal and Guide*, laid the blame for the internecine conflict between Hindus and Muslims at the doorsteps of the British. Hancock wrote that bad as the situation was in India sympathizers must not give in to "undue pessimism or surprise." While expressing hope in the quality of leadership India provided, he noted again that Gandhi was treading the path laid down by Jesus of Nazareth. "This little bewizened dreamer has taken a simple formula from the teachings of Jesus Christ and broken the back of the mightiest empire of modern times."[32]

Hancock emphasized that Britain was forced to leave India not because of India's superior physical might but because "Gandhi dared to exemplify the spirit of Jesus Christ." Then he picked up the familiar refrain, saying to his African-American readers that there was a lesson "in the Indian situation that should challenge under-privileged and defenseless groups everywhere." According to Hancock, "the only power in the world is moral power and against this armies and navies fight in vain." He came closer to home—he questioned the American claim to sit in the driver's seat in international affairs while the United States had "the millstone of color prejudice about her neck." He wrote, "The United States is busy lynching and segregating and disfranchising millions of her Negro citizens; thus what our country is doing speaks so loud that what she says in the parley of the nations cannot be heard." Much as he wanted the world to follow the moral path, Hancock was convinced that the Big Four (the United States, the United Kingdom, the Soviet Union, and France) were "disqualified to give the wo[r]ld moral leadership that today is the world's urgent need." The hope for the world lay elsewhere. Once again turning to India and Gandhi, he concluded, "One hopeful sign emanates from India where Mohandas Gandhi has given the world its greatest lesson in moral leadership since Jesus lived upon earth. India may be in travail but it points the way to the survival of mankind and shows the potency of moral leadership." The emphasis on the need for moral leadership and the nonviolent alternative were familiar themes for African-Americans. By continuing to place Gandhi and his movement in the context of Jesus, Hancock, like so many other interpreters, gave added weight to his argument.[33]

Within months of Indian independence, Gandhi was assassinated, on 30 January 1948, by Nathuram Vinayak Godse of the Hindu Mahasabha—an organization whose goal was Hindu supremacy. Many newspaper articles and editorials brought the news and its meaning to African-Americans, and they mourned the loss of this nonviolent warrior whose career they had followed with such interest for so long. The *Baltimore Afro-American*, in an editorial on 7 February 1948, called him a "man of peace," and observed that because the world had not fully understood the meaning of Gandhi's life, it will be "sometime before the world understands the full import of the tragic death." It noted that "the loss of his spiritual value in a troubled world is immeasurable." The editorial underscored the importance of Gandhi for African-American resistance when it declared that "to a large extent, Gandhi embodied the struggle of the darker peoples of the world for first-class citizenship." The editorial writer had no doubt that "the world is richer because he passed this way." In death as in his active public life, Gandhi became a subject of much attention.[34]

In the same edition, the *Baltimore Afro-American* printed a letter Gandhi had written in 1934 to Carl Murphy, the president of that newspaper's publishing company. In that letter, Gandhi had declared the practice of segregation in the United States "a negation of civili[z]ation." Without giving any details, the newspaper also suggested that it was Peter John Daniels, a colored tailor in South

Africa, "who introduced Gandhi to passive resistance." Later in February 1948, memorial services to honor the Mahatma were held in Washington, D.C.; "Washington Pays Tribute to Gandhi" was the headline of an item in the *Baltimore Afro-American*. Mary McLeod Bethune was among those who participated in the event.[35]

Gandhi's assassination was treated seriously and fully by the *Pittsburgh Courier* in its 7 February 1948 edition. In its main editorial the paper noted that in Gandhi the world had been "treated to the awesome spectacle of the birth and death of a god"; here was a man who "shared the god-traits . . . of Christ Himself." Moved and inspired by the life of the Mahatma, the editorial observed that though great individuals rise up in every generation, "a Gandhi is born only once in a thousand years." The essence of Gandhi, it argued, lay in his adherence to love, brotherhood, and peace, and not in his challenge to British rule. The paper also emphasized that for Gandhi "men of every race and clime, are the equal children of God," and it added, "Here was a heathen (if we must) more Christian than they, so Christian indeed, that they must stand in awe of him." To further stress Gandhi's nobility, the writer observed, "Of mankind, Gandhi asked nothing. To mankind, he gave all." This, the editorial went on, "is doubtless the essence of godhood, that in the giving of one's whole self one's being is expanded to encompass the yearning for good that is in all mankind." This inspiring interpretation, drawing upon and illuminating the religious dimension of Gandhi's life, would have been hard to surpass. On 7 February the *Pittsburgh Courier* carried a profile of the deceased leader by Frank Bolden, who had been its war correspondent in India. Bolden saw in Gandhi "a saint among politicians and a politician among saints." He suggested that Gandhi was like "another great man who died years ago on a cross, because He believed so much in the brotherhood of man." The *Pittsburgh Courier*, as at other times, emphasized that in the person of Gandhi Jesus of Nazareth had come alive for the twentieth century. Gandhi was the "Prince of Peace in our time." The image of a suffering saint at work for the healing of people and nations was central to the *Pittsburgh Courier's* reflections.[36]

Benjamin E. Mays wrote a piece for the *Pittsburgh Courier* honoring the life of "the great leader." He drew heavily on the conversation he had had with Gandhi in 1936. Love, he said, was the dominant force in Gandhian nonviolence. He concluded his eulogy with these words:

Gandhi saved the souls of millions. He helped to save India to freedom. He saved the untouchables by waging a non-violent war in their behalf. But he could not save himself from the assassin's bullet. He died practicing what he preached. The press states that when falling he gave the sign which meant "forgive." A Palestinian Jew died that way nineteen centuries ago.

By now, Mays, through the Morehouse connection, was even better situated than a decade earlier to communicate his news on Gandhi's nonviolence, his contribution to the independence of India, and his love for and concern for the the welfare of the Untouchables. The suggestion that Gandhi was the Jesus of the twentieth century could not have failed to impress Mays's readers.[37]

In February 1948, Gordon Hancock, in the *Norfolk Journal and Guide*, reflected on Gandhi's life, once again making a direct comparison between Jesus Christ and the departed Indian leader: "Well-informed and intelligent men the world over will truly mourn the passing of Mohandas Gandhi, the most picturesque figure to appear upon the earth since Jesus of Nazareth lived in the flesh." Turning to the question of the meaning of Gandhi for African-Americans, he observed,

NEGROES COULD—if they would—learn a lesson from Gandhi! In fact it would be tragic if they did not. Minority groups must rely upon powers beyond the ken of man! The back of the British Empire was not broken "by power and might" but by the faith of a little bewizened Hindoo, who dared to test the strength that lies beyond the domain of "power and might."

Jesus Christ employed this superhuman power and wrecked the Roman Empire; Gandhi employed it and hurled the British Empire from the pedestal of power. The all-important question for the subjugated peoples of color to fathom is, how far will they go in employing might and power for their deliverance, instead of appealing to the Supreme Court of Heaven by their righteous lives and their faithful prayers?

The method of Jesus and Gandhi, Hancock believed, was the only way out for a world in conflict; power and force were not going to solve the problems of anybody, African-Americans included.[38]

Charles H. Houston, a onetime vice-dean of Howard University's law school, had begun to play a major role in organizing the legal assault against segregation in the United States. In an article he contributed to the *Baltimore Afro-American* on 13 March he pointed out that the communal warfare among Hindus and Muslims had apparently quieted since Gandhi's death. He noted that the Mahatma, who "lived for peace and brotherhood," taught humanity "that violence breeds violence, and settles nothing." He was convinced that

> as long as Ghandi lived the fight for peace was Ghandi's fight. When Ghandi died by an assassin's bullet, the obligation to stand for peace and brotherhood became the intimate personal responsibility of every Indian with a social conscience, no matter what his religion, his station or his allegiance. We are witnessing a miracle; communal warfare stopped because the spiritual inspiration of a great soul makes the battlers put their weapons down.[39]

Houston, like many other African-American interpreters of Gandhi, had attributed more credit to Gandhi than was his due. In his lifetime and his death, Gandhi failed to bring about total harmony between Hindus and Muslims. Yet Houston was correct in highlighting the healing power of Gandhi and his way of nonviolent resistance.

As previously noted, African-American commentators were not unaware of the internal contradictions in the Indian situation (see Chapter 3). The Hindu practice of untouchability had been discussed by some observers. After independence, in the summer of 1948, when the Indian government moved its troops into the Muslim-ruled state of Hyderabad, some in the African-American community were disturbed. Taking note of the Indian military action, the *Baltimore Afro-American* took the Indian leaders to task. Alluding to Indian tradition of nonviolent resistance to Britain, the paper's editorial declared that "it would appear that India, which declared its independence a little more than a year ago, has quickly learned aggression as taught by the Christians who once ruled it." The desired and desirable message for African-Americans from out of India, then, was nonviolence and not violence; India was expected to follow the truth told and lived out by the Mahatma. When India erred, African-Americans were disappointed, and some said so.[40]

In the midst of the triumph and turmoil of Indian independence, Gandhi's death, and the Hindu-Muslim tragedy, African-Americans continued to follow events in India. One of the most important links in that period was Mordecai Johnson, president of Howard

University, a leader who touched many lives. By the late 1940s and early 1950s, Mordecai Johnson's focus had become sharper. In a certain sense, the process had been aided when, in 1949, the Indian Government invited him to visit India. On 21 November 1949, the *Washington Post* noted "Dr. W. Mordecai Johnson . . . plans to leave this week for India, where he will take part in a study of the methods of the late Mohandas K. Gandhi and the possibility of their wider use in achieving world peace." In December of that year, ninety-three participants from thirty-four countries attended the interfaith World Pacifist Meeting in India. Johnson, an eloquent spokesperson for world peace, was one of the participants. Yet, as William Robert Miller has argued, it was Gandhi, more than the cause of peace, which drew Johnson to India. Johnson was rooted in the Christian faith, and it was from the depths of that tradition that he was attracted to the Mahatma. After all, Gandhi's philosophy of nonviolence was compatible with the message of love in the teachings of Jesus. Gandhi's alternative offered a political instrument which had the potential of transforming society as well as meeting India's immediate goal of gaining independence. Indeed, so deeply affected was he by the Christ-like example of Gandhi that Johnson made it a practice, starting in the late 1920s, to share the wisdom and the way of Gandhi from every conceivable platform.[41]

During the visit, which lasted forty days, Johnson talked at length with Gandhi's followers. One of the most significant moments came one night while Johnson and world church leaders were in a discussion about the meaning of Gandhian nonviolence at Tagore's university at Santiniketan. During much of the discussion, the emphasis had been largely on nonviolence as a method of change rather than as a way of life. Before the session was over, the focus had shifted to the spiritual basis of Gandhian nonviolence, at the prompting of Manilal Gandhi (1892–1956), the Mahatma's second son:

> As I've sat and listened to you, more and more it has dawned upon me that you are working on the assumption that you can only intellectually understand my father's methods, what he hoped to do with it and how he worked it—you'll be able to work it too. . . . That's what I thought when I followed him in South Africa. I have been doing this for twenty years what you're doing now. But I think

I understand every method he used, but they won't work for me—
where he succeeded, I am a relative failure. . . . I have come to this
conclusion about it and I commend it to you for your thoughtful
consideration; that these methods and these tactics that you're talking about were the methods and tactics of a man of all but unparalleled purity of heart. It's not my lack of intellectual understanding
that has made me a failure. It is my lack of purity of heart.[42]

As a result of his encounters with a large group of Gandhians,
Johnson gained not only a deeper understanding of Gandhi's perspective on nonviolence but also a new zeal to communicate the
meaning and message of the Mahatma to African-Americans. Given
the power of his oratory (he was counted among the top ten speakers
in the country), Johnson was highly qualified to play that role. In
the words of Benjamin E. Mays, Johnson was "one of the great
prophets in the 20th century." Johnson was "a constant source of
inspiration from my own high school days," wrote Howard Thurman
in his autobiography. Many in the African-American community,
including Martin Luther King, Jr., were inspired by him to explore
the Gandhian alternatives seriously. For decades Johnson encouraged
students and church communities to learn from the example of
Gandhi. According to Mays, Johnson "was paving the way for
Martin Luther King, Jr., who got his first doctrine of non-violence
from Mordecai."[43]

As was to be expected, upon his return Johnson began a lecture
tour. As president of Howard and as a magnificent preacher-orator,
he was in demand as a speaker throughout black America. However,
as we now know, it was a sermon he gave early in 1950 at Fellowship
House, a relatively inconspicuous interracial community center in
Philadelphia, which went straight to the heart of the brilliant,
curious, and sensitive young seminarian Martin Luther King, Jr.

> As he listened to Mordecai Johnson, he found his skepticism melting
> before an oratorical onslaught. Why was Gandhi a great man? asked
> Johnson. On five counts. He had liberated India. He did it without
> firing a shot. He embraced the Untouchables as children of God
> and made a place for them in a society that had excluded them,
> segregated them. For his exemplary and saintly personal life alone,
> he was a great man. But the capstone of it all, said Johnson, was
> this: he had shown how to harness the redemptive power of love to
> social issuses, and through it, change had come. He had even, like

Jesus, died a redemptive death which abated the fearful strife between Hindus and Muslims that had raged after independence.[44]

Years later, reflecting on the impact of Johnson's sermon on him,
King wrote, "His message was so profound and electrifying that I
left the meeting and bought a half-dozen books on Gandhi's life
and works." With that encounter began King's serious study of
Gandhi and his method of nonviolence. King recalled that "as I
delved deeper into the philosophy of Gandhi my skepticism concerning the power of love gradually diminished, and I came to see
for the first time its potency in the area of social reform." He added
that "prior to reading Gandhi, I had about concluded that the ethics
of Jesus were only effective in individual relationship." In an important sense, therefore, Mordecai Johnson, continuing the fascinating Howard University connection, became a powerful link
between the post-King and the pre-King eras in the African-
American exploration of Gandhian nonviolence.[45]

By 1950, Mrs. Pandit was India's ambassador to the United
States. Johnson saw to it that Howard University awarded her an
honorary doctorate that year. With the words "it pleases me to
think that in honouring me you are expressing your admiration for
my country and the values she represents," she accepted the honorary
degree of Doctor of Laws. Pandit was deeply moved by the gesture.
In his citation, Mordecai Johnson said,

> We greet you today, VIJAYA LAKSHMI PANDIT, as Ambassador of
> India, it is true, but more than that as one of that noble company
> of men and women who, under the leadership of Mahatma Gandhi,
> have given the world the most magnificent demonstration of non-
> violent self-control and effective resistance in the history of mankind.

So the connections extended into the 1950s, deepened, and matured
as African-Americans continued to maintain their close interest in
the spirit of Gandhi. For example, Howard University stayed in
close touch with Indian national representatives in Washington,
D.C., even after Mrs. Pandit was succeeded in her ambassadorial
post by G. L. Mehta, and in 1953 Mehta was invited by the
university to participate in the ceremonies to observe the fifth anniversary of Gandhi's death.[46]

With his firm commitment to peace and a keen sense of history,
Mordecai Johnson was deeply interested in the new order which

was fast emerging in the post–World War II period. He had participated in the deliberations which led up to the formation of the United Nations. As president of Howard University and a leader of his community, he used several opportunities to bring home to African-Americans the significance of the revolutions which were taking place in the Third World. The fall convocation of Howard University, in September 1953, was another occasion when he turned to Gandhi to drive home a moral imperative of negotiation with the Soviet Union and the love of neighbor. Here again, Johnson urged that Gandhi could provide a valuable moral lesson for humankind. Deeply concerned as he was about the need for the United States to present a moral and humane alternative at home and abroad, Johnson pleaded for a rejection of the cold-war policy of hate and revenge. Disturbed at the anti-Soviet stance of the Eisenhower administration, and particularly at the views of Secretary of State John Foster Dulles, Johnson said, "We have reached the climax of hate. We now see that what the Scriptures of the world have always said—that they who take up the sword shall die by it." He made a plea for raising "international negotiations to the highest constructive power that human thought and human character is capable of."[47]

What was the way out? he asked. Not surprisingly, Johnson turned to Gandhi for an answer. He suggested that "the greatest example of successful international negotiation that this world has ever seen took place in your lifetime in India." British rule, even according to an enlightened Briton, he pointed out, was "one of the world's most brutal examples of political domination, exploitation and humiliation of a people in all history." The United States, he felt, would benefit from taking a leaf out of Gandhi's book. We must turn away from the "calculation of brutality and deception," he said. He reminded his audience of how at the worst of times Gandhi entered into negotiations "with as fine a courtesy [sic] as any human being ever accorded his best friend." Johnson also noted that every British negotiator testified that "never a single moment in negotiations with Ghandi were they ever able to lose sight of the fact that he was talking to a gentleman who was addressing him on the highest level of sincerity and honor that he was capable of."[48]

Johnson further argued that the United States and the Soviet

Union had invested so much in violence that they were headed for "insanity if we say we cannot negotiate with each other." According to Johnson, Gandhi saw no justification for the principle which demanded a diplomat be a deceptive scoundrel, "trained to say beautiful things while he knows that his nation has purposes that are different"; the Mahatma wanted the Indians to deal truthfully without exaggeration and propaganda. Gandhi, Johnson noted, returned British brutality with courtesy. Johnson urged the leaders of this nation to approach the Soviets in the manner and spirit of Gandhi. The meaning and the purpose of Gandhi's life he summed up in these words:

> There stood out above all intellectual content the clear and simple integrity of a human life that would rather die than to progress by deceit and violence against a single living human soul, and who looking at the future of India took the position that it would be better that all of us were dead than that we should embrutalize our [sic] ourselves than by killing our Indians in order to overcome their wills.

Thus, five years after the death of the Mahatma, the president of the nation's best-known African-American institution of higher education was invoking his name and his spirit in the quest for a more just and peaceful world. He called upon the United States to "rise from the spirit of violence, into the great statesmanship that Ghandi has set before us." Johnson said that "the most valuable all[y] to peace around any negotiating table in this world is the spirit of Mohandus Ghandi."[49]

In another speech, Johnson pointed out that he had not "wished to be a part of any movement which would tend to set up the educated people in an organized life apart from the masses of the people." Again he urged his listeners to learn from Gandhi. Johnson informed the gathering about how the Mahatma was grieved at the thought that the educated had "set themselves in the cities and exercised little or no concern about the economic and political needs of the great masses of more than three hundred million people that lived in the villages." Johnson was convinced that if educated African-Americans were to remove themselves from the masses "we should be unworthy of the education which we have received."[50]

On 26 January 1950 India became a republic, severing relations with the British Crown. The following July, Ram Manohar Lohia, an established Gandhian leader, came to the United States on a six-week lecture tour at the invitation of Stringfellow Barr, president of the Foundation for World Government. A longtime activist, Lohia had spent time in independent India's jails for participating in civil disobedience campaigns and, most recently, for organizing a march on Delhi to protest against the eviction of tillers by landlords. The march, in which some seventy-five thousand participated, and Lohia's subsequent arrest drew the attention of the Western press. While in the United States he gave twenty addresses, met with several activists, and spoke on one national radio forum. For our purposes, it is most important to see Lohia as another in the long series of Indian visitors who focused so much of their time and energy on building connections with America.

In contrast to Krishnalal Shridharani, who during the 1940s worked with groups in the East and the North, Lohia traveled throughout the country, including parts of the upper and deep South. Harris Wofford, a white graduate of Howard University's law school and a sympathetic student of Gandhian nonviolence, was in charge of the Lohia trip. Following the advice of Senator Hubert Humphrey, who had hoped that Lohia would "visit our people in their homes, their factories, their farms, and communities and that he will travel extensively beyond Washington and beyond New York," Wofford organized a trip that put Lohia on the road the same evening he landed in New York. Nashville, Tennessee, was his first stop. The students at Fisk University, an important African-American school, were his hosts. The following day he spoke at the concluding session of the university's well known annual Race Relations Institute. The institute had African-American and white participants from all over the country. Participants heard about "The Awakening of Asia and Africa." Lohia affirmed the African heritage of black people in this country and pleaded for solidarity with Africans who were fighting European powers for their own freedom.[51]

To Charles Johnson, president of Fisk (who in his closing remarks at the institute had spoken approvingly about the legal steps which were being taken to establish racial equality in the United States), Lohia recommended the use of Gandhian nonviolent direct action by African-Americans in their freedom struggle. The Indian leader wanted African-Americans to resist the system directly and non-violently and to be prepared to go to prison. This approach, he argued, had empowered Indians and won their freedom; he was convinced that it could work here in this country also. He urged African-Americans to do "a little jailgoing" rather than face indignities on a daily basis. Johnson, who was familiar with the Gandhian struggle from his visit to India, was not so sure: "No, we're not like India. Here we have the law and Constitution on our side. Besides, we're too weak a minority in America, just thirteen millions. It can never happen here." That was in 1951. University presidents were not all seers.[52]

After Fisk, Lohia headed for the interracial Highlander Folk School, which was attended by a number of key African-American social activists who helped prepare and open the way for Martin Luther King, Jr.'s leadership of the Southern nonviolent movement. (In 1932, Myles Horton, trained as an economist at the University of Chicago, was inspired to start this school by the example of Scandinavian folk schools for training farm, union, and community leaders.) It was here that Rosa Parks "discussed the idea of civil disobedience" in the summer of 1955, weeks before the start of the historic Montgomery bus boycott. At Highlander there was curiosity about Lohia's resort to civil disobedience in post-independence India. In response to the question about voluntary jailgoing, Lohia said,

> Well, under the British, it was natural. You threw their tea in the harbor, we burned some of their cloth. But mainly Gandhi invited us to get the British out by our own suffering, by refusing to obey them and going to jail. If we continue to use this system it is because there is still injustice. There is the usual way to remove injustices, through an election and a change of government every five years. But there is also the way of non-violent direct action, which includes the violation of unjust laws. For instance, we use this way of struggling against our unjust land tenures—what you call share-cropping.[53]

Lohia hammered home the relevance of Gandhian nonviolence beyond alien British rule and beyond Gandhi. In essence, his was a call for nonviolent resistance to unjust laws in all cases and at all times. It was a call which Rosa Parks and thousands upon thousands of African-Americans were to make their own in 1955 and beyond.

Marion Junction, Alabama, was Lohia's next stop. On the way, he learned the extent to which much of the African-American leadership was dependent on white interests. (Myles Horton, who also accompanied Lohia on the trip, described "the difficulty such Negro leaders had in satisfying both the increasingly militant people whom they were supposed to lead, and the whites on whom their jobs usually depended.") The Indian leader spoke to a group of whites and expounded on Gandhian philosophy and its relevance for ending African-American oppression in the United States. He wanted black Americans to adopt Gandhian ways and expressed his desire to meet black leaders. Local white leaders were quick to communicate the depth of their segregationist feelings and low esteem for African-Americans. Someone in the audience, Wofford recorded, told Lohia, "Down here in Alabama there are just nigras—no nigra leaders"; the same person added, "Why don't you talk to our nigras about all that [Gandhian nonviolence]. Come on and try—and I'll shoot you." During a visit to a 4-H club, Lohia was surprised to learn that the white women there had studied Gandhi. Even though he did not get to Birmingham, Lohia was able to gain some sense, albeit secondhand, of the intensity of racial discrimination there. He could understand what the city's police commissioner, Bull Connor, meant by the words "I ain't gonna have no niggers and whites segregating together in Birmingham."[54]

A week after starting his tour of the United States in New York, Lohia arrived at Howard University. He addressed the issues of caste, the United Nations, and the imperative that African-Americans adopt the cause of Africa. He also emphasized his belief in the efficacy of the way of Gandhian nonviolence. According to Lohia, nonviolence was a panacea for destroying the divisions which separate humanity.

> I believe that civil disobedience is a weapon of universal application. And I am not being oblique—I mean it can be used on the race question in this country. If I were an American, I would explore civil disobedience, by Negroes and Whites. I would do it more for the health of the non-Negro than of the Negro. I know that the Negro is a minority, but I believe that if there is an action with courage, there will be a response from other sections of the people, and the minority can be transformed into a majority. In any case, to the destruction of the caste system in all its forms we must dedicate our lives.

Lohia defined racism as a form of caste. His advocacy of nonviolence in the African-American struggle was forthright. He believed that passionate and determined adherence to nonviolence was essential to the creation of a just order. It was of no consequence that African-Americans were outnumbered by their white compatriots. After his speech, a young African-American who had been reading Gandhi told Lohia that he "was ready for civil disobedience" and wanted to know from the Indian leader what sort of "self-discipline" and "purification" practices he might enter into for the next stage. Lohia encouraged him "not to worry about preparations, just to go ahead and do the best he could."[55]

While on the east coast, Lohia took the message of nonviolent resistance to the Urban League. A league staff member, Bob Jones, took him through Harlem. He was told about the league's relief and rehabilitation work and the legal and legislative work of the NAACP. While appreciative of the league's empowerment work among ghetto residents, Lohia expressed the view that "the tempo was insufficient both for the demands of the world situation . . . and for the demands of the awakening Negro population in America." In a setting where he sensed violence in the air, he spelled out the methods of nonviolent direct action and "urged that peaceful resistance be applied, with American ingenuity, as an essential part of any approach to the racial problem."[56]

In response to Lohia's plea for the application of nonviolent resistance by African-Americans, Ed Lewis, the director of the league's project in Harlem, said that "he would like Lohia to explore this further with a group of representative Harlem leaders." Nine days later, Lohia went back to Harlem to discuss the relevance of civil disobedience with a number of African-American leaders the league had brought together. He saw in the moment a marvellous opportunity for further developing the concept of nonviolence. Not unlike Gandhi, Lohia believed that history had thrust African-Americans into an exemplary role to show the power of nonviolence. He argued that "by practicing non-violent direct action against segregation, by peacefully violating unjust racial laws wherever they exist, by willingly going to jail, the Negro—and the white who joined him—would thus strengthen the camp of peaceful change throughout the world." To those who insisted that nonviolence was not the part of the African-American tradition, Lohia provided the example of the Pathans of India's northwest frontier, who, he suggested, had a centuries-old tradition of violence. If they could adopt non-violence, then surely anyone could. According to Lohia, "No more violent person exists than the Pathan. He grows up with his gun. Yet they produced Abdul Gaffar Khan, whom we call the 'Frontier Gandhi,' who showed them that to fight non-violently was just as courageous, and more successful." He told of incidents when these Pathans maintained nonviolence even under machine gun fire and aerial bombardment. Lohia had another reason for urging African-Americans to explore nonviolence. Because "there is a great deal of violence underneath the surface in America," he warned them to prepare and develop the weapon of nonviolent resistance so as to avoid being surprised by events. Among the African-American leaders who had been invited to be with Lohia were representatives from the Brotherhood of Sleeping Car Porters. They informed the Indian leader about the march on Washington A. Philip Randolph had planned in the early 1940s.[57]

On his way to San Francisco, Lohia stopped in Laramie, Wyoming. There he met Taraknath Das (1884–1958), a fiery Indian activist who, when exiled by the British in the early part of the twentieth century, came to the United States and carried on his struggle against British rule from this country. Lohia's major responsibility on this stop was to give a formal address at the University of Wyoming's summer school conference. Inevitably, during question time the discussion turned to nonviolence and its relevance to the ongoing African-American struggle for freedom and justice. His audience wanted to know how people might best be educated in the way of nonviolence. To which Lohia said, "Education by activity in the subject to be taught, basic education we call it, is the newest way, and that is the way I suggest. Not manifestoes or speeches about non-violence, but practice!" As regards the workability of the method of nonviolent direct action in the African-American struggle for the reassertion of their fundamental rights, Lohia added,

> I want to see them go through a period of trial by practicing non-violent action. Let Negroes and whites resist racial injustices, go to jail, some even get killed. Then we will see an awakening of conscience in America, and in the world. This would encourage people like me everywhere, and reinforce the camp of peaceful change. A massive campaign, even of five hundred Negroes and five hundred

whites, would excite us all. We would say: look at that healthy democratic society; see how democracy works. And I may say that would do more good for the world and for the goodwill toward the U.S., than any amount of Point Four or E.C.A.[58]

The "period of trial by practicing non-violent action" was, of course, closer than Lohia likely knew. Meanwhile, members of the black community continued the now time-honored tradition of traveling to India to observe what might be called the breeding place of twentieth century nonviolent revolutionary action. Indeed, it was early in the 1950s that one of the most important of these bridge creating visitors arrived in Gandhi's land. James Lawson, son of an African-American Methodist minister, had been first introduced to the way of nonviolence by his mother when he slapped a white child for a racial slur. When he related the incident to his mother, she asked, "What good did that do, Jimmy?" The way of Jesus and the Sermon on the Mount were the predominant childhood influences of his youth. Lawson internalized biblical teachings during his college years through encounters with A. J. Muste and his radical peace witness, and he studied the history of the resistance movements against Nazism in Norway and Denmark. While Lawson was still a student, Gandhi's autobiography left a great impression on him. It convinced him of the validity and beauty of the way of nonviolence. The New Testament "infused all of my reading of Gandhi," he recalled. In the early 1940s he became interested in the nonviolent workshops which were then organized by Bayard Rustin of the FOR. Lawson was already a Gandhian-Christian conscientious objector when, in 1953, he left jail in the United States to go to India and serve out his alternative service term as a fraternal worker for his church.[59]

Lawson's official assignment was to teach and coach at Hislop College in Nagpur, India, but his deepest, unofficial, mission was to learn as much as he could from the followers of Gandhi about the way of nonviolent life and resistance. During his stay, which lasted into 1956, he met with such outstanding Gandhians as Vinoba Bhave, Gandhi's foremost disciple; J. C. Kumarappa, the leading Gandhian economist; and Asha Devi, a frontline Gandhian in the post-independence period. He also attended a variety of seminars, workshops, and conferences organized by Gandhian organizations such as the Serva Seva Sangh.[60] In a sense, Lawson was the last of the pre-Montgomery bridge builders to make the Indian pilgrimage, for while he was still on the subcontinent the African-Americans of Montgomery made their own new beginnings. They had found their own Gandhi deep in the heart of the Christian church, and from that point forward "watch the African-Americans" and "we need a Martin Luther King, Jr." would be watchwords of the world.

Predictably, it was not long after Lawson returned to the United States, in 1956, that he met King and accepted the new leader's invitation to come south and enter the struggle for the nonviolent transformation of American society. Within months the connections were complete and Lawson, bringing a wealth of experience with him, became one of the most powerful leaders of nonviolent revolution in the nation. Gandhi had predicted that "it could be through the African-American that the unadulterated message of nonviolence could be delivered to men everywhere." King, Lawson, and hundreds of their fellow leaders and teachers, and hundreds of thousands of their followers brought life to the Mahatma's prediction and created a natural conclusion to the long tradition of contact between African-Americans and Indians. Just as it was in the preceding decades, so also during the years from 1945 to 1955; African-American solidarity with the people of color, especially with India, came alive. Indeed, building on more than a generation of African-American interest in the Indian struggle and the Gandhian doctrine of nonviolence, a new crop of African-American activist-leaders eventually made revolutionary nonviolence a cornerstone of their own struggle. For when King said, "Christ furnished the spirit and motivation, while Gandhi furnished the method," he was doing much more than making a passing reference—he was pointing to the two major sources of energy, direction, and hope of the mid-twentieth-century African-American freedom movement.[61]

Conclusion:
Raising Up a Prophet

RESISTANCE TO OPPRESSION and injustice has remained a central feature of African-American life for more than three centuries. Throughout that time, whenever the opportunity was available, African-Americans paid serious attention to other freedom struggles, especially those of people of color, wherever they were carried on, from Haiti to the Philippines to India. It has been the aim of this study to demonstrate the attention given by African-Americans to the Gandhi-led, nonviolent independence struggle of the Indian people almost four decades before Martin Luther King, Jr., emerged on the scene.

The post–1954 movement led by African-Americans did not emerge out of an historical vacuum. African-American explorations into Gandhian philosophy and the techniques of nonviolent direct action in the pre-Montgomery years cleared the path for the creation of a major nonviolent revolution in the second half of the twentieth century. The ground for the coming of a black Gandhi and the making of a nonviolent struggle was assiduously prepared during those years. Whether it was the Montgomery bus boycott (1955–1956), the Prayer Pilgrimage (1957), the sit-ins in the early 1960s, the Freedom Rides (1961), the march on Washington (1963), or the Selma-Montgomery march (1965), Gandhi consciousness generated by the African-American press or by community leaders and earlier applications of nonviolent techniques became vital links in a chain which ultimately led to the maturation and success of the movement of the 1950s and 1960s. In many instances, the veterans of campaigns from earlier years became bridge builders, key participants, and trainers of the modern African-American movement. For a time some of them were also King's most important teachers and comrades in arms.

Consciousness of Gandhi and his movement began early in this century. It involved the activities of Indian nationalists who visited African-American communities in the United States, black leaders who visited Gandhi and India, African-American organizations whose leaders encouraged their people to be aware of the Indian struggle, and especially the African-American press, which kept a constant watch on "the little brown man" and his empire-shaking movement.

Gandhi appealed to black Americans because he, like them, was a member of an oppressed colored people. "We see how America and England live on the coloured races, exploit other people," Gandhi said. The two peoples, Indians under British rule and African-Americans in the United States, were denied their basic rights because of false notions of white supremacy—notions Gandhi had begun to question early in the twentieth century. He was also convinced that India's nonviolent struggle was "a struggle for the emancipation of all oppressed races against superior might." At the turn of the century, leaders such as W. E. B. Du Bois and Hubert Harrison helped to place the African-American struggle at the heart of the worldwide struggle of people of color. Marcus Garvey was also central to this development; indeed, it was important that Gandhi emerged as a major political and moral force on the world scene at the same time that Garvey rose to great prominence in this hemisphere. For Garvey, through the rich and broadly based na-tionwide network of the UNIA, actively turned African-American attention to Africa, India, and the struggles of oppressed people everywhere.[1]

It was at this time—the years immediately following World War I—that African-Americans began to take seriously Gandhi's lead-ership of the Indian movement, the method of nonviolence, his personal qualities, and the implications of his determined opposition to Britain. Over a period of decades, the two peoples became stronger in their sense of solidarity, and their struggles came closer together. For racial, material, and ideological reasons African-Americans identified themselves with Gandhi. He had a dark com-plexion and looked ordinary enough. "The little brown man," as they often called Gandhi, encouraged and inspired them because he dared to stand up against the mightiest of European empires.

African-Americans were also drawn to Gandhi because they too had been taught not to make distinctions between the personal and the public, the political and the religious, the sacred and the profane; all of life was viewed as a piece of the whole, inextricably connected. In addition to this shared religious value, the teachings of Jesus in the Sermon on the Mount presented another important meeting ground. Committed Hindu that he was, Gandhi never tired of drawing parallels between his movement and the one headed by Jesus. African-American leaders spoke of "the great power [Gandhi] has won through sincerity and love," and emphasized the need of taking him seriously because "he has Christ in him." For his part, Gandhi often reminded the world that the founder of Christianity was not only "the Prince of Peace" but also the first *satyagrahi* the world ever saw. African-American religious sensibilities certainly made it easier for them to move toward the creative adoption of the Gandhian method of nonviolent resistance.[2]

Also of great importance to many African-Americans was their sense that Gandhi offered an alternative mode of leadership for social struggles. They recognized that apart from his rural-based diet and dress, and his ability to encourage self-esteem in ordinary Indian people, it was Gandhi's love of humanity and his lack of double standards which made him a great spiritual and political leader. These qualities clearly set him apart from other politicians and made him seem to many African-Americans the model of a leader. Time and again, African-American writers raised the relevance and importance of his style of leadership for their struggle. The call for a "Black Gandhi" was made often, in a variety of ways and a variety of settings.[3]

Gandhi's outspoken stand against the practice of untouchability was another reason why he was so admired by the African-American community. Practitioners of untouchability were "Hindu Dyers," so named after General Dyer, who ordered the massacre of innocent protesters at Amritsar in 1919. Without reservations, African-American leaders lauded Gandhi for his denunciation of untouchability and for his attempts at bringing its victims, by encouraging intermarriage and interdining, into the mainstream of political and social life. Mays, who thought that the Hindu caste system was much worse than racism in the United States, stressed Gandhi's opposition to untouchability. At the same time, his encounter with Gandhi and India made Mays realize that he himself was "truly an untouchable in [his] own land." When Gandhi coined the term Harijan to describe the Untouchables, it had special resonance for African-Americans. Such affirmation was part of African-American tradition. They too were called "children of God" by their community elders; slave preachers used to end their sermons by telling their congregations, "You are not niggers! You are not slaves! You are God's children!" As the *Pittsburgh Courier* observed, "the Hindu, [Gandhi] sees, can with ill grace complain against the persecution and exploitation by the British overlords when he himself is more mercilessly exploiting and degrading one-sixth of his number, the Untouchables." The Indian leader's practice of carrying on the struggle against both the internal structures of oppression and external victimizers was a major factor in drawing African-Americans to Gandhi.[4]

The African-American community found much in Gandhi and his ways which was relevant to their struggle. They were forthright on this issue of connections; their interest in the Gandhian concept of nonviolent resistance was neither distant nor academic. In their quest to overcome racism and to create a just and humane social order for all people in the United States, African-Americans made serious efforts to understand fully the meaning of Gandhi's message. Indeed, a variety of African-American leaders advocated and experimented with the use of Gandhian methods prior to 1950.

The events of the Indian freedom struggle and Gandhi's leadership of that movement were given considerable prominence by African-American educators, church leaders, and the press. In the press, while there was no attempt to report all the major issues of the Indian struggle, certain critical events, such as the noncooperation movement (1920–1921), the civil disobedience campaign (1930–1931), Gandhi's leadership, and his unique message of love and nonviolence, were clearly and regularly communicated to the community. The African-American press reported on and interpreted the Indian situation to educate its readers. It also used developments in India to encourage and provide hope among its readers.

By the 1930s, the cruelties of international politics had provided another significant point of contact between black people and Gandhi, focused this time on the African-American response to the

Italian invasion of Ethiopia. It was not possible to read any African-American newspaper or journal of that time and not find a story, an editorial, or an essay about Ethiopia. The black press gave prominence to the stand taken by Gandhi in the matter. When, in 1935, Gandhi announced his strong opposition to Mussolini's invasion of Ethiopia and offered material help, he was again praised for his willingness to stand in solidarity with the great symbol of African and African-American connectedness.[5]

Considering the special place black Americans had in their hearts for Ethiopia, it is not surprising that they should have paid attention to Gandhi's expression of sympathy and the promise of material help for that beleagured African nation. What is even more striking is that even when there were pressing local issues—for example, at the height of the Scottsboro Affair—demanding unhampered attention, they did not ignore Gandhi and the Indian independence movement. In 1934 "two stories dominated the news as well as the daydreams of the people I met. One had to do with the demonstrations by Mahatma Gandhi and his followers in India; the other, the trials of the Scottsboro boys then in progress in Decatur, Alabama," writes Arna Bontemps in *Black Thunder*. The trial of the Scottsboro boys was an emotionally charged event of great significance for African-Americans. That Gandhi should concern blacks in Decatur at such a moment is suggestive of his impact.[6]

The meetings between Gandhi and African-Americans such as Howard Thurman and Sue Bailey Thurman, Edward Carroll Benjamin E. Mays, Channing Tobias, and William Stuart Nelson, and later journeys to India by such people as Bayard Rustin, Mordecai Johnson, and James Lawson provided strong witness to the lively interest of Afro-America in Gandhi and his movement. The journeys of such community leaders and activists as these were important in linking the two movements ideologically. There were strong personal bonds between many Gandhi watchers; at the same time, these leaders were part of a tradition of resistance and community. The network of relationships they maintained were inclusive of the worlds of the church and academia. Because of the powerful positions many of them held in these influential settings, they touched many lives—Thurman introduced James Farmer to Gandhi at Howard University, and Mays was a major influence in King's life.

Finally, long before the rise of Martin Luther King, Jr., a growing

162 RAISING UP A PROPHET

number of African-Americans not only grasped the relevance of the doctrine of nonviolence to their own situation in this country, but also sought to experiment with its uses. Building on the homegrown tactics of the labor movement and the conceptual framework of *satyagraha*, several new openings were sought. During the 1940s, inspired by persons like A. Philip Randolph, James Farmer, and Bayard Rustin, African-Americans explored the possibilities of applying Gandhian nonviolence in the United States. The Congress of Racial Equality (CORE) argued that its members were living by the teachings of the Sermon on the Mount and following the path laid down by Gandhi in South Africa and India. The adoption of Gandhian methods by the March on Washington Movement (MOWM) and the Gandhian-based work of CORE in the early 1940s provided new prospects for nonviolence in the United States. Randolph's threat to use civil disobedience "along Gandhian lines" against the military draft also kept the nonviolent alternative in focus. As a result of such explorations, important lessons in the practice of nonviolent direct action were learned for the future and the connections with India were deepened. In the post–1954 years, in many situations, the lessons thus learned were applied. Not only were some campaigns patterned on the earlier ones, but nonviolent trainers such as James Lawson and Bayard Rustin proved central to the ultimate success of the modern African-American freedom movement. These human and ideological links help to explain much of what happened in the years 1955–1968.

For several years before the Montgomery bus boycott, local leadership in Montgomery had prodded ministers of the church, without much success, to unite in the struggle. In the months leading up to the boycott, scores of people from the Women's Political Council had teamed up with E. D. Nixon to challenge boldly other aspects of segregation in Montgomery. In Mrs. Rosa Parks the community found not only a person of great courage and determination, but also a person who had considered the Gandhi alternative of civil disobedience in the summer of 1955. With her refusal, in December 1955, to cooperate with the system of segregation, she set in motion a chain of events which was to change much in the South and the rest of the nation. Somewhat unexpectedly, her initiative provided the missing link which enabled local church leaders to come together and opened the way for religion and religious institutions to be harnessed to the methodology of "passive resistance."

From A. Philip Randolph to James Farmer to Bayard Rustin, earlier attempts to apply Gandhian nonviolence to the African-American struggle lacked the vital religious dimension. It is not that this earlier generation of experimenters with nonviolence were not sensitive to this element in the African-American tradition or Gandhian philosophy. In the article "The Negro and Non-Violence," written in the fall of 1942, in which he argued that African-Americans possessed the qualities essential for nonviolent direct action, Rustin emphasized that this was so because they had learned to endure suffering without bitterness and also because they possess "a rich religious heritage" with the church at the center of their lives. He also argued that the alternative Gandhi had developed was "a workable and Christian technique for the righting of injustice and the solution of conflict" in the United States. To the extent that Rustin and others did not succeed, their failure was, at least in part, due to the fact that neither their efforts nor their own personal lives were rooted in the African-American church. By planting the seed of the Gandhian technique of nonviolent direct action in the dry bed of secularism, the pre–1955 experimenters could not fully avail themselves of the potential of the method or the latent energy of the people. It took another time, another leader, and another gathering of activists to bring together the spirit and the method of nonviolent direct action into a harmony that led to the transformation of the United States. And, at their best, it was this melding of the method and the spirit which Thurman and Mays, among the foremost advocates of Gandhian nonviolence, had in mind for America when they explored with Gandhi the relevance of the nonviolent alternative to the African-American struggle.[7]

Thus, the soil which had been prepared and nurtured for a generation and more by some of the key African-American leaders was ready not only to receive the seed of nonviolence, but also to bear fruit as never before. This happened when the man, the moment, and the message came together and became one. The man was Martin Luther King, Jr., and it happened even though King had no "great experience in handling nonviolent tactics," even though he was "not a confirmed believer in non-violence, totally, at the time that the boycott began." His real gifts lay where they were needed the most—in rooting the nonviolent struggle in the religious heart of the community. "King's genius," Lerone Bennett rightly argues, "was not in the application of Gandhism to the Negro struggle but in the transmuting of Gandhism by grafting it onto the only thing that could give it relevance and force in the Negro community, the Negro religious tradition." Like a magnet, King drew to the struggle in Montgomery and beyond those who had been steeled in the way of nonviolent resistance. Once again, the links from the past helped. Of the two key teachers, Glenn Smiley, a white Methodist minister, and Bayard Rustin, who advised King at the early and critical stage of the boycott, Rustin provided an important bridge between earlier African-American explorations into Gandhian nonviolence and what had begun to emerge in the days after December 1955. King, a newcomer to the field of nonviolent direct action, deepened his commitment to nonviolence enough to give up reliance on all forms of violence. As it was applied on a vast scale, the practical as well as philosophical aspects of nonviolence were fully understood and implemented. Thanks to King and his understanding of Christianity, there was now an emphasis on the redemptive power of nonviolence. He had learned the redemptive power of love from the tradition of his faith, and the notion of actively confronting evil with love from Gandhi.[8]

In an important sense, the MOWM also connected the pre–1955 era with the post-Montgomery movement. The idea of a march organized by African-Americans never died. The march which eventually took place in August 1963 was, of course, rooted in the MOWM; even more specifically, it sprang from prior conversations between Randolph and Rustin about how to organize a demonstration which would deal with unemployment in the African-American community. During the 1963 "March on Washington for Jobs and Freedom," Randolph's mediating role and Rustin's enormous skills as an organizer were key factors in pulling off the event. Despite the disappointment of Student Nonviolent Coordinating Committee (SNCC) activists in the march's failure to adequately address structural issues of racism and economic exploitation, the event was one of the major landmarks of the modern movement. The march captured the imagination of the nation and galvanized the African-American community into coalitions as never before.

Thus, the three and a half decades preceding the start of the post–World War II Southern freedom movement were years when a sizable group of influential African-American leaders watched closely the Indian experiment and explored the meaning of Gandhian nonviolence for their own struggle. The forerunners of the modern African-American movement never gave up their faith in the workability of Gandhian nonviolence in the United States. They demystified the myth of nonviolence. It fell to Martin Luther King, Jr., to move beyond his own earlier preparation in Gandhian nonviolence, transmuting it through the great power of the African-American church and making it a reality in the struggle for a just community in this country.

King, then, was part of the decades-old tradition of the African-American search for meaning in the Gandhi-led Indian freedom movement. When from out of Montgomery he led a nonviolent struggle, King did more than just build on that tradition. He provided a bridge between two eras and between Gandhi-inspired activists and church-centered followers of Jesus. The convergence between the new and the older generation of nonviolent activists set in motion energy which helped to transform the nation.

Notes

Introduction

1. See Juan Williams, *Eyes on the Prize: America's Civil Rights Years,
   1954–1965* (New York: Viking, 1987); Clayborne Carson et al.,
   Eyes on the Prize: A Reader and Guide (New York: Penguin Books,
   1987); Henry Hampton, *Eyes on the Prize, Part I (1954–1965) and
   Part II (1964–1985)* (Boston: Blackside, 1987 and 1990), distributed
   by Public Broadcasting Service Video, Alexandria, Virginia.
2. Gandhian methods of nonviolent resistance have guided peace activists in many parts of the world for decades. In the early 1950s, Gandhian nonviolence was adopted in Ghana and South Africa;
   participants in the recent resistance campaigns in Israel, the Philippines, China, and Eastern Europe have applied Gandhian techniques
   in their struggles. See Mubarak Awad, "Nonviolence and Peace Perspectives in the Israeli-Palestinian Conflict," lecture at the Iliff School
   of Theology, 23 January 1989, sound cassette CST–1086, Ira J. Taylor Library, Denver. Awad, one of the key organizers of the Palestinian resistance which began in the Israeli-occupied West Bank in
   December 1987, has been inspired, in part, by Gandhian nonviolence. On the Philippines, see Hildegard Goss-Mayr, "When Prayer
   and Revolution Become People Power," *Fellowship* 53 (March 1987),
   9. Before his assassination, Benigno Aquino, Jr., explored the use of
   Gandhian methods in his challenge to the dictatorship of Ferdinand
   Marcos. According to Goss-Mayr, "While in prison, [Aquino] read
   the Gospel and Gandhi and began to understand that a politician must
   serve the people. He decided then that if he ever had the chance to assume responsibility for his country, he would try to be a politician
   who worked with nonviolence and served the people rather than himself." Also see Jose C. Blanco, S. J., "Revolutionary Thoughts, Preparation for Nonviolence," *Fellowship* 53 (March 1987), Robert

Shaplen, "A Reporter at Large: From Marcos to Aquino—I and II,"
New Yorker, 25 August and 1 September 1986. The role of the religious community in guiding and leading the Philippine people into
adopting nonviolence is emphasized by both Blanco and Shaplen. The
1986 successful nonviolent civilian resistance to Marcos was, in part, a
result of the nonviolent training carried out in the Philippines by the
International Fellowship of Reconciliation (IFOR), a pacifist organization of long standing, which has always been sympathetic to the vision and method of Gandhi and has done a great deal to make it a
reality in the United States and around the world. For the impact
Gandhi had on the pro-democracy movement in China, see Shen Tong
with Marian Yen, *Almost a Revolution* (Boston: Houghton Mifflin Co.,
1990), 89; and Han Minzhu and Hua Sheng, eds., *Cries for Democracy:
Writings and Speeches from the 1989 Chinese Democracy Movement* (Princeton: Princeton University Press, 1990), 377–78. On Poland, see
Adam Michnik, *Letters from Prison and Other Essays*, trans. Maya Latynski (Berkeley, Los Angeles: University of California Press, 1985), 88–
89. Michnik writes that "the ethics of Solidarity, with its consistent
rejection of the use of force, has a lot in common with the idea of nonviolence as espoused by Gandhi and Martin Luther King, Jr."

3. Martin Luther King, Jr., *Stride Toward Freedom: The Montgomery Story*
   (New York: Harper & Brothers, 1958), 85.

4. Gunnar Myrdal, *An American Dilemma: The Negro Problem and Modern
   Democracy* (New York: Harper & Brothers, 1944), 2: 908–10; Ibid.,
   911; Ibid., 744, 912. See Jack Lyle, ed., *The Black American and the
   Press* (Los Angeles: Ward Ritchie Press, 1968), 3–4. Armistead S.
   Pride argues that for almost 150 years the African-American press
   has "been instrumental in keeping alive the discontent of Negroes
   scattered over the country." See Myrdal, *An American Dilemma*, 914,
   909. He argues that World War I "provided the tide of protest upon
   which the press rose in importance and militancy," and that the
   African-American press "made the Negroes fully conscious of the
   inconsistency between America's war aims to 'make the world safe
   for democracy' and her treatment of this minority at home." Also
   see Maxwell R. Brooks, *The Negro Press Re-examined: Political Content
   of Leading Negro Newspapers* (Boston: Christopher Publishing House,
   1959); Martin E. Dann, ed., *The Black Press, 1827–1890: The Quest
   for National Identity* (New York: Putnam, 1971); Henry G. La Brie,
   III, ed., *Perspectives of the Black Press: 1974* (Kennebunkport, Maine:
   Mercer House Press, 1974); Odessa B. Baker, "Metaphors of Self-
   Identity as Contained in the Black Press from 1827 to the Present"
   (Ph.D. diss., Harvard University, 1978); Walter C. Daniel, *Black*

Journals of the United States: Historical Guides to the World's Periodicals and Newspapers (Westport, Conn.: Greenwood Press, 1982); Henry Lewis Suggs, ed., *The Black Press in the South, 1865–1979* (Westport, Conn.: Greenwood Press, 1983).

5. Myrdal, *An American Dilemma*, 923; Brewton Berry in Brooks, *The Negro Press Re-examined*, 11–12.

6. "The Value of a Negro Newspaper," *Atlanta Daily World*, 22 January 1932, 6. Also see "White Professor Calls Afro A Radical Newspaper," *Baltimore Afro-American*, 9 July 1920, 1, 4; "Best Friend of the Race," *Baltimore Afro-American*, 20 May 1921, [9?]; "Why We Need Our Own Home Newspaper," *Norfolk Journal & Guide*, 29 April 1922, 4; "Kelly Miller Says," *Baltimore Afro-American*, 21 February 1925, 9; "Newspaper Logic," *Chicago Defender*, 6 June 1925, [10?]; "The White Press," *Chicago Defender*, 10 October 1925 [12?]; "Congratulate Us," *Chicago Defender*, 8 May 1926, [8?]; "The Sale Price of Negro Newspapers," *Norfolk Journal & Guide*, 15 January 1927, [12?]; William M. Kelley, "Negro Press 100 Years Old Today," *New York Amsterdam News*, 16 March 1927, Magazine Section [14?]; "Negro Newspapers Have A Moral and Social Value—Nannie Burroughs, Radical Press Needed—Crosswaith," *Norfolk Journal & Guide*, 29 March 1930, Part Two, 2; "The Biased Associated Press," *Norfolk Journal & Guide*, 26 July 1930, 10; James Weldon Johnson, "A Noted Writer Says Newspapers are Creators of Modern Conventions," *Norfolk Journal & Guide*, 16 May 1931, 4; Kelly Miller, "The Progress of Negro Journalism in America," *New York Amsterdam News*, 21 October 1931, 8; "Save the Crisis!," *New York Amsterdam News*, 30 March 1932, 8; Miller, "Kelly Miller Says," *Atlanta Daily World*, 27 October 1932, 2; "Five Years Old Today," *Atlanta Daily World*, 3 August 1933, 1; G. James Fleming, "Emancipation and the Negro Press," *Crisis* 45 (July 1938): 213–16; "The Power of the Press," *Atlanta Daily World*, 19 August 1940, 6; Vincent Tubbs, "Full Democracy Has Been Battle Cry of Editors Ever Since First Paper Was Printed," *Baltimore Afro-American*, 19 September 1942, [11?].

7. Gandhi returned to India from South Africa in 1915. He entered national politics in 1916. His first national campaign was launched in 1919 against the Rowlatt Act. The noncooperation movement (1921–22) and the Salt Satyagraha (1930–31) were the other major confrontations between Gandhi and the British rule. Questions of *khadi* (homespun) and village industries, Hindu-Muslim unity, and removal of untouchability were a part of the Indian leader's internal reform package. See Judith M. Brown, *Gandhi's Rise to Power: Indian Politics, 1915–1922* (New York: Cambridge University Press, 1972),

xiii–xvi, 1–51; Judith M. Brown, *Gandhi and Civil Disobedience: The Mahatma in Indian Politics, 1928–1934* (New York: Cambridge University Press, 1977), xiii–40. Brown has amply demonstrated the significance of Gandhi's resistance campaigns and his place in the overall scheme of the national movement for India's freedom.

8. See Benjamin E. Mays, *Born to Rebel: An Autobiography by Benjamin E. Mays* (New York: Charles Scribner's Sons, 1971), 155–60; D. G. Tendulkar, *Mahatma: Life of Mohandas Karamchand Gandhi* (Delhi: Publications Division, Ministry of Information and Broadcasting, Government of India, 1961), 4:141–42.

9. See Benarsidas Chaturvedi and Marjorie Sykes, *Charles Freer Andrews: A Narrative* (New York: Harper & Brothers, 1950), 238; Hugh Tinker, *The Ordeal of Love: C. F. Andrews and India* (New York: Oxford University Press, 1979), 234–40; Thurman, *With Head and Heart: An Autobiography of Howard Thurman* (New York: Harcourt Brace & Jovanovich, 1979), 105–07; Elizabeth Yates, *Howard Thurman: Portrait of a Practical Dreamer* (New York: John Day Co., 1964), 94–95. It is well worth noting that Madeleine Slade was not a mere appendage to the Mahatma, an impression conveyed by Richard Attenborough's film *Gandhi*. Slade was a determined, strong-willed, and able spokesperson of the Gandhian movement. She appeared as such to Howard Thurman and the students at Howard University. See Thurman, *With Head and Heart*, 106. The role of Lala Lajpat Rai in building bridges between India and America during the first and second decades of the twentieth century was very significant. So also was the work of persons such as Taraknath Das and Haridas Muzumdar in the interwar years. For the contributions Das and Muzumdar made, see Manoranjan Jha, *Civil Disobedience and After: The American Reaction to Political Developments in India During 1930–1935* (Delhi: Meenakshi Prakashan, 1973). See James Farmer, *Freedom... When?* (New York: Random House, 1965), 54–57; idem, *Lay Bare the Heart: An Autobiography of the Civil Rights Movement* (New York: New American Library, 1985), 74, 93–95, 112; August Meier and Elliott Rudwick, *CORE: A Study in the Civil Rights Movement, 1942–1968* (New York: Oxford University Press, 1973), 6; Harris Wofford, *Lohia and America Meet*, (Maryland, n.p., n.d.) and idem, *Of Kennedys and Kings: Making Sense of the Sixties* (New York: Farrar Strauss Giroux, 1980), 110.

1. *The Awakening of a Global Alliance*

1. John H. Bracey, Jr., August Meier and Elliott Rudwick, eds., *The Afro-Americans: Selected Documents* (Boston: Allyn Bacon, 1972), 388;

W. E. Burghardt Du Bois, *The Souls of Black Folk: Essays and Sketches*, 3d ed. (Chicago: A. C. McClurg & Co., 1903), 13; Du Bois, "The Color Line Belts the World," in *Writings by W. E. B. Du Bois in Periodicals Edited by Others*, comp. and ed. Herbert Aptheker, (Millwood, New York: Kraus-Thomson Organization, 1982), 1:330; Andrew G. Paschal, ed., *A W. E. B. Du Bois Reader* (New York: Macmillan Publishing Co., 1971, 1974), 284.

2. Julius Lester, ed. *The Seventh Son: The Thought and Writings of W. E. B. Du Bois* (New York: Random House, 1971), 2:299–300. See also Kelly Miller, *Race Adjustment and the Everlasting Stain* (New York: Arno Press and the New York Times, 1968), part 2, 295–98, for another perspective on the unity of the struggle of darker peoples of the world.

3. Philip S. Foner, ed., *The Voice of Black America: Major Speeches by Negroes in the United States, 1797–1971* (New York: Simon & Schuster, 1972), 731, 733.

4. Vincent Harding, *The Other American Revolution* (Los Angeles: Center for Afro-American Studies, University of California; Atlanta: Institute of the Black World, 1980), 93. See also Herbert Aptheker, *A Documentary History of the Negro People in the United States, 1910–1932*, (Secaucus, New Jersey: Citadel Press, 1977), 3:208–15

5. Harding, *The Other*, 93; John Hope Franklin, *From Slavery to Freedom: A History of Negro Americans*, 5th ed. (New York: Alfred A. Knopf, 1980), 345.

6. Hubert H. Harrison, *When Africa Awakes: The "Inside Story" of the Stirrings and Strivings of the New Negro in the Western World* (New York: Porro Press, 1920), 97–98; Ibid., 95. In a resolution he wrote for the Liberty League in 1917, Hubert H. Harrison (1883–1927) clearly saw the indivisibility of the African-American struggle in the United States and the struggles of the colonial peoples. He called for an end to the violation of the Thirteenth, Fourteenth, and Fifteenth Amendments and the restoration of the "rights of the 250,000,000 Negroes of Africa." Also see J. A. Rogers, ed., *World's Great Men of Color*, vol. 2 (New York: 1946; Colliers Books, 1972), 432, 437. According to Rogers, Harrison "was not only perhaps the foremost Afro-American intellect of his time, but one of America's greatest minds." Such a gifted speaker was he that Harlemites gathered in large numbers to hear him. He had a profound influence on African-American leaders as diverse as Marcus Garvey, A. Philip Randolph, and Chandler Owen. Rogers writes that though Harrison was "fluent on almost any subject, he was best in topics dealing with world problems in relation to the darker races." In this context, also see Jervis Anderson, *This Was Harlem: A Cultural Portrait, 1900–*

1950 (New York: Farrar Straus Giroux, 1981, repr., 1987), 122. Anderson writes that "Garvey's fortunes began to improve in June of 1917, when Hubert Harrison, the eldest and most learned of the radical group invited him to share a platform at the Bethel A.M.E. Church, on West 132 Street." See also Manning Marable, *Black American Politics: From the Washington Marches to Jessie Jackson* (London: Verso, 1985), 58. The impact of worldwide freedom movements has been underscored by Marable. He argues that "radical nationalist movements outside the African Diaspora have frequently served to inspire and promote the development of similar movements among Blacks." He is convinced that Indian nationalism presents closer parallels to the African-American struggle than others. For Harrison's profound awareness of the worldwide exploitation of the darker peoples based on race, see Harrison, *When Africa Awakes*, 119–20, 101.

7. See Stanley A. Wolpert, *A New History of India*, 2d ed. (New York: Oxford University Press, 1982), 286–300.

8. Thanks to the New England transcendentalists, especially to the writings of Walt Whitman, Henry David Thoreau, and Ralph Waldo Emerson, Indian thought had become part of American consciousness. Before the century was out, the universalist perspective in Indian thought was emphasized once again. This time, the communicator of "the Indian Way" was Swami Vivekananda (1863–1902). Through his presence and spiritual insights (his message of universalism), he won the hearts of audiences at the Parliament of World Religions in Chicago (1893). Vivekananda stayed on until 1895, and helped to establish Vedanta centers in a number of metropolitan areas. He became an instant celebrity. Life-size posters of the Indian swami were displayed at Chicago's World Fair. See Vincent Sheean, *Lead, Kindly Light* (New York: Random House, 1949), 338–47. Also see Binoy K. Roy, *Socio-Political Views of Vivekananda* (New Delhi: People's Publishing House, 1970). For a complete account of Vivekananda's addresses at the World Parliament of Religions, see John Henry Barrows, ed. *The World Parliament of Religions: An Illustrated and Popular Story of the World's First Parliament of Religions, Held in Chicago in Connection With the Columbian Exposition of 1893* (Chicago: Parliament Publishing Co., 1893), 1:118, 120; 2:968–78. See also Jha, *Civil Disobedience and After*, 13; Wolpert, *A New History of India*, 272. The immediate antecedents of increased anti-British revolutionary activity can be traced to the first "War of Indian Independence" (1857). The revolt by the *sepoys* (soldiers) lasted well into 1858. The British responded to this challenge by tightening their grip on the country. Shaken by the extent of opposition to its rule, Whitehall

assumed direct control over Indian affairs. As the century moved toward its close, emergent nationalist forces also became visible, outspoken, and confrontational. On the *Ghadr*, see Haridas T. Muzumdar, *Asian Indians' Contributions to America* (Little Rock, Arkansas: Gandhi Institute of America, 1986), 3.

9. N. G. Rathore, "Indian Nationalist Agitation in the United States: A Study of Lala Lajpat Rai and the India Home Rule League of America, 1914–1920" (Ph.D. diss., Columbia University, 1965), 73–74. According to Rathore, Rai saw his role as that of a nationalist ambassador and acknowledged the importance of American influence in the world. Though not always successful, Rai established contacts and used them to advantage for the cause of Indian freedom. Also see Herbert Aptheker, ed., *The Correspondence of W. E. B. Du Bois, Vol. 1: Selections, 1877–1934* (Amherst: University of Massachusetts Press, 1973), 385–86. On the occasion of Rai's death in 1928 in India, caused by police beatings, Du Bois sent a message to *People*, an English daily of Lahore, India which in part read: "It was my good fortune to know Lala Lajpat Rai while he was in exile in America during the great War. . . . I hope that the memory of Lala Lajpat Rai will be kept green in India, and that out of the blood of his martyrdom very soon a free colored nation will arise." Indian interest in Washington and Carver was not confined to Rai. Gandhi followed the work of the founder of Tuskegee Institute closely. Indeed, his interest in Washington goes back at least to 1903. See K. Swaminathan, ed. *The Collected Works of Mahatma Gandhi* (hereafter *CWMG*), 90 vols. (New Delhi: Government of India, Ministry of Information and Broadcasting, 1958–1984), 3:437–40. And Gandhi kept in touch with Carver. See "Says Gandhi Gets Strength from Peanuts, Scientist Gave Mahatma Diet of Peanut Milk," *Norfolk Journal & Guide*, 24 April 1937, 20; *CWMG* 75:292.

10. Vijaya Chandra Joshi, ed. *Lajpat Rai: Autobiographical Writings*, 1st ed. (Delhi: University Publishers, 1965), xvii. On his extended stay in this country, Rai also wrote *Young India, England's Debt to India*, and *The Political Future of India*.

11. Muzumdar, *Asian Indians' Contributions*, i, 3. From 1920 onwards, Muzumdar spoke about Gandhian nonviolence from many platforms and participated in a great many forums. In a letter of 14 December 1988 to the author, Muzumdar emphasized how he used the public platform to spread the message of Gandhi and work for Indian independence.

12. Anderson, *This Was Harlem*, 120. See Philip S. Foner, *History of Black Americans: From Africa to the Emergence of the Cotton Kingdom*

(Westport, Conn.: Greenwood Press, 1975), 21. According to Foner, "Woodson, Du Bois, and Marcus Garvey caused numbers of black Americans of the post–World War I generation to draw strength from their African heritage." See also Franklin, *From Slavery to Freedom*, 355. According to Franklin, even Garvey's detractors agreed that UNIA membership was at least half a million.

13. Randall K. Burkett, *Black Redemption: Churchmen Speak for the Garvey Movement* (Philadelphia: Temple University Press, 1978), 4. Also see Edmund David Cronon, *Black Moses: The Story of Marcus Garvey and the Universal Negro Improvement Association* (Madison, Wis.: University of Wisconsin Press, 1955), 45. There is no agreement about the circulation figures of *The Negro World*. Cronon places the estimates somewhere between 60,000 and 200,000. In August 1920, *The Negro World* put its circulation at 50,000. Robert A. Hill, ed., *The Marcus Garvey and Universal Negro Improvement Association Papers* (hereafter *MGUNIA*) (Berkeley: University of California Press, 1983), 2: 500. The FBI report cited above noted that "Garvey . . . opened his speech by calling the negroes of America a bunch of fools for wanting to work for white folks, when the 4[0]0,000,000 negroes could after being organized solidly, demand the freedom and independence of Africa, the same as the Irish are fighting for Ireland and the Hindu for India." *MGUNIA* 2: 340. Also see *CWMG* 25: 26.

14. *MGUNIA* 3: 49. Also see Amy Jacques Garvey, *Garvey and Garveyism* (New York: Octagon Books, 1978), 68. For the possible impact the UNIA conventions might have had on the African-American community, see Cronon, *Black Moses*, 62; John Henrik Clarke, ed., *Marcus Garvey and the Vision of Africa* (New York: Vintage Books, 1974), 95.

15. "Marcus Garvey to Mahatma Gandhi," 1 August 1921, in *MGUNIA* 3: 587.

16. *MGUNIA* 4: 52, 51.

17. Ibid., 4: 184, 379.

18. Ibid., 4: 333, 334.

19. Ibid., 4: 444, 451, 452.

20. Ibid., 4: 567. From a "Speech by Marcus Garvey," delivered at New York on 12 March 1922. (The *Negro World* published the speech in its entirety. In its edition of 6 May 1922, the paper also gave a detailed account of the arrest of Gandhi and published the Indian leader's statement in the court.) *MGUNIA* 4:568.

21. From Haridas Muzumdar's letter of 26 December 1988 to the author.

22. *MGUNIA* 4: 573 n. 1, 891.

23. See Marable, *Black American Politics*, 59.

2. *"Watch the Indian People"*

1. Langston Hughes, *Fight For Freedom: The Story of the NAACP* (New York: Norton, 1962), 25, 65, 24. Hughes argues that the NAACP engaged in an "intensive publicity campaign by means of press releases and pamphlets exposing acts of racial injustice and setting forth the Association's objectives." The first issue of its official organ, *The Crisis*, appeared in November 1910. According to Hughes, "Dr. Du Bois was considered the dean of Negro writers and the foremost intellectual of his race. Thousands of young Negro men and women have been guided and inspired by his example as writer, editor, speaker, teacher, and interpreter of the race problem." Also see James S. Tinney and Justine J. Rector, eds., *Issues and Trends in Afro-American Journalism* (Washington, D.C.: University Press of America, 1980), 74, 71–72. Tinney and Rector write that *The Crisis*, which was "clearly written and produced for literate Blacks, consisted of several monthly features, e.g., 'Along the Color Line,' . . . 'Opinion,' a section in which Du Bois wrote about significant events from the point of view of various newspapers . . . 'Postscripts,' 'As the Crow Flies [*sic*].' " The importance of this journal is further underscored by the authors when they argue that "Du Bois' incomparable editorials are in themselves an important piece of black American History."

2. See Louis Fischer, *The Life of Mahatma Gandhi* (New York: Harper & Row, 1950; Harper paperback, 1983), 176.

3. Ibid., 185–86. Fischer writes, "The road by which Gandhi arrived at the center of the Indian political world was tortuous. It started at Jallianwalla Bagh; no matter where he went the echo of General Dyer's fusillade pursued him [Dyer ordered the killing of innocent men, women, and children at Amritsar]." Also see Brown, *Gandhi's Rise to Power*, xiii–51, 352–60. Also see "The Looking Glass," *Crisis* 20 (August 1920): 187–89. The journal's account, which was decidedly critical of Dyer's actions, drew heavily upon reports and essays in the *Nation, Young India*, and the liberal *Manchester Guardian* of Britain. After Rai left, *Young India* was edited by his friend, J. T. Sunderland. The *Crisis* report gave details of Dyer's atrocities, and readers were told that the findings of the Hunter Commission, appointed by the British government to inquire into the shooting of unarmed civilians at Amritsar, were a whitewash.

4. "The Woes of India," *Crisis* 22 (May 1921): 27.

5. "India's Saint," *Crisis* 22 (July 1921): 124–25. Also see Basa[n]ta Koomar Roy, "Blessed India, Great Britain's Dixie," in *Chicago Defender*, 15 April 1922, 15. In this article, which was accompanied

by several photographs, Roy noted how even some members from princely households, had fallen under the spell of Gandhi, changed their frivolous ways, and joined the freedom movement. India, he argued, was restless for change. Roy spent the greater part of his life in the United States and did much of his writing from there.

6. "An Open Letter from Gandhi," *Crisis* 22 (August 1921): 170. So as not to leave any doubt, *The Crisis* underscored Gandhi's disenchantment with the British when it added that "experience has taught Gandhi that he need expect nothing from the Englishman's fine words, so he is staking his all on the far-famed British love of fair play." Fischer, *The Life*, 191. *Crisis* 22 (August 1921):170.

7. "The Boycott in India," *Crisis* 22 (October 1921): 270–72.

8. Reverdy C. Ransom, "Gandhi, Indian Messiah and Saint," *A.M.E. Church Review* 38 (October 1921): 87–88.

9. A. L. Jackson, "Mahatma Gandhi," *Chicago Defender*, 24 December 1921. The *Chicago Defender* also noted that, in 1857 India had unsuccessfully experimented with the violent overthrow of the British. John Haynes Holmes (1879–1964) was a well-known pacifist and Unitarian minister, one of the founder members of the National Association for the Advancement of Colored People. From 1918 onwards, when he first became aware of Gandhi's method of nonviolent resistance, Holmes used the pulpit and his pen (he wrote several pamphlets and books about the Mahatma) to inform and educate Americans about the life and thought of Gandhi. His *My Gandhi* (New York: Harper & Brothers, 1953), with all its mythologizing of the Mahatma, will go down as one of the most outstanding personal accounts of the meaning and message of Gandhi. For a corrective to Holmes's view, see James D. Hunt, "The Mythologization of Gandhi," n.p., 14 October 1989. Holmes's sermon "Who Is the Greatest Man in the World Today?" was given on 10 April 1921. *The Community Pulpit* series 1920–21, no. xix, 21.

10. Du Bois, "Opinion," *Crisis* 23 (January 1922): 104.

11. "Gandhi and India," *Crisis* 23 (March 1922): 203–07. This essay borrowed extensively from Gilbert Murray's item in the *Hibbert Journal* and from the London *Nation*. The *Nation* argued that Gandhi "has India at his feet" and that he was "a human being in touch with the divine."

12. Fischer, *The Life*, 200–04. Fischer describes the specific events leading up to Gandhi's arrest and draws attention to the fact that Gandhi was totally opposed to any violence in the event of his arrest. For a fuller account of the proceedings of the trial (popularly known as "the Great Trial"), see Homer A. Jack, ed. *The Gandhi Reader: A*

Source Book of His Life and Writings (New York: 1956; Grove Press, 1961), 197–212. Gandhi pleaded guilty and recounted how a series of British betrayals, beginning with the introduction of the Rowlatt Act and the willful killings of unarmed women, children, and men at the Jallianwala Bagh, led him to oppose the British Empire. He also defined his philosophy of nonviolence and listed the duties and responsibilities of a nonviolent resister. His courageous stand coupled with utter frankness moved one and all, so much so that Justice C. N. Broomfield, after announcing the jail sentence, "got up, bowed, and departed." We may safely argue that both the conduct and outcome of the trial had worldwide repercussions. The African-American response captured something of the significance of the event. "Sedition Growing in India," *Norfolk Journal & Guide*, 18 March 1922, 4. See Suggs, *The Black Press*, 402, 407, 399. The *Norfolk Journal & Guide* was founded in 1910. By 1920, the paper became "the largest colored weekly in Virginia." During the second World War, its circulation reached the 70,000 mark. P. B. Young, Sr., the founder-editor of *Norfolk Journal & Guide*, was well connected in the African-American community. His home was "the favorite meeting place of James Weldon Johnson, Joel Spingarn, William Pickens, Walter White, and other prominent members of the NAACP whenever they visited the Tidewater area." (Johnson, Pickens and White played an important role in keeping Gandhi and the India connection alive.) Also see A. L. Jackson, "The Onlooker," *Chicago Defender* 25 (March 1922): 12. The paper reported that "the arrest of Mahatma Gandhi by the British India government . . . is enough to make the world sit up and take notice. Gandhi has appeared to hold the whip hand in India so far, especially since he refused to be coerced or tricked into violence and rebellion, which would lend some thread of justification for the use of troops."

13. "The Mystic Gandhi Imprisoned," *Norfolk Journal & Guide*, 1 April 1922, 4.

14. Du Bois, "Opinion," *Crisis* 23 (April 1922): 247; *Crisis* 24 (June 1922): 82–83.

15. Lala Lajpat Rai, "Gandhi and Non-Cooperation," *A.M.E. Church Review* 39 (October 1922): 80.

16. "Gandhi in Prison is Able Force, British Expect Silent Revolt in India by Non-Co-operation," *Chicago Defender*, 3 June 1922, 14. See Fischer, *The Life*, 217–18.

17. "The Looking Glass," *Crisis* 26 (May 1923): 36. Blanche Watson also contributed articles to the white press.

18. E. Franklin Frazier, "The Negro and Non-Resistance," *Crisis* 27

(March 1924): 213, 214. Also see Valentine Nieting, "Black and White," *Crisis* 28 (May 1924): 16–19. A couple of months later, Gandhi became the focus in an article Valentine Nieting wrote. His essay was woven around the insights of an Indian student he came to know at Columbia University. Nieting recounted the glory of India, the wisdom of Tagore, and how the Indian student gave up his ambition to do Ph.D. studies and instead joined Gandhi's movement. The story was accompanied by a photograph of Gandhi with the caption "Gandhi, Prophet of India, After Two Years in Prison."

19. Du Bois, "Opinion," *Crisis* 28 (June 1924): 58, 58–59, 59.
20. "Gandhi Orders All of His Aids to Produce," *Chicago Defender*, 10 January 1925, part 2, 1.
21. Du Bois, "As the Crow Flies," *Crisis* 35 (January 1928): 3.
22. "The Far Horizons," *Crisis* 35 (January 1928): 34. The review of Gandhi's autobiography was a reprint of the piece which appeared in July 1927 in *Current Thought*.
23. Du Bois, "As the Crow Flies," *Crisis* 36 (January 1929): 5; "The Browsing Reader," *Crisis* 36 (May 1929): 175.
24. Mary Church Terrell, "Up-to-date," *Chicago Defender*, 9 February 1929, part 2, 2. Terrell (1863–1954) was an educator-activist. During the years 1895–1901 and 1906–1911, she served on the Board of Education in the nation's capital. She was an office-bearer of the International Council of Women of Darker Races—an organization which promoted better understanding among women of color everywhere—in the early 1920s. A committed suffragist, Terrell was a major civil rights activist. In her long and active life she spread her views through talks and addresses to church and university communities, and through articles in journals and newspapers.
25. Gandhi, "To the American Negro, A Message From Mahatma Gandhi," *Crisis* 36 (July 1929): 225. The cover of the journal carried the banner "A Message From Gandhi." The message itself was dated 1 May 1929. Two years later, Du Bois urged Gandhi again to send a word of encouragement for the African-American people, who, Du Bois wrote, "were tremendously interested at the effort of the Indian people to achieve independence and self-government." Also see Du Bois's letter of 30 October 1931 to Mohandas Karamchand Gandhi, W. E. B. Du Bois Papers, Widener Library, Harvard University, microfilm reel 36 frame 51.
26. *New York Amsterdam News*, 19 July 1929, [20?].
27. Du Bois, "Opinion," *Crisis* 24 (May 1922): 27. Also see Du Bois, "Opinion," *Crisis* 24 (June 1922): 55. Du Bois pointed out that the disinherited of the world were on the move.

3. *"We Need a Gandhi"*

1. Horace Alexander, *Gandhi Through Western Eyes* 1969; repr. Philadelphia, Pa.: New Society Publishing, 1984), 56–57; Fischer, *The Life*, 252–57.

2. Du Bois, "As the Crow Flies," *Crisis* 37 (April 1930): 113; Du Bois, "As the Crow Flies," *Crisis* 37 (May 1930): 149.

3. Julius J. Adams, "World Unrest," in "Sidelights," *Chicago Defender*, 22 March 1930, 14; Frank R. Crosswaith, "Sidelights," *Chicago Defender*, 1 February 1930, 14. Also see *New York Amsterdam News*, 15 March 1930, [24?].

4. Kelly Miller, "Passive Resistance of Gandhi," *New York Amsterdam News*, 2 April 1930, [20?]. Miller (1863–1939), a trained sociologist and mathematician, was a highly respected faculty person at the renowned Howard University. He was a regular contributor to the African-American press and author of several books, including *From Servitude to Service* (1905), *Race Adjustment* (1910), and *Out of the House of Bondage* (1914).

5. Miller, "Passive Resistance of Gandhi," *New York Amsterdam News*, 2 April 1930, [20?].

6. Miller, "A Living Sacrifice," *New York Amsterdam News*, 23 April 1930, [24?].

7. George S. Schuyler, "Views and Reviews," *Pittsburgh Courier*, 10 May 1930, 12. Schuyler (1895–1977) was a columnist for the *Pittsburgh Courier* during the years 1924–1949. He was business manager of the *Crisis* from 1937 to 1944. Schuyler also worked closely with Randolph on *The Messenger*. As an author, he is better known for *Racial Intermarriage in the United States* (1930), *Slaves Today* (1931), and *Black No More* (1971).

8. *Crisis* 37 (July 1930): 246.

9. Ibid.

10. O. R. Burns, "How'd Sox Come Out Today," in "Observations," *Chicago Defender*, 20 September 1930, 14.

11. For a summary of British propaganda in the early 1930s, see Jha, *Civil Disobedience and After*, 104–08; Du Bois, "Postscript," *Crisis* 37 (August 1930): 281.

12. "Browsing Reader," *Crisis* 37 (October 1930): 341. The U.S. edition of Gregg's book was published in 1935. Two years later, Reinhold Niebuhr advocated the relevance of Gandhi's concept of satyagraha for overcoming racism in the United States. See Niebuhr, *Moral Man and Immoral Society: A Study in Ethics and Politics* (New York: Scribner's & Sons, 1960).

13. " 'Ghandi [sic] Most Like Christ,' Says Proctor," *Pittsburgh Courier*, 14 February 1931, 10.

14. Du Bois "Postscript," *Crisis* 38 (January 1931): 29.

15. "Britain Bid to Gandhi," *Norfolk Journal & Guide*, 7 February 1931, 8. Also see Fischer, *The Life*, 275. At a fundamental level, Gandhi succeeded in furthering the national cause. The Salt Satyagraha campaign shattered British confidence in its ability to rule India. After an initial refusal, the viceroy agreed to meet with Gandhi. The two signed an agreement (Gandhi-Irwin Pact) which met no concrete Indian demands but brought civil disobedience to an end. Also see Nandy, *The Intimate Enemy: Loss and Recovery of Self Under Colonialism* (New Delhi: Oxford University Press, 1983), 104–07. For African-American responses to this important development and Gandhi's role in it, see the editorial "Gandhi Triumphs," *Norfolk Journal & Guide*, 14 March 1931, 8. The editorial summed up the salient features of the agreement between Gandhi and the viceroy, and indicated the necessity of having Gandhi in any future negotiations between India and Britain. The writer felt sure that the Indian leader would "receive the approval and applause of the world as the most unselfish, sincere and consecrated leader of this generation." "May his tribe increase," the paper concluded. Also see "Gandhi Wins Long Fight with Britain," *Chicago Defender*, 7 March 1931, 13. The paper reported that the "war" between Britain and India ended "when the British acceded to all the demands of the 'Holy Man' and entered into peace negotiations with him."

16. "If We Had a Ghandi [sic]," *Pittsburgh Courier*, 28 February 1931, 10.

17. Gordon Hancock, "Wanted: A Black Reformer," in "Between the Lines," *Norfolk Journal & Guide*, 14 March 1931, 8. Hancock (1884–1970) was one of the key leaders of the NAACP. He used the African-American press to instill race pride. He wrote his autobiography, *Bursting Bonds*, in 1923. *The New Negro*, published in 1916, contains Hancock's reflections on the political and social aspects of life. See also Raymond Gavins, *The Perils and Prospects of Southern Black Leadership: Gordon Blaine Hancock, 1884–1970* (Durham, North Carolina: Duke University Press, 1977).

18. Schuyler, "Views and Reviews," *Pittsburgh Courier*, 12 September 1931, 10.

19. "Schuyler on Ghandi [sic]," in "What the People Think," *Pittsburgh Courier*, 19 September 1931, 2. The correspondent recommended Lala Lajpat Rai's *England's Debt to India*.

20. Ibid.

21. Du Bois, "As the Crow Flies," *Crisis* 40 (October 1931): 332; "Mahatma Gandhi On Voting," *Pittsburgh Courier*, 26 September 1931, 10.

22. "Gandhi and Economics," *Pittsburgh Courier*, 3 October 1931, 10. African-Americans used the weapon of economic boycott on a fairly regular basis. The appropriateness or lack of it was debated in the columns of the African-American press. For instance, see Kelly Miller, "Boycott Seen as Effective Weapon in Hands of Group," *Baltimore Afro-American*, 23 December 1933, [17?]; Vere E. Johns and George S. Schuyler, "To Boycott or not to Boycott?" *Crisis* 41 (September 1934): 258–60, 274; "Italy, Abyssinia and Harlem," *New York Amsterdam News*, 16 February 1935, 8; "Italy and Ethiopia," *New York Amsterdam News*, 2 March 1935, 8; "Making Your Jobs," *New York Amsterdam News*, 18 May 1934, 8. Also see "Boycott Italian Goods," *Chicago Defender*, 29 June 1935, 3. African-Americans organized boycotts of Italian goods when Mussolini invaded Ethiopia.

23. Du Bois, "The Wide, Wide World," *New York Amsterdam News*, 7 October 1931, 8.

24. Du Bois, "The Wide, Wide World," *New York Amsterdam News*, 14 October 1931, 8.

25. Drusilla Dunjee Houston, "That Little Man Gandhi," *Chicago Defender*, 12 December 1931, [14?].

26. Du Bois, "The Wide, Wide World," *New York Amsterdam News*, 28 October 1931, 8.

27. *Chicago Defender*, 14 November 1931, 2.

28. See Fischer, *The Life*, 297. When Gandhi reached the shores of India in December 1931, he said, "I have come back empty-handed, but I have not compromised the honor of my country."

29. *Chicago Defender*, 16 January 1932, 4.

30. "Imprisonment of Gandhi," *Chicago Defender*, 23 January 1932, [14?].

31. Pickens, "Gandhi-ism and Prayer Will Not Solve Negro's Problem," in "Reflections," *New York Amsterdam News*, 10 February 1932, 8.

32. Ibid., 8–9.

33. "Liberty Leads India," *New York Amsterdam News*, 27 April 1932, 8.

34. Du Bois, "As the Eagle Soars," *Crisis* 41 (May 1932): 150.

35. See *Pittsburgh Courier*, 3 January 1931, 1. Gandhi's usage of the term *Harijan* gained currency even in the press. The *Pittsburgh Courier* pointed out that "Ghandi [*sic*] is a colored man who is leading a

revolution against the English. 'All human beings are the children of God.' "

36. For instance, see Schuyler, "Views and Reviews," *Pittsburgh Courier*, 1 October 1932, 10.

37. "Gandhi's Plan to Starve Self Not New as Political Weapon," *Atlanta Daily World*, 20 September 1932, 4. Also see Suggs, *The Black Press*, 127. W. A. Scott II started the *Atlanta Daily World* in 1928. Given its Atlanta base, this first African-American daily, "became a newspaper with national significance." The *Atlanta Daily World* enjoyed a "monopoly on the black news market in Atlanta that was not seriously challenged until 1960."

38. "India, Dixie Compared by GOP, Campaigner Compares 'Untouchable' and South's Negroes," *Atlanta Daily World*, 4 October 1932, 1. William E. King was also a member of the Colored Voters Planning Board.

39. "Ghandi [*sic*] Staggers the Imagination," *Norfolk Journal & Guide*, 1 October 1932, 6. See also Fischer, *The Life*, 320–21.

40. "Gandhi the Great," *Pittsburgh Courier*, 1 October 1932, 10. The editorial also suggested that in comparison to Gandhi "names like Mussolini, Stalin, Von Hindenburg, Herriot, De Valera, MacDonald, Hitler, Venizelos, Mustapha Kemal, Hoover and Lenin sink into insignificance."

41. Schuyler, "Views and Reviews," *Pittsburgh Courier*, 1 October 1932, 10; 3 January 1931, 1. See Thurman, *With Head and Heart*, 20, for the special meaning the term "Children of God" might have held even for twentieth-century African-Americans; in his autobiography, he noted that slave preachers used to end their sermons by telling the congregation, "You are not niggers! You are not slaves! You are God's children!"

42. Hancock, "Our Negro 'Untouchable' " in "Between the Lines," *Norfolk Journal & Guide*, 8 October 1932, 6.

43. Du Bois, "As the Crow Flies," *Crisis* 39 (November 1932): 342; "Foreign News," *Crisis* 39 (November 1932): 351.

44. "Will a Gandhi Arise?" *Chicago Defender*, 5 November 1932.

45. Ibid.

46. Hancock, "This Man Gandhi," in "Between the Lines," *Norfolk Journal & Guide*, 24 June 1933, 6.

47. Cleveland G. Allen, "Will Gandhi Movement Help Race?" *Chicago Defender*, 16 September 1933, 11.

48. "Dr. Kirby Page Lauds Ghandi [*sic*] as an Example," *Norfolk Journal & Guide*, 17 March 1934, 10; "Gandhi Strikes a Snag," *Pittsburgh Courier*, 22 September 1934, 10. Kirby Page (1890–1957) was a

well-known white pacifist writer-activist. He was an author, evangelist, and one of the leading pacifists of the interwar years. Page visited India and knew Gandhi. The two corresponded over a period of several years. See *CWMG* 37: 276; Ibid., 66: 250–51; Ibid., 69: 121–23. *Living Courageously* (1936) and *Now Is the Time to Prevent a Third World War* (1946) were among the several books Page authored.

49. Harding, *There Is a River: The Black Struggle for Freedom in America* (New York: Harcourt Brace & Jovanovich, 1981), 85.

50. " 'India Cannot Ignore Mussolini's Threat Against the Colored People,' Gandhi," *Pittsburgh Courier*, 3 August 1935, 1.

51. "Schuyler Reveals Gandhi's Power," *Pittsburgh Courier*, 3 August 1935, 1, 4.

52. "Gandhi Urges India to Aid Ethiopia If War Begins," *Baltimore Afro-American*, 3 August 1935, [5?]; "Ghandi [*sic*] Backs Ethiopia," *Atlanta Daily World*, 4 August 1935, 1; "India Rallies to Gandhi's Summons," Ibid.

4. *Journey West, Journey East*

1. Chaturvedi and Sykes, *Charles Freer Andrews*, 38, 41; Fischer, *The Life*, 113. Also see Hugh Tinker, *The Ordeal of Love: C. F. Andrews and India* (Oxford: Oxford University Press, 1979), 18–30.

2. Chaturvedi and Sykes, *Charles Freer Andrews*, 95, 110. For Gandhi's deeply held feelings for Andrews, see *CWMG* 16: 295–96; Ibid., 58: 348; Ibid., 71: 394; Ibid. 84: 383–84. Andrews's *India and the Simon Report* (1930) was one of the books on Howard Thurman's reading list as he prepared to go to India. See Howard Thurman's letter of 13 February 1935 to Elizabeth Harrington, in Howard Thurman Papers, Mugar Memorial Library, Boston University (hereafter cited as HT Papers), Box 65, India Miscellaneous Folder.

3. Tinker, *The Ordeal*, 236; Ibid., 234; Ibid., 229; Candadai Seshachari, *Gandhi and the American Scene: An Intellectual History and Inquiry* (Bombay: Nachiketa Publications, 1969), 47, 50–54; Jha, *Civil Disobedience*, 183–84, 208–09. For the American interest in Gandhi and Andrews's efforts in spreading the message of the Indian leader in the United States, see J. T. Sunderland, "Rev. C. F. Andrews in America," *Modern Review* 47 (June 1930): 682–84. See also *CWMG* 40: 168–69 for the contributions Sarojini Naidu and C. F. Andrews made during their tour of the United States in countering the impact of Mayo's work.

4. Chaturvedi and Sykes, *Charles Freer Andrews*, 238; *Baltimore Afro-American*, 16 March 1929, 4; Chaturvedi and Sykes, *Charles Freer*

Andrews, 238; Tinker, *The Ordeal*, 234. In their work, Sykes and Chaturvedi provide an abridged and paraphrased version of the *Tuskegee Messenger*'s observations. Chaturvedi and Sykes, *Charles Freer Andrews*, 238. See also Alain Locke's letters of 26 December 1929 and 6 March 1930 to C. F. Andrews and of 28 December 1929 to Sue Bailey Thurman, in Alain Locke Papers, Moorland-Spingarn Research Center, Howard University (hereafter cited as AL Papers), Box Andi-Ban.

5. C. F. Andrews, "Christianity and Race Prejudice," *Crisis* 36 (August 1929): 271, 284, 271. Also see Chaturvedi and Sykes, *Charles Freer Andrews*, 102.

6. "A Message from the American Negro from Rabindranath Tagore," *Crisis* 36 (October 1929): 333, 334. The journal carried a fine photograph of the Indian poet. While it introduced Tagore as a colored person, *The Crisis* was quick to note that the Indian poet represented the universal spirit which "has risen to something quite above the artificial limitations of race, color and nation." Also see Tinker, *Ordeal*, 235 and Michael Winston, interview with author, 2 December 1986, Howard University, Washington, D.C., author's files. Winston suggests that African-American "interest in India pre-dated Gandhi." And he adds that out of a sense of solidarity and pride in the achievements of a person of color, many African-Americans hung photographs of Tagore in their homes even before they heard of Mahatma Gandhi. African-Americans were drawn to the Indian poet for "the lyricism of his poetry," and because he was the first nonwhite to win the Nobel Prize for Literature (1913). Also see *Crisis* 40 (July 1931): 224; *Crisis* 40 (November 1931): 391. For the quality and depth of attention given to Tagore and his vision for an undivided humanity, see *Crisis* 39 (December 1932): 372. For information about Tagore's 1929 and other visits to the United States, see Sujit Mukherjee, *Passage to India: The Reception of Rabindranath Tagore in the United States, 1912–1941* (Calcutta: Bookland, 1964).

7. *The Hampton Script*, 8 March 1930, 1, 4. When we consider Andrews's deep concern for the colored peoples of the world, for example, his collaboration in South Africa in 1914 with Gandhi on behalf of the racial minority, his outspoken stand from the pulpit for the racially oppressed people everywhere, and his mission to the Caribbean, where he spent several months in 1929, it is likely that he made a positive impression on the African-American community at large.

8. C. F. Andrews, *Mahatma Gandhi's Ideas: Including Selections from His Writings* (New York: Macmillan & Co., 1930), 8. Also see Chaturvedi and Sykes, *Charles Freer Andrews*, 233. Andrews is quoted as having

said that his book "may . . . be sufficiently lucid and popular to be read by average people, both in Europe and America."

9. Kenneth L. Smith and Ira G. Zepp, *Search for the Beloved Community: The Thinking of Martin Luther King, Jr.* (Valley Forge, Pa.: Judson Press, 1974), 48; Andrews, *Mahatma Gandhi's Ideas*, 37, 128.

10. "Gandhi Hits U.S. Bar," *Baltimore Afro-American*, 16 June 1934, 1. The item also carried a photograph with the banner "Color No Worry to Him." For a fuller understanding of Gandhi's position on the issue of intermarriage between races and castes, see *CWMG* 65: 134–38, 182–84.

11. "Students to Hear Gandhi Follower," *Atlanta Daily World*, 27 October 1932, 2. Vithalbhai Patel was not second in line to succeed Gandhi, as the paper suggested. While in the United States, Patel expressed his sympathy and support for the Mahatma. Gandhi recognized Patel's contribution during the latter's tour of the United States. For the high esteem in which Gandhi held Patel, see *CWMG* 58: 167 and Ibid., 61: 118–19. Also see *Pittsburgh Courier*, 9 March 1929, 2. In 1929, T. Ninan Jacob, an educator from India, spoke to the students and faculty at the Atlanta group of African-American colleges. Over and above what he said on education, Jacob talked about Gandhi's sacrificial and determined opposition to British tyranny.

12. "Hindu Leader Speaks Here This Tuesday," *Atlanta Daily World*, 14 January 1934, 1; "Noted Hindu Speaks Here This Sunday," *Atlanta Daily World*, 24 February 1934, 1; "Hindu Leader to Speak Here at Four O'clock," *Atlanta Daily World*, 25 February 1934, 1. A photograph of Parekh accompanied the news item. The caption also highlighted that the visitor from India was a "personal friend of Mahatma Gandhi."

13. Sue Bailey Thurman, audiotaped interview with author, 5 March 1989, Denver, author's files. See "The Student Conference at Mysore, India," *Crisis* 36 (August 1929): 267, 280–82, for Derricotte's account of her India trip and regrets about not meeting with Gandhi and Tagore. Thurman, *With Head and Heart*, 116; "India Report," HT Papers, Box 65, India Miscellaneous Folder.

14. Thurman, *With Head and Heart*, 78. These times were pregnant with new meanings and opportunities for Thurman. As he wrote, "These studies finally culminated in the Ingersol Lecture on Immortality which I gave at the Harvard Divinity School in 1947, and the publishing of *Deep River* in 1955. The required courses allowed me to explore fully with the students the mind of Jesus as found in the Gospels." See also Thurman, *With Head and Heart*, 12, 60–61; and

Jean Burden, "Howard Thurman," *Atlantic Monthly* 192 (October 1953): 40–41.

15. See Thurman's letter dated 13 February 1935 to Elizabeth Harrington, HT Papers, Box 65, India Miscellaneous Folder. Thurman requested the loan of the following books from Elizabeth Harrington of the National Student Council of the YWCA: Vincent A. Smith, *The Oxford History of India* (1923); H. D. Griswold, *Religion of the Rigveda* (1923); Haridas T. Muzumdar, *Gandhi Versus the Empire* (1932); Claude Halstead Van Tyne, *India in Ferment* (1923); James B. Pratt, *India and Its Faiths: A Traveler's Record* (1915); C. F. Andrews, *India and the Simon Report* (1930). Thurman's letter dated 14 June 1935 to Miss Mabel E. Simpson of Ingomar, Montana, HT Papers, Box 65, India Miscellaneous Folder. Simpson was deeply rooted in the Christian tradition, had strong views against racism in the United States and within the churches, and was a great admirer of Howard Thurman. Simpson kept herself abreast of events related to Gandhi and his movement. She was a subscriber to *Harijan*, a journal Gandhi edited. Delighted at what she read about the report of the conversation the African-American delegation had with Gandhi in the *Harijan*, she wrote a very touching letter to Thurman. Also see Simpson's letter of 24 April 1936 to Howard Thurman, HT Papers, Box 65, India Miscellaneous Folder. Simpson wrote, "In every line of its [*Harijan*] several pages I could see that you had got that which I had prayed you might—prayed for years that God would send you to get—true understanding of that marvelous movement which our brother and friend, Gandhiji, truly says is the Kingdom of God. Like many of the rest of us you took your little gift from our rich native land and returned loaded down with jewels a hundredfold—but why marvel; that is the rate of interest Jesus specified isn't it? I simply wept as I read." Thurman's letter to Simpson, 14 June 1935, HT Papers, Box 65, India Miscellaneous Folder. Mabel Simpson also corresponded with Gandhi. For example, see *CWMG* 63: 55–56.

16. Thurman, *With Head and Heart*, 105.

17. Ibid., 111.

18. "Prof. Thurman Heads Group Going to India," *Norfolk Journal & Guide*, 28 July 1934, 1; *Norfolk Journal & Guide*, 4 August 1934, 8; "Student Delegation to India Next October," *Crisis* 42 (July 1935): 219. Initially, Grace Hamilton, and not Mrs. Carroll, was to be the fourth member of the team.

19. See Madeleine Slade, *Gandhi's Letters to a Disciple* (New York: Harper & Brothers, 1950), 156; *CWMG* 58: 358. Originally, Madeleine

Slade had planned to go to Britain and speak about Gandhi and his message. Her decision to include the United States in her tour developed later. Thurman, *With Head and Heart*, 105–06.

20. "Gandhi Praised by English Girl Before Audience in D.C.," *Baltimore Afro-American*, 27 October 1934, 2.

21. "Gandhi's British Assistant Touring U.S. to Laud Work of India's Humble Saint," *Atlanta Daily World*, 18 October 1934, 4. Also see *CWMG* 60: 18.

22. Thurman, *With Head and Heart*, 107.

23. "H. U. Men Refuse Jim Crow On Philadelphia," *Baltimore Afro-American*, 3 May 1930, 3. See also "Howard's International House," *New York Amsterdam News*, 18 July 1928. On the occasion of the university's decision to set up an "international house," the *New York Amsterdam News* praised Howard's plans to set up a house for overseas students, and argued that "a project that brings the darker peoples of the world together in closer sympathy and co-operation cannot fail to bring them new strength and power." The paper noted that Howard University had as many as 165 overseas students. See Thurman, *With Head and Heart*, 106–07; Michael R. Winston, interview with author, 2 December 1986, Howard University, Washington, D.C., author's files. During his visit to Howard University, Louis Fischer, Gandhi's biographer, was "surprised to find that the School had more interest in India than in Africa."

24. Schuyler, "Views and Reviews," *Pittsburgh Courier*, 29 March 1930, 10. The ever-changeable Schuyler dismissed Johnson's remarks as "unadulterated nonsense." He argued that communism had more to offer to African-Americans than Gandhian methods, which were likely to remain ineffective against British might. He equated Christianity with superstition and said that it had done "more to hinder the Negro's advancement than any one single thing." Interestingly enough, in the 1960s, at the height of the Southern nonviolent movement, the practice of donning cheap homemade overalls was adopted by Student Non-Violent Coordinating Committee activists.

25. Thurman, *With Head and Heart*, 107.

26. See Muriel Lester, *It Occurred to Me* (New York: Harper & Brothers, 1937); *Dare You Face Facts?* (New York: Harper & Brothers, 1940); *It So Happened* (New York: Harper & Brothers, 1947). Quote from Thurman, *With Head and Heart*, 108.

27. "Thurmans, Carrolls, Embark for India," *Baltimore Afro-American*, 5 October 1935, 5; Thurman, *With Head and Heart*, 128–30.

28. Thurman, *With Head and Heart*, 131–32.

29. D. G. Tendulkar, *Mahatma* 4: 49.

30. Ibid., 50.
31. Elizabeth Yates, *Howard Thurman*, 108; Thurman, *With Head and Heart*, 134. Thurman does not recall the singing of "We are Climbing Jacob's Ladder." Yates does. Tendulkar, *Mahatma* 4: 50–51. Over a period of decades, Gandhi continued to receive many invitations to visit the United States. As events turned out, he never did. About these invitations, see *CWMG* 29: 416; Ibid., 30: 95–96; Ibid., 58: 399–403. For a discussion of Holmes's influence in dissuading Gandhi from visiting the United States, see Lloyd Rudolph in Sulochana Raghavan Glazer and Nathan Glazer, eds., *Conflicting Images: India and the United States* (Glenn Dale, Md.: Riverdale Co., 1990).
32. About the attention given to Naidu, see *Chicago Defender*, 3 November 1928, part 2 [12?]; *Chicago Defender*, 17 May 1930, part 2 [22?]; *Pittsburgh Courier*, 17 May 1930, 9; *Chicago Defender*, 31 January 1931, [22?] *Chicago Defender*, 19 September 1931, part 2 [22?]. Also see the news item, "India's Woman Leader Leaves for South Africa," *Chicago Defender*, 29 May 1937, 24. Throughout, Naidu's close working relations with Gandhi were emphasized. See also *CWMG* 35: 441–42; 37: 272–73, 279–80.
33. Thurman, *With Head and Heart*, 90. Also see "A Pilgramage of Friendship" in HT Papers, Box 65, India Miscellaneous Folder. It said, in part, "On returning to America they will speak to students in all parts of the country, particularly to Student Christian Movement conferences, reporting their experiences, in the interest of greater understanding and fellowship." See also Phenola and Edward Carroll, audiotaped interview with author, 18 April 1987, Baltimore, Maryland, author's files.
34. "Dr. Thurman to Lecture at Olivet," *Chicago Defender*, 11 April 1936, 12; "Thurman Finds Indian, Negro Problem Same, Tells Howard Faculty of His Talk With Mahatma Ghandi [*sic*]," *Norfolk Journal & Guide*, 9 May 1936. Thurman said that "for years I have been fascinated and moved by the continuous line of its historic civilization, from very early movements in the far off past to the flowering of soul force in the Gandhi movement." See G. James Fleming, "Preacher-at-Large," *Crisis* 46 (August 1939): 233, 251, 253. In this essay, Fleming gave some idea of the inspirational role Thurman played within the African-American community.
35. "Lauds Gandhi in Stirring Chapel Talk," *Atlanta Daily World*, 4 November 1936, 1. It is likely that the Thurmans visited with their longtime friends, the Rev. Martin Luther King, Sr., and Mrs. Alberta Williams King. The Kings and the Thurmans were good friends.

Alberta Williams King and Sue Bailey Thurman knew each other
from their high school days.

36. "Howard Professor speaks on India," *Baltimore Afro-American*, 23
January 1937, 13; "Mrs. Thurman Talks on India at Oberlin," *Baltimore Afro-American*, 27 February 1937, [19?]. Also see *New York Amsterdam News*, 23 January 1937. In an item about Thurman's
lecture tour (between 24 January and 6 February 1937) to Canada,
the *New York Amsterdam News* of 23 January 1937 drew attention to
the delegation Thurman led to the "Ghandi [*sic*]-land."

37. Sue Bailey Thurman, audiotaped interview with author, 24 April
1987, Washington, D.C., and 5 March 1989, Denver, author's file.
The scholarship fund named after Juliette A. Derricotte was initiated
by Sue Bailey Thurman to encourage African-American women students to study in India. Mrs. Thurman undertook speaking engagements to raise funds for a number of students. Tagore's ashram school,
Santiniketan, was an important focus of the India program. Derricotte
looked after the African-American student section of the National
YWCA. According to Mrs. Thurman, Derricotte helped to open the
way for African-Americans to explore India and other parts of the
world. For Derricotte's impressions about India, see "The Student
Conference at Mysore, India," *Crisis* 36 (August 1929): 267, 280–
82; "As American Educators Were Greeted by Ghandi [*sic*]," *Norfolk
Journal & Guide*, 11 December 1937, 5; "A Charming Visitor Draws
India's Holy Man Out of Seclusion," *Chicago Defender*, 13 August
1938, 24. For Gandhi on MacSwiney, see *CWMG* 22:2.

38. "Sue Bailey Thurman will be Heard at A. U. Monday," *Atlanta Daily
World*, 17 July 1938, 1.

39. "Sails for Indian Study," *Atlanta Daily World*, 5 May 1939, 1; "India
Calm, Hindu Fun, Say Derricotte Fellows," *Baltimore Afro-American*,
18 November 1939, 9. In her report, McCree gave a graphic picture
of the condition of peasants in India, and the grace and beauty of
classical Indian dancing and singing. At a personal level, she also
conveyed an idea about what it meant for her and Bush to be students
at Visva-Bharati, learning a new language and managing daily routine
in a different culture.

40. Mays, *Born to Rebel*, 134–35; Rayford W. Logan and Michael R. Winston, eds., *Dictionary of American Negro Biography* (New York: W. W.
Norton & Co., 1982), 593. In 1943, Tobias was elected to serve on the
board of trustees of the NAACP. Three years later, he became the first
African-American director of the board of the prestigious Phelps-
Stokes Fund, a foundation set up to further educational opportunities
for African-Americans. In addition, he held many government posi-

tions; he was a member of Harry Truman's Committee on Civil Rights (1946). The African-American press kept its readers abreast of the developments in Tobias's career. His activities and personal accomplishments were closely followed in sections of the press.

41. "Sails for India," *Chicago Defender*, 7 November 1936, 14; "To Go Abroad," *Baltimore Afro-American*, 14 November 1936, 17; Mays, *Born to Rebel*, 155.

42. "Interview To Prof. Mays," *CWMG* 64: 221–22. See also Mays, *Born to Rebel*, 156.

43. *CWMG* 64: 222; Ibid., 223.

44. *CWMG* 64: 223, 224, 225; Mays, "Gandhi and Non-Violence," *Norfolk Journal & Guide*, 22 May 1937, 8. Mays shared many of these ideas with the readers of the paper. Here was a detailed, penetrating analysis of Gandhi's concept of nonviolence.

45. "Mays Back From YMCA Conference," *Baltimore Afro-American*, 6 March 1937, 9; Mays, "Gandhi and Non-Violence," *Norfolk Journal & Guide*, 22 May 1937, 8.

46. Mays, "Gandhi Rekindled Spirit of Race Pride in India, Dr. Mays Finds," *Norfolk Journal & Guide*, 29 May 1937, 9, 19; Mays, "The Color Line Around the World," *Journal of Negro Education* 6 (April 1937): 134–43. See "Gandhi Re-kindled Spirit of Race in India, Dr. Mays Finds," *Norfolk Journal & Guide*, 29 May 1937, 9, 19. Also see Muriel Lester, *It Occurred to me*, 139–40. The degree to which Gandhi had enabled the Indian people to overcome fear is graphically recorded there in the words of a British magistrate.

47. Mays, "What are the Differences Between Gandhi and Nehru; Dr. Mays Asks, Gives Answer," *Norfolk Journal & Guide*, 5 June 1937, 9, 19.

48. "Until Then," *Norfolk Journal & Guide*, 12 June 1937, 8.

49. Mays, "The Color Line Around the World," *Journal of Negro Education* 6 (April 1937): 141.

50. Andrews, *Mahatma Gandhi's Ideas*, 177. When George Joseph, an Indian Christian follower of Gandhi, undertook nonviolent direct action, he was beaten and arrested by the local police. According to C. F. Andrews, an eyewitness to the struggle, Gandhi's involvement marked "the turning point in the campaign against 'untouchability.' "

51. "India Wants National Independence, Says Dr. Channing H. Tobias," *Chicago Defender*, 6 March 1937, 24.

52. "India Wants National Independence, Says Dr. Channing H. Tobias," *Chicago Defender*, 6 March 1937, 24. "Interview To Dr. Tobias," *CWMG* 64: 229–30. Also see Rayford Logan and Michael

Winston, *Dictionary of American Negro Biography*, 594, which contains
a part of this interview. Except for minor differences, the text Logan
and Winston use is identical. Influenced as he was by Gandhian
nonviolence, it is important to note that by the time the Second
World War ended, Tobias had begun to entertain reservations about
the applicability of nonviolence in certain situations. In the *Dictionary
of American Negro Biography*, Logan and Winston note that "in 1945
[Tobias] did not believe that Gandhi's pacifism was the proper course
in all circumstances. Instead, he favored the more aggressive attitude
of Nehru who 'does believe that we cannot get social change by
waiting for it. We must stand for the right and make it come.' "

5. *Exploring Gandhian Techniques*

1. See Herbert Garfinkel, *When Negroes March: The March on Washington
   Movement in the Organizational Politics for FEPC* (Glencoe, Ill.: Free
   Press, 1959), 15–36; Hughes, *Fight for Freedom*, 83. North American
   Aviation stated that it would employ African-Americans only as
   janitors and a Kansas aviation firm advertised that only "white American citizens" need apply.
2. Garfinkel, *When Negroes March*, 135; Lerone Bennett, Jr., *Confrontation: Black and White*, (Chicago: Johnson Publishing Co., 1965),
   174.
3. Bennett, *Confrontation*, 174. See also Garfinkel, *When Negroes March*,
   38–42; Jervis Anderson, *A. Philip Randolph: A Biographical Portrait*
   (New York: Harcourt Brace Jovanovich, 1973), 247–48; "What the
   People Say," a letter by Helen S. Davis, *Chicago Defender*, 9 May
   1942, [14?]. A. Philip Randolph, "Let the Negro Masses Speak,"
   Norfolk Journal & Guide, 15 March 1941, 8. Also see Garfinkel, *When
   Negroes March*, 49–51, 112.
4. Randolph, "Why not Issue the Executive Order?", *Norfolk Journal
   & Guide*, 12 April 1941, 8. Also see Ernest E. Johnson, "First Lady
   Confers with Randolph and White in New York," *Atlanta Daily
   World*, 18 June 1941, 1.
5. "President Confers with Walter White and A. P. Randolph," *Atlanta
   Daily World*, 22 June 1941, 1. See also Garfinkel, *When Negroes
   March*, 60–61 and Anderson, *A. Philip Randolph*, 255–59.
6. "Randolph's Speech Explains why He Called off March," *New York
   Amsterdam News*, 19 July 1941, 15.
7. Anderson, *A. Philip Randolph*, 262; "A. Philip Randolph, Leader,"
   New York Amsterdam News, 12 July 1941, 14; Anderson, *A. Philip
   Randolph*, 263.

8. "Color Call to America—Attention!!!: An Editorial," *New York Amsterdam News*, 4 April 1942, 1, 6; "Readers Praise 'Call to America' Editorial," *New York Amsterdam News*, 11 April 1942, [7?]; Letter by Thomas E. Wilson, "India, a Deadly Parallel," *New York Amsterdam News*, 11 April 1942, [7?]; Letter by Rebecca West, "Should go Further," *New York Amsterdam News*, 11 April 1942, [7?].

9. Garfinkel, *When Negroes March*, 8; George F. McCray, "12,000 in Chicago Voice Demands for Democracy," *Chicago Defender*, 4 July 1942, 1, 3; "Randolph Urges Fight to Save FEPC Status," *Chicago Defender*, 15 August 1942, 1, 2.

10. Randolph, "Freedom on two Fronts, March on Washington Leader sees Danger of Race Losing the Peace," *Chicago Defender*, 26 September 1942, magazine section, 15.

11. Ibid.

12. See Garfinkel, *When Negroes March*, 9, 133–38. So as to win maximum support, the convention met in July 1943, and its name was changed to "We are Americans Too." It was during this period that the protest form of a "prayer meeting," without much success, was experimented with in New York. (The idea of the "Prayer Pilgrimage for Freedom," which took place in 1957, is rooted in this earlier practice.) "Randolph to Adopt Gandhi Technique, Non-violent Disobedience May be Used," *Chicago Defender*, 9 January 1943, 4.

13. Randolph, "Movement Will Help Win War—Randolph," *Baltimore Afro-American*, 6 February 1943, 11.

14. Du Bois, "As the Crow Flies," *New York Amsterdam News*, 13 March 1943.

15. Ralph T. Templin, "Letters from Amsterdam News Readers," *New York Amsterdam News*, 29 May 1943, [10?]. Also see Ralph T. Templin, *Democracy and Nonviolence: The Role of the Individual in World Crisis* (Boston: An Extending Horizons Book, Porter Sargent Publisher, 1965). During his missionary work in India, Templin came to know Gandhi. For his support of the Gandhian movement, he and others, including Jay Holmes Smith, were expelled by the British in 1940. Templin notes that the ad hoc Committee on Nonviolent Direct Action which Smith founded in New York in 1940 "directly influenced A. Philip Randolph and other leaders who later inspired, founded, and led other movements, such as CORE and the Journey of Reconciliation." *Democracy and Nonviolence*, 296–97. Harlem Ashram, where Templin and Smith were based, was known to James Farmer and others from FOR. In 1943, Farmer moved into the ashram, partly because it was inexpensive to stay there. Also see James Farmer, *Lay Bare the Heart*, 149–52.

16. "Randolph Explains His Civil Disobedience Project," *Baltimore Afro-American*, 29 May 1943, 5.

17. Randolph, "A Reply to My Critics: Randolph Blasts Courier as 'Bitter Voice of Defeatism,' " *Chicago Defender*, 12 June 1943, 13.

18. Randolph, "A Reply to My Critics: Randolph Tells Philosophy Behind 'March' Movement," *Chicago Defender*, 19 June 1943, 13.

19. Randolph, "A Reply to My Critics: Randolph Tells Technique of Civil Disobedience," *Chicago Defender*, 26 June 1943, 13.

20. Ibid.

21. Randolph, "A Reply to My Critics: Should Negroes March on Washington—If So, When?", *Chicago Defender*, 3 July 1943, 13.

22. "Randolph Blames Roosevelt for U.S. Wave of Rioting," *Chicago Defender*, 10 July 1943, 1, 4.

23. "Non-Violence Policy Urged to Get Rights," *Baltimore Afro-American*, 10 July 1943, 7; B. M. Phillips, "Whites Barred from March on Washington Movement," *Baltimore Afro-American*, 10 July 1943, 7.

24. Bishop C. L. Russell, "What the People Say," *Chicago Defender*, 31 July 1943, [14?]; John Robert Badger, "World View," *Chicago Defender*, 24 July 1943, 15. Also see Badger, "World View," *Chicago Defender*, 10 and 17 July 1943, for his critique of Randolph's vision and leadership.

25. Garfinkel, *When Negroes March*, 145–46, 135. According to Garfinkel, "it was to the Gandhian movement in India that Randolph turned for his inspiration. The Indian struggle for Independence from Britain had been of interest to Negroes for a long time. This was more than anti-colonialist sympathy, for Gandhi's preaching against the caste system was bound to have implications for Negroes in America. Indeed, the very weapon of *satyagraha*, variously translated as passive resistance or civil disobedience, had originated in South Africa where Indians and Negroes were lumped together as 'blacks.' Gandhi had not objected to this as such or sought to raise the status of Indians above Negroes. Rather, in his first imprisonment in Johannesburg, 'Gandhi set an example by putting on clothes assigned to Negro convicts.' Thenceforth, his activities were followed very closely by the American Negro press." Gandhi adopted "Negro clothing" after his last imprisonment and not first; and it was a version of indentured Indian clothing. See Hunt, "Gandhi and the Black People of South Africa," *Gandhi Marg* 11 (April/June 1989): 21.

26. Aldon D. Morris, *The Origins of the Civil Rights Movement: Black Communities Organizing for Change* (New York: Free Press, 1984; paperback, 1986) x–xi.

27. Bennett, *Confrontation*, 179.
28. Garfinkel, *When Negroes March*, 136; Bayard Rustin, audiotaped interview with author, 9 April 1987, A. Philip Randolph Institute, New York, author's files. See August Meier and Elliott Rudwick, *Along the Color Line: Explorations in the Black Experience* (Urbana, Ill.: University of Illinois Press, 1976), 346, 345. They argue that "Randolph's approach flowed from his past as a radical Marxist and trade unionist." They further point out that even the vocabulary (e.g., "mass action," "monster mass meetings," and "march on Washington,") Randolph used to energize the African-American community was derived from the labor movement, and write, "The really innovative elements in the history of direct-action strategies during the early 1940's came not from Randolph, but from the Gandhi-inspired pacifists who founded the Congress of Racial Equality."
29. For the significance of the role E. D. Nixon played, see Taylor Branch, *Parting the Waters: America in the King Years, 1954–63* (New York: Simon and Schuster, 1988; 1989), 121; Howell Raines, *My Soul Is Rested: Movement Days in the Deep South Remembered* (New York: G. P. Putnam's Sons, 1977), 43–51; King, *Stride Toward Freedom*, 38–39, 44–46.
30. See Raines, *My Soul*, 27. Those who worked with Farmer in Chicago were mostly pacifists and socialists. According to Farmer, they were "graduate students at the University of Chicago . . . who were similarly studying Gandhi." See also Meier and Rudwick, *CORE*, 5–6. Years later, Bernice Fisher, another founding member of CORE, recalled, "all of us were afire with the ideas of Gandhian nonviolence." George Houser, son of a white Methodist minister, was also a founding member of CORE. After World War II, he helped to organize the Journey of Reconciliation and formed the Committee on Africa. Meier and Rudwick underscore the fact that it was no mere accident that Houser and Farmer came together. They were both members of the youth movement of the Methodist Church which, according to A. J. Muste, was "the most progressive of our Protestant Youth Movements."
31. Raines, *My Soul*. See also Farmer, *Lay Bare the Heart*, 142, 146, 74, 75.
32. Ibid., 75; Raines, *My Soul*, 27; Farmer, *Lay Bare the Heart*, 75, 95; Farmer, *Freedom . . . When?*, 54. Initially, the Chicago group was known as the Chicago Committee of Racial Equality.
33. See Krishnalal J. Shridharani, *War Without Violence: A Study of Gandhi's Method and Its Accomplishments* (New York: Harcourt, Brace &

Co., 1939); Gene Sharp, *Gandhi as a Political Strategist: With Essays on Ethics and Politics* (Boston: Porter Sargent Publishers, 1979), 315–18.

34. See Branch, *Parting the Waters*, 171; Shridharani, *War Without Violence*, xxxv–vi.

35. Farmer, *Freedom . . . When?*, 55; Raines, *My Soul*, 28; Meier and Rudwick, *CORE*, 13, 11. Also see Farmer, *Lay Bare the Heart*, 93, 112–13.

36. Raines, *My Soul*, 32, 32–33.

37. James Farmer, audiotaped interview with author, 24 November 1986, author's files; Raines, *My Soul*, 34.

6. *African-American Solidarity*

1. George Padmore, "Walter White to Interview Eboue, Selassie, Gandhi," *Chicago Defender*, 29 January 1944, 1. See Walter White, *A Rising Wind* (Garden City, New York: Doubleday, Doran & Co., 1945), 31. White writes that "it is my hope to visit India on this trip." Also see Walter White, *How Far the Promised Land?* (New York: Viking Press, 1955), 4–7. The account of the Indian visit, with which the book opens, suggests that White got to India sometime after Gandhi's death. A sizeable body of literature now exists about the African-American press and the important role played by some of the leaders of the major black-owned and black-controlled journals and newspapers. It would be helpful to have a detailed study of the work and contribution of African-American war correspondents.

2. Deton J. Brooks, "Defender Reporter Visits Gandhi," *Chicago Defender*, 16 June 1945, 1. See also *CWMG* 80: 209.

3. Frank E. Bolden, "Meet the 'Great Soul,' I talk to Gandhi," *Baltimore Afro-American*, 18 August 1945, 5. See "Frank Bolden, NNPA War Correspondent Back Home," *Baltimore Afro-American*, 15 September 1945, 1, 2; "Bolden, Divide India, National Unity Can't Work, Says Moslem Chief," 25 August 1945, 15; 13 October 1945, [19?]. During his two-year stay as a war correspondent for the National Negro Press Association in Iran and the China-Burma-India theater, Frank Bolden contributed several items on Gandhi, the prospects of Indian independence, and the condition of African-American soldiers in India.

4. Bolden, *Baltimore Afro-American*, 18 August 1945, 5.

5. Ibid. For Gandhi's interviews with foreign correspondents, see Fischer, *The Life*, 409–10.

6. Padmore, "Gandhi Urges Justice for Colored Peoples," *Chicago Defender*, 28 April 1945, 1.

7. Anne Guthrie, *Madame Ambassador: The Life of Vijaya Lakshmi Pandit* (New York: Harcourt, Brace & World, 1962), 125. With Gandhi's blessings and the sponsorship of the Committee for Indian Freedom and the India League, Pandit attended the San Francisco Conference. For the work of India League, see White, "People, Politics and Places," *Chicago Defender*, 24 February 1945, 11. White noted that India League had the support of such "distinguished and influential Americans" as Pearl S. Buck (an Asia watcher and distinguished author), John Haynes Holmes (a pacifist and leading minister of the Unitarian Church), Louis Fischer (writer and biographer of Gandhi), William Shirer (a well-known journalist), and noted Indians like Krishnalal Shridharani.

8. Metz T. P. Lochard, "Colonial Issue Still Hot Potato at Parley," *Chicago Defender*, 12 May 1945, 5; Du Bois, "Du Bois, White Run from Photo with India Stooges," *Chicago Defender*, 12 May 1945, 5.

9. Guthrie, *Madame Ambassador*, 129; White, *How Far*, 5–6. *Crisis* 56 (December 1949): 388. During Nehru's U.S. visit, he took the time to meet with noted African-American leaders such as Mary McLeod Bethune, William Hastie, Arthur B. Spingarn, Robert C. Weaver, Albert M. Greenfield, and Lester Granger in Harlem, where he raised "searching inquiries about the Negro's growing political independence and power." In July 1949, Mrs. Pandit was asked to present Ralph Bunche with the prestigious Spingarn Medal.

10. White, "Portrait of Madam Pandit," in "People, Politics and Places," *Chicago Defender*, 30 June 1945, [13?]; Du Bois, "The Winds of Time," *Chicago Defender*, 14 July 1945, [13?].

11. "India Protests to UN About Rank South Africa Jim Crow," *New York Amsterdam News*, 29 June 1946, 4.

12. See Guthrie, *Madame Ambassador*, 130. "India, South Africa Set for Color Bar Test in UN, . . . " *Baltimore Afro-American*, 2 November 1946, 14. See Padmore, "India War on S. Africa Asked Over Color Ban," *Chicago Defender*, 25 November 1944, 2. As early as 1944, Padmore gave the background of India's quarrel with South Africa and stated that the color bar was applied "more stringently [there] than in any other part of the British Empire." He noted that "as a retaliatory measure, India may enforce economic sanctions against South Africa and recall her High Commissioner from the Union [of South Africa]." Also see "Churchill and Colonies," *Baltimore Afro-American*, 16 March 1946, 4. The tense debates over the future of Southwest Africa and treatment of Indians in South Africa continued

throughout the rest of the year in the UN. Neither the Indians nor African-Americans took the public postures and protestations of Western powers at face value. For example, Winston Churchill's "Iron Curtain" speech at Fulton, Missouri, which in many ways signaled the start of the Cold War between the United States and its West European allies and the Soviet Union and its allies in Eastern Europe prompted the *Baltimore Afro-American* to ponder on the hidden meaning behind the British leader's proposal for the continuation of the alliance between Britain and the United States. The editorial warned that such an arrangement was bound to lead to the continuation of imperialism.

13. "One For 'Our Side,' " *New York Amsterdam News*, 14 December 1946, 10; *Crisis* 54 (February 1947): 35. For African-American press coverage of third world nations' responses to South Africa's racist policies, see "Resolution to Abolish Discrimination to be Considered by UN General Assembly," *Baltimore Afro-American*, 23 November, 1946, 10. Third World nations steadfastly opposed the racist policies of South Africa. When, in November 1946, Egypt proposed a resolution in which it called upon the UN to end racial and religious persecution, the *Baltimore Afro-American* not only carried the story, but also used the opportunity to share with its readers the perspectives of a radical writer, Saul K. Padover. Padover argued that, "today the non-white and dependent peoples of the world are stirring with revolt and resentment; sooner or later they will achieve liberation and equality of status." His observation that "a stable and strong India and China will give racism and 'white supremacy' a staggering blow, the effects of which will be felt even in the United States," must have given the readers additional hope. Also see "Weak Antibias Motion Passed by UN Assembly," *Baltimore Afro-American*, 30 November 1946, 1, 8. Finally, the UN adopted a woefully weak resolution on human rights.

14. "Slav States Join India, Condemn Racism in S.A.," *Baltimore Afro-American*, 7 December 1946, 15; "U.N. Gives Smuts Mild Censure," *Baltimore Afro-American*, 14 December 1946, 10.

15. A. M. Wendell Malliet, "S. Africa Rebuke High Spot of UN," *New York Amsterdam News*, 21 December 1946, 1, 28; "Farewell 1946," *New York Amsterdam News*, 28 December 1946, 8.

16. Michael Carter, "Head of Indian Delegation to UN Is Colored Too," *Baltimore Afro-American*, 15 February 1947, magazine section, 9.

17. See Alexander, *Gandhi Through Western Eyes*, 128. In a statement Attlee made in the House of Commons, he said that "India must

choose what will be her future constitution. I hope that the Indian people may elect to remain within the British Commonwealth. . . . But if she does so elect it must be by her own free will. . . . If, on the other hand, she elects for independence, in our view she has a right to do so. . . . We are very mindful of the rights of minorities, and minorities should be able to live free from fear. On the other hand, we cannot allow a minority to place a veto on the advance of the majority." Quotes in text from Ralph Matthews, "Drama in Asia: India's Partition may Prolong British Stay," *Baltimore Afro-American*, 21 June 1947, 11. Matthews lauded the "apostolic figure of Mahatma Gandhi and his theories of civil disobedience" and added that "as one of the darker races constituting one-fifth of the world's population, we are naturally interested in seeing India relieved from subjugation and domination by white exploiters."

18. "Mohandas K. Gandhi, Picket," *Baltimore Afro-American*, 25 January 1947, magazine section, 4.

19. William Stuart Nelson, "Our Mission in India," American Friends Service Committee, Foreign Service Bulletin 4 (June 1947) 42, in William Stuart Nelson Papers, Moorland-Spingarn Research Center, Howard University (hereafter cited as WSN Papers), Box 3. See also Nelson, "The Relevance of Gandhi Today," 1975, 5, WSN Papers, Box 7; Nelson, 23 September 1947, WSN Papers, Box 22. Also see Robbins W. Barstow's letter of 6 June 1946 to Benjamin E. Mays, Press Release of the India Famine Emergency Committee of 12 June 1946, Mays's letter of 7 August 1946 to Pearl S. Buck, and Buck's letter of 13 August 1946 to Mays, all in Benjamin E. Mays Papers, Moorland-Spingarn Research Center, Howard University (hereafter cited as BEM Papers), Box 3, Folder I–L, Folder 2, 1946–47. In the summer of 1946, the India Famine Emergency Committee also organized a mission to India. The committee, headed by Buck, nominated Mays as one of the four members to help in the task of the mission. Because of illness, Mays had to withdraw his name. Also see Locke's letter of 1 February 1949 to M. Ramaswamy and Cedric Dover's letter and enclosures of 7 June 1948 to Locke; the extract from Nehru's letter of 23 June 1948 to Cedric Dover, and note from Cedric Dover to the Prime Minister [of India], in AL Papers, Moorland-Spingarn Research Center, Howard University. In subsequent years, especially in those immediately following Indian independence, Locke expressed the hope of going to India. Dover wrote to Nehru that the Government of India might invite Du Bois, Locke, Frazier, and some others to teach and participate in the nation-building efforts there.

20. Nelson, 23 September 1947, WSN Papers, Box 22[+]; press release of 23 September 1947; Cathy Perlmutter, "Dr. William S. Nelson, Theologian, Dies at 81," *Washington Star*, 30 March 1977. For Nelson's links with King and modern African-American movement, see Rayford W. Logan, *Howard University: The First Hundred Years, 1867–1967* (New York: New York University Press, 1968; repr. 1969), 543–44. Logan writes that "several years before Dr. Martin Luther King, Jr., gained world renown for his advocacy of nonviolence based upon the teachings of Mohandas K. Gandhi, Dr. William Stuart Nelson had begun to study and teach the philosophy of this great Indian leader." In 1958, Howard University, with the support of Taraknath Das, a Gandhi-follower based in the United States, also established the Gandhi Memorial Lecture. On 6 November 1966, King delivered the seventh annual lecture in this series.

21. Nelson, "The Relevance of Gandhi Today," 5, WSN Papers, Box 7; American Friends Service Committee, Philadelphia, press release of 28 January 1947, WSN Papers, Box 12, 1; "Gandhi Interprets God to Dr. Nelson," *Baltimore Afro-American*, 1 February 1947, 14. In "The Relevance," he has a slightly different version: "To the hungry God is food, to the naked God is clothing, to the homeless God is shelter." He also added that "our mission was clear: no sermons, no attempt to solve the difficult issues between Hindus and Muslims. Thousands of men, women and children were hungry, naked, homeless. Our problem was somehow to see that they were provided with food, clothing and shelter." See also Nelson Biodata, January 1947, WSN Papers, Box 12.

22. American Friends Service Committee, Philadelphia, press release, 28 January 1947, 2, WSN Papers, Box 12. Also see Blanche and Stuart Nelson's letter to Lela Mills, 9 March 1947, 3, WSN Papers, Box 11.

23. Nelson, "The Relevance," 2, WSN Papers, Box 7.

24. Alain Locke, review of *Bases of World Understanding* by W. Stuart Nelson, in *Journal of Religious Thought* 8 (Autumn/Winter 1950–51): 86–87.

25. "Hindus Interested in Problems of All Oppressed, Natives of India Ask About Negro in United States," *Norfolk Journal & Guide*, 29 November 1947, 17.

26. Nelson, "Visit to India," 21 March 1958, 1, 2, 3. WSN Papers, Box 12.

27. "Proposed North Carolina Collegiate Workshop on 'Problems in Interstate Travel,'" 1947, FOR Papers, Swarthmore College Peace Collection, Swarthmore College, Pennsylvania (hereafter cited as FOR

Papers). Such was the commitment of FOR to the removal of segregation in interstate travel that it even organized workshops to
educate and train college students so that they might "take an active
part in eradicating injustice to minority groups in their communities." The call for strict adherence to "non-violence in word and deed
in dealing with tension and in making racial progress" was emphasized. Rustin, *Down the Line: The Collected Works of Bayard Rustin*
(Chicago: Quadrangle Books, 1971), 13, 50. Also see Ollie Stewart,
"Seven Arrests, Near Riot Mark Bus Tour," *Baltimore Afro-American*,
26 April 1947, 1, 2, 7. Meetings were held at Raleigh, Chapel Hill,
Greensboro, and Asheville to explain the purpose of the trip.

28. Rustin, *Down the Line*, 14. The eight African-Americans in the group
were: Dennis Banks, a musician from Chicago; Andrew Johnson, a
law student from Cincinnati; Conrad Lynn, a New York-based civil
rights attorney; Wallace Nelson, a free-lance lecturer; Bayard Rustin;
Eugene Stanley, a teacher at Agriculture and Technical College,
Greensboro, North Carolina; William Worthy, an official of the New
York council of FEPC; Nathan Wright, a church social worker from
Cincinnati. The eight white participants in the Journey of Recon-
ciliation were Louis Adams and Ernest Bromley, Methodist ministers
from North Carolina; Joseph Felmet of the Southern Workers Defense
League; George Houser, executive secretary of CORE; Homer Jack,
executive secretary of the Chicago Council Against Race and Religious
Discrimination; James Peck of the Workers Defense League; Worth
Randle, a biologist from Cincinnati; and Igal Roodenko, a printer.
Also see Ollie Stewart, "Journey of Reconciliation Knocks Props From
Under Weak J.C. System," *Baltimore Afro-American*, 26 April 1947,
7; James Peck, "Not So Deep are the Roots," *Crisis* 54 (September
1947): 273–74, 282. James Peck (1914–), is a white radical peace
activist. In 1961, he was nearly killed for participating in the Free-
dom Ride. Peck has authored several books, including, *We Who Do
Not Kill* (1958), *Cracking the Color Line: Nonviolent Direct Action,
Methods of Eliminating Racial Discrimination* (1962), *Underdogs Versus
Upperdogs* (1969).

29. Rustin, *Down the Line*, 50. For the impact of the Journey of Reconciliation on the Freedom Rides, see Meier and Rudwick, *CORE*,
39; Raines, *My Soul*, 34.

30. Du Bois, "The Freeing of India," *Crisis* 54 (October 1947): 301.

31. "Shoe on the Other Foot in India," *Baltimore Afro-American*, 23 August 1947, [4?]. Also see "How Many Will Die in India," *Baltimore
Afro-American* editorial 20 September 1947, [4?].

32. Hancock, "India's Plight Blamed on Great Britain's Years of Ex-

ploitation, The People Give the World Its Best Lesson in Power of Moral Leadership," in "The Point," *Norfolk Journal & Guide*, 20 September 1947, 7.

33. Ibid.

34. "Gandhi, Man of Peace," *Baltimore Afro-American*, 7 February 1948, 4.

35. "Letter from Gandhi," *Baltimore Afro-American*, 7 February 1948, 7; "Washington Pays Tribute to Gandhi," *Baltimore Afro-American*, 21 February 1948, 12.

36. "Mohandas K. Gandhi," *Pittsburgh Courier*, 7 February 1948, [6?]; Frank E. Bolden, "India Loses Its Apostle of Peace," *Pittsburgh Courier*, 7 February 1948, 1, 4; "National Leaders Mourn Gandhi," and ". . . On the Sands of Time," *Pittsburgh Courier*, 7 February 1948, 4, 1.

37. Mays, "Non-Violence," *Pittsburgh Courier*, 28 February 1948, [6?]. Also see Mays, Releases to *Pittsburgh Courier* (28 February 1948), "I Talked with Gandhi," BEM Papers, Box 2.

38. Hancock, "Mohandas Gandhi Ends Gloriously," in "The Point," *Norfolk Journal & Guide*, 14 February 1948, 9. Also see Sirdar J. J. Singh, "Mahatma Gandhi—India's Bapu," *Crisis* 55 (March 1948): 82–3, 91. In March 1948, J. J. Singh, an Indian nationalist who worked for Indian independence from his base in the United States, contributed an article to mark Gandhi's death. Singh wrote that Gandhi rid Indians of their fear of the British.

39. Charles H. Houston, "The Highway," *Baltimore Afro-American*, 13 March 1948, [4?].

40. "Indians Are Apt Students," *Baltimore Afro-American*, 25 September 1948, [4?].

41. See William Robert Miller, *Martin Luther King, Jr.: His Life, Martyrdom, and Meaning for the World* (New York: 1968; Discus Edition 1969), 29; Mordecai Johnson, "Gandhi's Purity of Heart," in Mordecai Wyatt Johnson Papers, Moorland-Spingarn Research Center, Howard University (hereafter cited as MWJ Papers), Box 1 +, 1 and 2. Nelson helped to pave the way for Mordecai Johnson to visit India as a guest of the Government of India. Also see P. L. Prattis Scrapbook, Howard University Library. In 1949, Prattis, executive editor of the *Pittsburgh Courier*, also went to India. Of his visit, which materialized with the help of Mrs. Pandit, whom he came to know personally in San Francisco in 1945, he wrote: "The friends I made in New Delhi and other cities have been a source of both pride and enlightenment to me." Writing in March 1949, Mrs. Pandit, then India's ambassador to the Soviet Union

introduced Prattis to Jawaharlal Nehru in these words: "As an
American Negro he is very interested in the role which he thinks
India is destined to play on behalf of the coloured peoples of Asia
and elsewhere and wishes to contact leaders of public opinion in
India." Also see Crystal Bird Fauset, Scrapbook 4, Howard University Library, item 33–5, folder 1. Early in 1950, Fauset, a
writer, visited India on the personal invitation of Mrs. Pandit and
the government of India.

42. Johnson, "Gandhi's Purity of Heart," June 1964, MWJ Papers, Box
    1+, 1 and 2.
43. Mays, "The Relevance of Mordecai Wyatt Johnson for Our Times,"
    27 January 1978, [2?] and 4, BEM Papers, Box 2. See Thurman,
    With Head and Heart, 87, 106. According to Thurman, "again and
    again in public addresses [Johnson] paid authentic tribute to the
    journey into freedom chartered by this 'little brown man.' "
44. Miller, *Martin Luther King, Jr.*, 30.
45. King, *Stride Toward Freedom*, 96.
46. "President Johnson's Citations," *Howard University Bulletin*, 1 Feb-
    ruary 1950, 26; Guthrie, *Madam Ambassador*, 141. For additional
    information about Pandit's connections with African-Americans, see
    Baltimore Afro-American, 28 February 1953. In a photograph the paper
    carried, it showed, among others, Johnson, Nelson, and Merze Tate.
    Tate, who was a professor of history at Howard, kept in touch with
    the developments in post-independent India. She was a regular con-
    tributor to the *Journal of Religious Thought*. Her review of Hallam
    Tennyson's, *The Walking Saint* is of particular relevance here. In her
    review, she focused on the application of Gandhian nonviolence under
    the leadership of one of the Mahatma's closest followers and col-
    leagues, Vinoba Bhave.
47. Johnson, "Presidential Address Given at the Formal Opening of
    School Exercises," Howard University, 22 September 1953, 4–5,
    MWJ Papers, Box 8. Also see "Pattern for Peace," The University
    of Chicago Round Table, no. 645 (Chicago, Ill.: University of Chi-
    cago, 1950), 1. Johnson outlined some of his perspectives on the
    Korean war, East-West relations, and the creation of a plan for solving
    some of the immediate problems facing the world. At the outset, he
    called upon the Western powers to "give up entirely the political
    domination, economic exploitation, race and color discrimination and
    humiliation, of the Asiatic and African peoples." Also see Johnson,
    "The Heart of the Matter," (Reprint from *Progressive*, March 1952),
    Vertical File, Box 1, Howard University Library. Johnson often urged
    his nation to provide moral leadership at home by ending racism and
    abroad by standing in unity with the colonial people in their struggles

for freedom. Johnson impressed on his country's leadership the necessity to be on the right side of worldwide revolutionary movements. He was convinced that such a moral posture was the most appropriate answer to the challenge of Communism. At another level, he appealed to the leaders in his country to recognize the humanity of the enemy. Gandhi had a lesson to teach: "that in dealing with the most ruthless enemy, we must conceive that even he is capable of acting in response to the noblest human motives."

48. Johnson, "Presidential Address," 5, 9–10.
49. Ibid., 13–14, 24–25.
50. Johnson, transcript of an address, undated, 3–4, MWJ Papers, Box 6.
51. Wofford, *Lohia and America Meet*, 7–9.
52. Wofford, *Of Kennedys and Kings*, 111. Also see Wofford, *Lohia and America Meet*, 11.
53. Quoted in Wofford, *Of Kennedys and Kings*, 113; Wofford, *Lohia and America Meet*, 13.
54. Ibid., 18, 26; Wofford, *Of Kennedys and Kings*, 111.
55. Wofford, *Lohia and America Meet*, 37–39.
56. Ibid., 49.
57. Ibid., 49, 66–67.
58. Ibid., 86, 87.
59. See transcript of James Lawson's class presentation of 1 March 1988 at the Iliff School of Theology, and James Lawson, audiotaped interview with author, 2 March 1988, author's files. Also see Branch, *Parting the Waters*, 143.
60. After Gandhi's death, his former co-workers formed an all-India organization (Serva Seva Sangh) to carry forward his work. Serva Seva Sangh is still actively engaged in rebuilding the nation on Gandhian lines.
61. Thurman, *With Head and Heart*, 132; King, *Stride Toward Freedom*, 85. As a major trainer in the method of nonviolence in the late 1950s and 1960s, Lawson was deeply conscious of the specifics of Gandhian techniques. In the nonviolent training workshops he organized in Nashville and other places, he followed Gandhi's outline. Lawson said that "I may have changed the language, which I did . . . but basically it [was Gandhi's] outline." James Lawson, audiotaped interview with author, 3 April 1988, author's files.

Conclusion

1. *CWMG* 85: 342; 83: 12.
2. Hortense Powdermaker, *After Freedom: A Cultural Study in the Deep*

South (New York: Viking Press, 1939; Russell & Russell, 1968), 248.

3. For a discussion of the leadership question in general, see "We Have No Leaders," *Chicago Defender*, 13 November 1926, part 2, 1; Miller, "Is the Negro Race Looking for a Moses," in "My Opinion," *New York Amsterdam News*, 30 May 1933, 6; Miller, "The Second Generation of Negro Leadership," in "Kelly Miller Says," *Atlanta Daily World*, 29 January 1938, 4; "The Race and Its Leadership," *Atlanta Daily World*, 23 February 1938, 6; Lucius C. Harper, "Why We Have No Leader of National Repute," in "Dustin' Off the News," *Chicago Defender*, 3 June 1939, 1, 2.

4. *CWMG* 19: 288; Mays, *Born to Rebel*, 158–59; Thurman, *With Head and Heart*, 20. For the importance Thurman and Mays attached to Gandhi's position on untouchability, also see Thurman's sermon, "Men Who've Walked With God," Ira J. Taylor Library, The Iliff School of Theology, Denver, sound cassette, CST–1093; and Mays, *Born to Rebel*, 157. The African-American press followed the debate over untouchability with great interest. "Gandhi the Great," *Pittsburgh Courier*, 1 October 1932, 10. See "Gandhi Strikes a Snag," *Pittsburgh Courier*, 22 September 1934, [10?]; Harry Paxton Howard, "The 'Negroes' of India," *Crisis* 49 (December 1942): 377–78, 392–93; Howard, "Aryan Versus 'Untouchables' in India," *Crisis* 50 (January 1943): 19–20, 30. In his full-length essay, Schuyler described the origins of the caste system, its current practice, and a number of pointed comparisons between the conditions facing African-Americans and the untouchables in India. Paxton detailed the basis of the caste system within Hinduism and also addressed the contradictions in Gandhi's position.

5. There were scores of editorials, articles, reports, and letters to editors expressing concern and support for Ethiopia in the African-American press in 1935, the year Italy invaded Ethiopia. Of special interest are: J. A. Rogers, "Italy Over Abyssinia," *Crisis* 42: (February 1935), 38–39, 50; "Ethiopia Thrown to the Wolves?", *Crisis* 42 (February 1935): 48; "Ethiopia's Hands," *New York Amsterdam News*, 26 January 1935, 8; Padmore, "Ethiopia and World Politics," *Crisis* 42 (May 1935): 138–39 and 156–57; Rogers, "Ruminations," *New York Amsterdam News*, 18 May 1935, 8; "Boycott Italian Goods," *Chicago Defender*, 29 June 1935, 3; "Trust God and Give 'em Hell," *Norfolk Journal & Guide*, 3 August 1935, 1; "The Glory of Ethiopia," *Norfolk Journal & Guide*, 21 September 1935, 8; Harold Preece, "War and the Negro," *Crisis* 42 (November 1935): 329 and 338.

6. Arna Bontemps, *Black Thunder: Gabriel's Revolt, Virginia, 1800* (New

York: MacMillan Co., 1936; Boston: Beacon Press, 1968). See also Charles H. Nichols, ed., *Arna Bontemps-Langston Hughes Letters, 1925–1967* (New York: Dodd, Mead & Co., 1980), 80, 103, 487.

7. For a discussion about the preparations for the Montgomery bus boycott, see Joanne Grant, ed., *Black Protest: History, Documents, and Analyses, 1619 to the Present* (New York: Fawcett Publications, 1968), 279; Wofford, *Of Kennedys and Kings*, 112; Grant, *Black Protest*, 276–80; August Meier, Elliott Rudwick, and Francis L. Broderick, *Black Protest Thought in the Twentieth Century*, 2d ed., (New York: 1965; MacMillan Co., 1986), 237–38.

8. See Raines, *My Soul*, 53; Lerone Bennett, Jr., *What Manner of Man: A Biography of Martin Luther King, Jr.* (Chicago: Johnson Publishing Co., 1964; 1968; 1976), 4. In his letter of 19 March 1987 to the author, Glenn E. Smiley also stressed the view advanced by Bennett.

Bibliography

PRIMARY SOURCES

Journals and Newspapers

A. M. E. Church Review, Atlanta, Georgia.
Atlanta Daily World, Atlanta, Georgia.
Baltimore Afro-American, Baltimore, Maryland.
Chicago Defender, Chicago, Illinois.
The Crisis, New York, New York.
Journal of Religious Thought, Washington, D.C.
Journal of Negro History, Washington, D.C.
Journal of Negro Education, Washington, D.C.
The Negro World, New York, New York.
New York Amsterdam News, New York, New York.
Norfolk Journal & Guide, Norfolk, Virginia.
Pittsburgh Courier, Pittsburgh, Pennsylvania.

Papers and Archival Materials

Alain L. Locke Papers, Moorland-Spingarn Research Center, Howard University, Washington, D.C.
Fellowship of Reconciliation Papers, Swarthmore College Peace Collection, Swarthmore, Pennsylvania.
Mordecai Wyatt Johnson Papers, Moorland-Spingarn Research Center, Howard University, Washington, D.C.
Benjamin E. Mays Papers, Moorland-Spingarn Research Center, Howard University, Washington, D.C.
Howard Thurman Papers, Mugar Memorial Library, Boston University, Boston, Massachusetts.
William Stuart Nelson Papers, Moorland-Spingarn Research Center, Howard University, Washington, D.C.

Interviews and Correspondence

Edward and Phenola Valentine Carroll, 18 April 1987.
St. Clair Drake, 9 and 26 March, 15 April, and 13 May 1987.
James Farmer, 24 November 1986.
James Lawson, Jr., 1 and 2 March 1988.
George Makechnie, 24 March 1987.
Haridas T. Muzumdar, 14 December 1988.
Bayard Rustin, 9 April 1987.
Glenn Smiley, 19 March 1987.
Sue Bailey Thurman, 24 April 1987, 5 March 1989.
Michael R. Winston, 2 December 1986.

SECONDARY SOURCES

Alexander, Horace. *Gandhi Through Western Eyes*. New York: 1969. Reprint, Philadelphia: New Society Publishers, 1984.

Anderson, Jervis. *A. Philip Randolph: A Biographical Portrait*. New York: Harcourt Brace Jovanovich, 1973.

———. *This Was Harlem: A Cultural Portrait, 1900–1950*. New York: Farrar Strauss Giroux, 1981. Reprint, 1987.

Andrews, Charles F. *Mahatma Gandhi's Ideas: Including Selections from His Writings*. New York: Macmillan Co., 1930.

Andrews, Charles F., ed. *Mahatma Gandhi at Work: His Own Story Continued*. New York: Macmillan Co., 1931.

Aptheker, Herbert, ed. *A Documentary History of the Negro People in the United States, 1910–1932*. Vol 3. Secaucus, New Jersey: Citadel Press, 1977.

———, ed. *The Correspondence of W. E. B. Du Bois*. 3 vols. Amherst: University of Massachusetts Press, 1973–1978.

Aptheker, Herbert, comp. and ed. *Writings by W. E. B. Du Bois in Periodicals Edited by Others*. Vol. 1. Millwood, New York: Kraus-Thomson Organization, 1982.

Awad, Mubarak, "Nonviolence and Peace Perspectives in the Israeli-Palestinian Conflict." 23 January 1989, Ira J. Taylor Library, The Iliff School of Theology, Denver. Sound cassette CST–1086.

Baker, Odessa B. "Metaphors of Self-Identity as Contained in the Black Press from 1827 to the Present." Ph.D. dissertation, Harvard University, 1978.

Barrows, John-Henry, ed. *The World Parliament of Religions: An Illustrated and Popular Story of the World's First Parliament of Religions, Held in Chicago in Connection with the Columbian Exposition of 1893*. 2 vols. Chicago: Parliament Publishing, 1893.

Bell, Inge Powell. *CORE and the Strategy of Nonviolence.* New York: Random House, 1968.

Bennett, Lerone, Jr. *What Manner of Man: A Biography of Martin Luther King, Jr.* Chicago: Johnson Publishing Co., 1964; 1968; 4th rev. ed., 1976.

————. *Confrontation: Black and White.* Chicago: Johnson Publishing Co., 1965.

Blanco, Jose C., S.J. "Revolutionary Thoughts, Preparation for Nonviolence." *Fellowship* 53 (March 1987): 12–15.

Bontemps, Arna. *Black Thunder: Gabriel's Revolt, Virginia, 1800.* New York: 1936. Boston: Beacon Press, 1968.

Bracey, John H., August Meier, and Elliott Rudwick, eds. *The Afro-American Selected Documents.* Boston: Allyn Bacon, 1972.

Branch, Taylor. *Parting the Waters: America in the King Years, 1954–63.* New York: Simon & Schuster, 1988; 1989.

Brooks, Maxwell R. *The Negro Press Re-Examined: Political Content of Leading Negro Newspapers.* Boston: Christopher Publishing House, 1959.

Brown, Judith M. *Gandhi's Rise to Power: Indian Politics, 1915–1922.* New York: Cambridge University Press, 1972.

————. *Gandhi and Civil Disobedience: The Mahatma in Indian Politics, 1928–1934.* New York: Cambridge University Press, 1977.

Burden, Jean. "Howard Thurman." *Atlantic Monthly* 192 (October 1953): 39–44.

Burkett, Randall K. *Black Redemption: Churchmen Speak for the Garvey Movement.* Philadelphia: Temple University Press, 1978.

Carson, Clayborne, Jr. "Toward Freedom and Community: The Evolution of Ideas in the Student Nonviolent Coordinating Committee, 1960–1966." Ph.D. dissertation, University of California, Los Angeles, 1975.

Carson, Clayborne, David J. Garrow, Vincent Harding, and Darlene Clark Hine, eds. *Eyes on the Prize: A Reader and Guide.* New York: Penguin Books, 1987.

Chatfield, Charles, ed. *The Americanization of Gandhi: Images of the Mahatma.* New York: Garland Publishing Co., 1976.

Chaturvedi, Benarsidas, and Marjorie Sykes. *Charles Freer Andrews: A Narrative.* With a Foreword by M. K. Gandhi. New York: Harper & Brothers, 1950.

Clarke, John Henrik, ed. *Marcus Garvey and the Vision of Africa.* New York: Vintage Books, 1974.

Cronon, Edmund David. *Black Moses: The Story of Marcus Garvey and the Universal Negro Improvement Association.* Madison, Wis.: University of Wisconsin Press, 1955.

Daniel, Walter C. *Black Journals of the United States: Historical Guides to the World's Periodicals and Newspapers.* Westport, Conn.: Greenwood Press, 1982.

Dann, Martin E., ed. *The Black Press, 1827–1890: The Quest for National Identity.* New York: Putnam, 1971.

Duberman, Martin Baum. *Paul Robeson.* New York: Alfred A. Knopf, 1988.

Du Bois, W. E. Burghardt. *The Souls of Black Folk: Essays and Sketches.* 3d ed. Chicago: A. C. McClurg & Co., 1903.

Farmer, James. *Freedom . . . When?* New York: Random House, 1965.

————. *Lay Bare the Heart: An Autobiography of the Civil Rights Movement.* New York: New American Library, 1985.

Fischer, Louis. *The Life of Mahatma Gandhi.* New York: Harper & Row, 1950; Harper paperback, 1983.

Foner, Philip S. *History of Black Americans: From Africa to the Emergence of the Cotton Kingdom.* Contributions in American History, No. 40. Westport, Conn.: Greenwood Press, 1975; 2d printing, 1976.

Foner, Philip S., ed. *The Voice of Black America: Major Speeches by Negroes in the United States, 1797–1971.* New York: Simon & Schuster, 1972.

Franklin, John Hope. *From Slavery to Freedom: A History of Negro Americans.* 5th ed., rev. and enl. New York: Alfred A. Knopf, 1980.

Gandhi, Mohandas Karamchand. *An Autobiography: The Story of my Experiments with Truth.* Translated from the Gujarati by Mahadev Desai. Washington, D.C.: 1948. Boston: Beacon Press, 1957.

Garfinkel, Herbert. *When Negroes March: The March on Washington Movement in the Organizational Politics for FEPC.* Glencoe, Ill.: Free Press, 1959.

Garrow, David J. *Bearing the Cross: Martin Luther King, Jr., and the Southern Christian Leadership Conference.* New York: William Morrow & Co., 1986.

————. "The Intellectual Development of Martin Luther King, Jr.: Influences and Commentaries." *Union Seminary Quarterly Review* 60 (1986): 5–20.

Garvey, Amy Jacques. *Garvey and Garveyism.* 1970. New York: Octagon Books, 1978.

Gavins, Raymond. *The Perils and Prospects of Southern Black Leadership: Gordon Blaine Hancock, 1884–1970;* Durham, North Carolina: Duke University Press, 1977.

Glazer, Sulochana Raghavan, and Nathan Glazer, eds. *Conflicting Images: India and the United States.* Glenn Dale, Md.: Riverdale Co., 1990.

Goss-Mayr, Hildegard. "When Prayer and Revolution Become People Power." *Fellowship* 53 (March 1987): 8–11.

Grant, Joanne, ed. *Black Protest: History, Documents, and Analyses, 1619 to the Present*. New York: Fawcett Publications, 1968.

Gregg, Richard B. *The Power of Nonviolence*. Philadelphia: J.B. Lippincott Co., 1935.

Guthrie, Anne. *Madame Ambassador: The Life of Vijaya Lakshmi Pandit*. New York: Harcourt, Brace & World, 1962.

Hampton, Henry. *Eyes on the Prize, Part I (1954–1965) and Part II (1964–1985)*. Boston: Blackside, 1987 and 1990. Distributed by Public Broadcasting Service Video, Alexandria, Va.

Harding, Vincent. *The Other American Revolution*. Los Angeles: Center for Afro-American Studies, University of California. Atlanta: Institute of the Black World, 1980.

———. *There Is a River: The Black Struggle for Freedom in America*. New York: Harcourt Brace & Jovanovich, 1981.

Harrison, Hubert H. *When Africa Awakes: The "Inside Story" of the Stirrings and Strivings of the New Negro in the Western World*. New York: Porro Press, 1920.

Hill, Robert A., ed. *The Marcus Garvey and Universal Negro Improvement Association Papers*. 8 vols. Berkeley: University of California Press, 1983–1991.

Hill, Ruth Edmonds, ed. *Women of Courage: An Exhibition of Photographs By Judith Sedwick*. Cambridge, Mass.: Radcliffe College, 1984.

Hine, Darlene Clark, ed. *The State of Afro-American History: Past, Present, and Future*. Baton Rouge, La.: Louisiana State University Press, 1986.

Holmes, John Haynes. *My Gandhi*. New York: Harper & Brothers Publishers, 1953.

Houser, George H., and Bayard Rustin. *We Challenged Jim Crow! A Report on the Journey of Reconciliation, April 1947*. New York: Fellowship of Reconciliation, 1947.

Houser, George H. *CORE: A Brief History*. New York: CORE, 1949.

Hughes, Langston. *Fight for Freedom: The Story of the NAACP*. New York: Norton, 1962.

Hunt, James D. *Gandhi in London*. With a Preface by Stephen Hay. New Delhi: Promilla and Co., Publishers, 1978.

———. *Gandhi and the Nonconformists: Encounters in South Africa*. New Delhi: Promilla and Co., Publishers, 1986.

———. "Gandhi and the Black People of South Africa." *Gandhi Marg* 11 (April/June 1989): 7–24.

———. "The Mythologization of Gandhi." N.p., 14 October 1989.

Jack, Homer A., ed. *The Gandhi Reader: A Source Book of His Life and Writings*. New York: Grove Press, 1961.

Jha, Manoranjan. *Civil Disobedience and After: The American Reaction to Political Developments in India During, 1930–1935.* Delhi: Meenakshi Prakashan, 1973.

Joshi, Vijaya Chandra, ed. *Lajpat Rai: Autobiographical Writings.* Delhi: University Publishers, 1965.

King, Martin Luther, Jr. *Stride Toward Freedom: The Montgomery Story.* New York: Harper & Brothers, 1958.

La Brie, Henry G. III, ed. *Perspectives of the Black Press: 1974.* Kennebunkport, Maine: Mercer House Press, 1974.

Lester, Julius, ed. *The Seventh Son: The Thought and Writings of W. E. B. Du Bois.* 2 vols. New York: Random House, 1971.

Lester, Muriel. *It Occurred to Me.* 3d ed. New York: Harper & Brothers Publishers, 1940.

Logan, Rayford W. *Howard University: The First Hundred Years, 1867–1967.* New York: New York University Press, 1968; reprint 1969.

Logan, Rayford W., and Michael R. Winston, eds. *Dictionary of American Negro Biography.* New York: W.W. Norton & Co., 1982.

Lyle, Jack, ed. *The Black American and the Press.* Los Angeles: Ward Ritchie Press, 1968.

Lynd, Staughton, ed. *Nonviolence in America: A Documentary History.* Indianapolis, Ind.: Bobbs-Merrill and Co., 1966.

Marable, Manning. *Black American Politics: From the Washington Marches to Jessie Jackson.* London: Verso, 1985.

Mays, Benjamin E. *Born to Rebel: An Autobiography by Benjamin E. Mays.* New York: Charles Scribner's Sons, 1971.

Meier, August, and Elliott Rudwick. *CORE: A Study in the Civil Rights Movement, 1942–1968.* New York: Oxford University Press, 1973.

————. *Along the Color Line: Explorations in the Black Experience.* Urbana, Ill.: University of Illinois Press, 1976.

Meier, August, Elliott Rudwick, and Francis L. Broderick. *Black Protest Thought in the Twentieth Century.* 2d ed. New York: 1965; Macmillan Co., 1986.

Michnik, Adam. *Letters from Prison and other Essays.* Translated by Maya Latynski. Berkeley, Los Angeles: University of California Press, 1985.

Miller, Kelly. *Race Adjustment and the Everlasting Stain.* New York: Arno Press and the New York Times, 1968.

Miller, William Robert. *Martin Luther King, Jr.: His Life, Martyrdom, and Meaning for the World.* New York: Weybright & Talley, 1968; Discus edition, 1969.

Minzhu, Han, and Hua Sheng, eds. *Cries for Democracy: Writings and Speeches from the 1989 Chinese Democracy Movement.* Princeton: Princeton University Press, 1990.

Morris, Aldon D. *The Origins of the Civil Rights Movement: Black Communities Organizing for Change.* New York: Free Press, 1984; 1986.

Mukherjee, Sujit. *Passage to India: The Reception of Rabindranath Tagore in the United States, 1912–1941.* Calcutta: Bookland, 1964.

Myrdal, Gunnar. *An American Dilemma: The Negro Problem and Modern Democracy.* 2 vols. With the assistance of Richard Sterner and Arnold Rose. New York: Harper & Brothers Publishers, 1944.

Muzumdar, Haridas T. *Asian Indians' Contributions to America.* Little Rock, Ark.: Gandhi Institute of America, 1986.

Nandy, Ashis. *The Intimate Enemy: Loss and Recovery of Self Under Colonialism.* New Delhi: Oxford University Press, 1983.

Nichols, Charles H., ed. *Arna Bontemps-Langston Hughes Letters: 1925–1967.* New York: Dodd, Mead & Co., 1980.

Niebuhr, Reinhold. *Moral Man and Immoral Society: A Study in Ethics and Politics.* New York: Scribner's Sons, 1960.

Paschal, Andrew, G., ed. *A W. E. B. Du Bois Reader.* With an Introduction by Arna Bontemps. New York: Macmillan Publishing Co., 1971.

Pfeffer, Paula. "A. Philip Randolph: A Case Study in Black Leadership." Ph.D. dissertation, Northwestern University, 1980.

Powdermaker, Hortense. *After Freedom: A Cultural Study in the Deep South.* New York: 1939; Russell & Russell, 1968.

Powell, Adam Clayton, Jr. *Adam by Adam: The Autobiography of Adam Clayton Powell, Jr.* New York: Dial Press, 1971.

Rai, Lajpat. *The United States of America: A Hindu's Impressions and a Study.* Calcutta: R. Chatterjee, 1916.

Raines, Howell. *My Soul Is Rested: Movement Days in the Deep South Remembered.* New York: G. P. Putnam's Sons, 1977.

Rathore, N. G. "Indian Nationalist Agitation in the United States: A Study of Lala Lajpat Rai and the India Home Rule League of America, 1914–1920." Ph.D. dissertation, Columbia University, 1965.

Reddick, Lawrence D. *Crusader Without Violence: A Biography of Martin Luther King, Jr.* New York: Harper & Brothers, 1959.

Rogers, J. A., ed. *World's Great Men of Color.* 2 vols. New York: 1946; Collier Books, 1972.

Roy, Binoy K. *Socio-Political Views of Vivekananda.* New Delhi: People's Publishing House, 1970.

Rustin, Bayard. *Down the Line: The Collected Writings of Bayard Rustin.* Chicago: Quadrangle Books, 1971.

Seshachari, Candadai. *Gandhi and the American Scene: An Intellectual History and Inquiry.* Bombay: Nachiketa Publications, 1969.

Shaplen, Robert. "A Reporter At Large: From Marcos to Aquino—I and II." *New Yorker*, 25 August and 1 September 1986: 33–73; 36–64.

Sharp, Gene. *Gandhi as a Political Strategist: With Essays on Ethics and Politics.* With and Introduction by Corretta Scott King. Boston: Porter Sargent Publishers, 1979.

Sheean, Vincent. *Lead, Kindly Light.* New York: Random House, 1949.

Shridharani, Krishnalal J. *War Without Violence, A Study of Gandhi's Method and its Accomplishments.* New York: Harcourt Brace & Co., 1939.

Slade, Madeleine. *Gandhi's Letters to a Disciple.* With an Introduction by John Haynes Holmes. New York: Harper & Brothers Publishers, 1950.

Smith, Kenneth L., and Ira G. Zepp. *Search for the Beloved Community: The Thinking of Martin Luther King, Jr.* Valley Forge, Pa.: Judson Press, 1974.

Suggs, Henry Lewis, ed. *The Black Press in the South, 1865–1979.* Westport, Conn.: Greenwood Press, 1983.

Sunderland, J. T. "Rev. C. F. Andrews in America." *Modern Review* 47 (June 1930): 682–84.

Swaminathan, K., ed. *The Collected Works of Mahatma Gandhi.* 90 vols. New Delhi: Government of India, Ministry of Information and Broadcasting, 1958–1984.

Templin, Ralph T. *Democracy and Nonviolence: The Role of the Individual in World Crisis.* Boston: An Extending Horizons Book, Porter Sargent Publisher, 1965.

Tendulkar, D. G. *Mahatma: Life of Mohandas Karamchand Gandhi.* 4 vols. Delhi: Publications Division, Ministry of Information & Broadcasting, Government of India, 1961.

Thurman, Howard. *With Head and Heart: An Autobiography of Howard Thurman.* New York: Harcourt Brace & Jovanovich, 1979.

———. "Men Who've Walked with God." Ira J. Taylor Library, The Iliff School of Theology, Denver. Sound cassette CST–1093.

Tinker, Hugh. *The Ordeal of Love: C. F. Andrews and India.* New York: Oxford University Press, 1979.

Tinney, James S., and Justine J. Rector, eds. *Issues and Trends in Afro-American Journalism.* Washington, D.C.: University Press of America, 1980.

Tong, Shen. With Marian Yen. *Almost a Revolution.* Boston: Houghton, Mifflin Co., 1990.

White, Walter F. *A Rising Wind.* 1st ed. Garden City, N.Y.: Doubleday, Doran & Co., 1945.

———. *How Far the Promised Land.* New York: Viking Press, 1955.

Williams, Juan. *Eyes on the Prize: America's Civil Rights Years, 1954–1965.* New York: Viking, 1987.

Yates, Elizabeth. *Howard Thurman: Portrait of a Practical Dreamer.* New York: John Day Co., 1964.

Wofford, Harris. *Of Kennedys and Kings: Making Sense of the Sixties.* New York: Farrar Strauss Giroux, 1980.

————. *Lohia and America Meet.* Maryland: n.p., n.d.

Wolpert, Stanley A. *A New History of India.* 2d ed. New York: Oxford University Press, 1982.

INDEX